music 4.1

music PRO
guides

music 4.1

A Survival Guide for
Making Music in the Internet Age

Bobby Owsinski

Hal Leonard Books
An Imprint of Hal Leonard Corporation

Published in 2016 by Hal Leonard Books
An Imprint of Hal Leonard Corporation
7777 West Bluemound Road
Milwaukee, WI 53213

Trade Book Division Editorial Offices
33 Plymouth St., Montclair, NJ 07042

All illustrations by Bobby Owsinski except the following: 5-1 from Shidlas; 9-2 from Square, Inc.

Printed in the United States of America

Book design by John J. Flannery

Library of Congress Cataloging-in-Publication Data

Names: Owsinski, Bobby, author.
Title: Music 4.1 : a survival guide for making music in the Internet age /
 Bobby Owsinski.
Description: Montclair : Hal Leonard Books, 2016. | Series: Music pro guides
 | Includes bibliographical references and index.
Identifiers: LCCN 2015047632 | ISBN 9781495045219 (pbk.)
Subjects: LCSH: Music trade--Technological innovations. | Music and the
 Internet. | Internet marketing.
Classification: LCC ML3790 .O968 2016 | DDC 780.68/8--dc23
LC record available at http://lccn.loc.gov/2015047632

ISBN: 978-1-4950-4521-9

www.halleonardbooks.com

Contents

Introduction

Welcome to the fourth edition of *Music 3.0: A Survival Guide for Making Music in the Internet Age.* As you've probably noticed, it's now called Music 4.1; that's because the industry has continued to change at a record pace and has now reached the next level of evolution.

I originally decided to write this book precisely because the music world was changing so much. Oh, it's always been evolving, but the speed of the industry's remodeling has increased at a rate previously unimagined. It would be nice to say that this change was brought about by a leap in musical creativity, but that's not the case. This metamorphosis has been caused by technology.

The Internet has brought us so many conveniences and so many new ways of living our lives, having fun, and communicating with those we know and don't know that we sometimes don't appreciate how quickly it's all come about. It's also brought us so many choices in the way we make music and ultimately make it available that, unfortunately, it's also left most artists and music makers dazed and confused with all the seemingly endless options. What should I do? How can I do it? Who are my customers and fans? What do they want from me? How do I reach them? How do I take advantage of all these choices? How am I going to make money? These are all questions that an artist might have asked previously, but the relevance and urgency of these questions have only increased with the current times.

I came up with the concept of the original *Music 3.0* edition after writing a post on my production blog (bobbyowsinski.blogspot.com; there's now also music3point0.blogspot.com) in which I discussed the current woes of not only the music business, but especially the artists who are just trying to do the thing they love most—play music.

I know that some artists have grand ambitions to be the next Justin Timberlake, Christina Aguilera, Jay-Z, Coldplay, or any number of bestselling acts. Sometimes artists crave fame a lot more than they yearn to make the kind of music that will attract and keep fans for the long term. These type of musicians seem to burn out of the business the fastest after they realize how much work they really have to put in.

The vast majority of artists aren't like that. They love what they do and are supremely happy when they find others who love what they do too. For them, just being able to make music without having to work a job on the side is considered a success. If that describes you, I hear you and feel you. Reading this book might not get you there, but it can set you on your way. Knowledge is power—and that phrase has never been truer than in the current music stage that I call "Music 4.1." The possibilities for what can happen to your music are endless, but you've got to know how to take advantage of them before you can put them into action.

Throughout this book, I'll refer to various stages of music, like Music 4.0 as M4.0 or "M four oh." It has a nice ring and rolls off the tongue well. But you're probably wondering, "How did we get to M4.1? And what were M1.0 and 2.0?" I'll go over all that in depth in Chapter 1, but briefly, here's how I delineate the various stages of the music business:

Music 0.5: The embryonic stage of the music business, predating recorded music, when the product was limited to sheet music and piano rolls and the song was much more important than the artist.

Music 1.0: The first generation of the music business as we know it today, in which the product was vinyl records, the artist had no direct contact with the record buyer, radio was the primary source of promotion, the record labels were run by record people, and records were bought from retail stores.

Music 1.5: The second generation of the music business, when the product was primarily CDs, labels were owned and run by large conglomerates, MTV caused the labels to shift from artist development to image development, radio was still the major source of promotion, and CDs were purchased from retail stores.

Music 2.0: The third generation of the music business, which signaled the beginning of digital music and during which piracy ran rampant due to peer-to-peer networks. The industry, however, took little notice, because CD sales were still strong from radio promotion.

Music 2.5: The fourth generation of the music business, in which digital music became monetized thanks to iTunes and, later, others such as Amazon MP3. CD sales plunged, the music industry contracted, and retail stores closed.

Music 3.0: The fifth generation of the music business, in which the artist could communicate, interact, market, and sell directly to the fan. Record labels, radio, and television became somewhat irrelevant, and single songs were purchased more often than albums.

Music 3.5: The sixth generation of the music business, when YouTube and other online video platforms become the new radio, and the digital side of the business began to slowly morph from one of downloads to streaming.

Music 4.0: The seventh generation of the music business, where streaming became the preferred music delivery method for the consumer, making it profitable on a wide scale and increasing revenue for artists, songwriters, publishers, and labels.

Music 4.1: The generation of the music business where record labels and publishers are forced to adjust to the new business model brought about by streaming distribution.

This book is an aggregation of concepts about the new music business in the so-called Internet Age, which I've been following for some time. It contains the guiding insights of some of the brightest minds in the music industry about where the industry has been, where it is now, and where it's going. With so much information available, I wanted to do what I do best—collect it, organize it, and present it in a way that everyone can understand.

As with my other books, I sought out the help of some of the most respected voices from the cutting edge of different aspects of the music business, and I've included selected quotes from them along the way.

Let me briefly introduce these respected experts to you:

Dae Bogan has considerable experience in both music and social media marketing, starting out in event production for major brands such as Chipotle, Dell, Blackberry, Virgin Mobile, and Def Jam, and then becoming vice president of marketing for Shiekh shoes and their Shiekh music artists program. His current company, Chazbo Music, provides in-store video music entertainment services by programming custom-curated channels for businesses, music, and lifestyle.

Richard Feldman is a very successful songwriter and producer who has both Platinum and No. 1 records and a Grammy award to his credit. He now leads a publishing venture focused on evergreen music compositions, a music library with Time Warner Cable and Fox Sports, and a successful music placement agency, Artists First Music. As a past president of the American Independent Music Publishers Association, Richard brings a unique perspective to publishing as a musician, producer, songwriter, and businessman.

An expert on entertainment analytics, **Larry Gerbrandt's** Media Valuation Partners advises its clients on the economics of media and content on traditional and emerging technology platforms. Formerly a senior vice president with research giant Nielsen Analytics, Gerbrandt provides a wealth of experience in entertainment market research that we're pleased we could tap for this book.

Shan Dan Horan is the president of indie label Artery Recordings after his previous position of director of the New Media Department at Century Media Records. He's also a talented music video director and photographer for his own company (ShanDanVideo.com), a skill set that's quite in demand these days, when YouTube is the king of music distribution and discovery.

Bruce Houghton started his highly influential Hypebot blog because he wanted to better understand the changes in the music business in order to help educate the clients of his Skyline Music agency. Since then, Bruce's blog has become a must-read for anyone at any level in the music industry. His keen observations come from being not only a highly prominent blogger but also a booking agent working in the industry trenches every day.

Ariel Hyatt and her socially based Cyber PR agency have been guiding artists, bands, and musicians through the worlds of Facebook, YouTube, Twitter, and other social media platforms since their birth. Ariel was one of the first publicists to incorporate these tools into her skill set, and she's one of the few true experts in the field of online publicity and social media.

One of the pioneers of search engine optimization (SEO) and marketing, **Gregory Markel**'s company Infuse Creative touts major entertainment clients like Gibson Musical Instruments, New Line Cinema, the National Geographic Channel, Led Zeppelin, the Rolling Stones, the television show *24*, and many more. As a recording artist and great singer, formerly signed to Warner Brothers, Markel has a deep empathy for the plight of today's artist and provides an abundance of good advice.

One of the most respected and beloved executives in the music industry, **Rupert Perry** held a variety of executive positions with EMI for 32 years. He went from vice president of A&R at Capitol to president of EMI America to managing director of EMI Australia and, later, of EMI Records UK to president and CEO of EMI Europe to, finally, the worldwide position of vice president of EMI Recorded Music. Rupert is well up on the latest technology and trends within the music business and shares some surprising contrasts between the old business and the one we're in right now.

Jacob Tell founded Oniracom, a new breed of company that provides a full line of digital media services to artists, labels, and management. Helping artists in the digital space since before YouTube, MySpace, or Facebook, Jacob has watched the development of social networking and learned how an artist can best take advantage of it along the way. Now 12 years old, Oniracom has branched from its core business of web development, social media marketing, and community management for artists into branding and design.

Michael Terpin is the founder of SocialRadius, a social media marketing company focused on outreach and strategy. The projects his firm has worked on include the outreach for recording artist Will.i.am's *Yes We Can* video for the Obama presidential campaign (which won

Emmy, Global Media, and Webby awards) and social media event marketing for music events like Live8, LiveEarth, the Green Inaugural Ball, and the David Lynch Foundation. Terpin also founded Marketwire, one of the world's largest international newswires.

Dan Tsurif is head of digital strategy and an artist manager at Mercenary Management, where he handles the day-to-day management for The Casualties, Nekroantix, and Black Label Society.

While you read this book, be aware that there is one basic concept that it subtly follows. It's an idea I've lived by for some time, and it helps to clarify an artist's intent (which is now more important than ever) if kept in mind.

> **Art is something you do for yourself.**
> **A craft is something you do for everyone else.**

You'll see as you read this book that it's really important to know whether what you're doing is really an art or a craft because that will determine your level of involvement in the many jobs required to advance your career as an artist. If you're making music just for yourself, all the rules change—as does your level of commitment to the muse itself.

As I said before, the music business is changing rapidly and, though it may seem painful now, it will ultimately change for the better. There will be a lot of the old guard who will fall by the wayside, but it's probably time that happened anyway (perhaps it's long overdue). Consumers are more selective and sophisticated in their tastes and about technology, and that's something everyone in the industry should not only be aware of but also cater to. It's the only way to survive in today's music world.

Keep in mind that there are many, many issues that reach out to us in M4.1, but things change so quickly that this book would be obsolete before it even got on the retail shelves if it were too specific in certain areas. I won't discuss the legal issues of copyright, I won't evaluate individual distributors and social networks beyond some generalities, and I won't discuss the relative merits of a particular website or service. Once again, things could all change so quickly that you'd get no value from the book if it were that detailed. I'll look mostly at the big picture, but drill down where it's appropriate.

This book looks at how to use Music 4.1 to its utmost. If you're an artist, you've got to be aware of all your options—both traditional and online. This book will show you who controls today's music industry; who the new movers and shakers are; how to grow, market to, sell to, and interact with your fan base; how to utilize the new concepts that power M4.1; and what you need to do to harness the potential of M4.1, all without spending so much time online that you aren't left with time to make music.

It seems like a lot of information, but if you want to control your destiny in the new music industry, this book will show you how.

This fourth edition includes the latest updated info whenever possible. There's some philosophy, some how-to's, and some predictions, but it's all based on excellent information from expert sources, some of whom you'll meet in this book.

Keep in mind that this book is not only for the musician but also for other members of the music industry. Everyone must understand his or her options and challenges in order to survive in this new business environment. Hopefully, you'll find this book to be an invaluable tool as you go forth into this new world.

BOBBY OWSINSKI BIBLIOGRAPHY

These other publications might be of particular interest to readers of this book:

Social Media Promotion for Musicians (ISBN 978-0-9888391-1-3—BOMG Publishing)

The Mixing Engineer's Handbook, Third Edition (ISBN 128542087X—Thomson Course Technology)

The Recording Engineer's Handbook, Third Edition (ISBN 1285442016—Course Technology PTR)

The Audio Mastering Handbook, Second Edition (ISBN 978-1598634495—Course Technology PTR)

The Drum Recording Handbook, with DVD (with Dennis Moody) (ISBN 978-1423443438—Hal Leonard)

How to Make Your Band Sound Great, with DVD (ISBN 978-1423441907—Hal Leonard)

The Studio Musician's Handbook, with DVD (with Paul ILL) (ISBN 978-1423463412—Hal Leonard)

The Music Producer's Handbook, with DVD (ISBN 978-1423474005—Hal Leonard)

The Musician's Video Handbook, with DVD (ISBN 978-1423484448—Hal Leonard)

Mixing and Mastering with T-RackS: The Official Guide (ISBN 978-1435457591—Course Technology PTR)

The Touring Musician's Handbook (ISBN 978-1423492368—Hal Leonard)

The Ultimate Guitar Tone Handbook (ISBN 978-0739075357—Alfred Publishing)

The Studio Builder's Handbook (ISBN 978-0739077030—Alfred Publishing)

Abbey Road to Ziggy Stardust [with Ken Scott] (ISBN 978-0739078587—Alfred Publishing)

The Audio Mixing Bootcamp with DVD (ISBN 978-0739082393—Alfred Publishing)

Audio Recording Basic Training with DVD (ISBN 978-0739086001—Alfred Publishing)

The PreSonus StudioLive Mixer Handbook (ISBN 978-1470611286—Alfred Publishing)

Deconstructed Hits (3 volumes)—Alfred Publishing

You can get more info and read excerpts from each book by visiting the excerpts section of bobbyowsinski.com.

BOBBY'S ONLINE COACHING PROGRAMS

101 Mixing Tricks—101mixingtricks.com
Music Prosperity Breakthrough—musicprosperitybreakthrough.com

BOBBY'S ONLINE CONNECTIONS

Bobby's Website—bobbyowsinski.com
Bobby's Music Production Blog—bobbyowsinski.blogspot.com
Bobby's Music Industry Blog—music3point0.blogspot.com
Bobby on Forbes—forbes.com/sites/bobbyowsinski
Bobby on Facebook—facebook.com/bobby.owsinski
Bobby on Twitter—@bobbyowsinski
Bobby on YouTube—youtube.com/polymedia

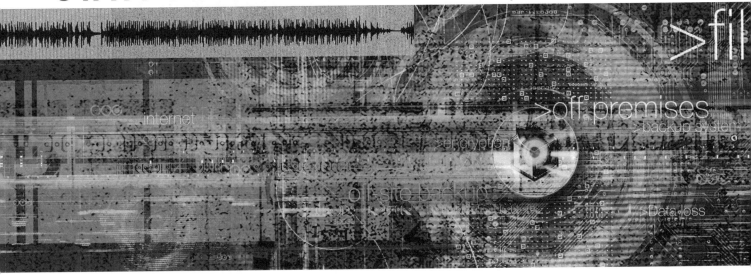

The Life Stages of the Music Industry

The history of the music business can be broken down into distinct stages. Each stage is readily apparent once you know what to look for, although the exact beginning and ending points may not be. In order to understand the significance of the stage termed *Music 4.1* (we'll call it M4.1, pronounced "em-four-one," from now on), it's important to look closely at the other stages to spot the changes, and the opportunities, that present themselves.

One thing to remember is that what we all have come to think of as the "music business" is mostly based on popular ("pop") music, meaning music that's aimed at reaching the largest number of people possible. This popularity used to be measured exclusively by sales activity, but now even the charts of unofficial industry bible *Billboard* magazine use digital streaming and YouTube views to generate their rankings. In fact, charts such as *Billboard*'s Social 50 and the Ultimate Chart (ultimatechart.com), which go a step further and take all social media into account as well, are now becoming a serious force in measuring the true popularity of an artist.

So as you read about the following stages of the music business, keep in mind that the way success is determined has changed through the years as new products, sales, and measurement technologies were introduced.

MUSIC 0.5: THE PRECURSOR BUSINESS

In the days before recorded music, the music business was a different animal indeed. This was an industry centered around sheet music, which is how music was disseminated to the public. Thus, the only way music was heard was to buy sheet music and perform it live in your home, so the original music industry promoted the song, not the artist.

Although this industry really started in the 18th century, by the late 19th century, the center of this industry was the music publishers of New York's "Tin Pan Alley" district. When player pianos, the first big leap in music delivery, were introduced, the publishers created the system of what we now call "promotion" to get their songs included on player rolls, the mechanism that allowed the pianos to play by themselves. Promotion soon became an essential part of the music business that exists to this day.

New Technology Drives the Business

Various new music technology delivery systems were soon created, changing the focus of the industry more to the artist. The first record player, the Gramophone, was introduced in 1890. In the 1920s, radio was introduced, and music delivery quickly grew as new popular songs and the artists who recorded them could rapidly spread to a wide audience. The late 1920s then gave us motion pictures with sound ("talkies"), which soon became another source of music dissemination.

In 1932, the first record store in the United States came into existence ("George's Song Shop" in Johnstown, Pennsylvania), and in 1941, the first store of what would become the largest chain of record stores ever, Tower Records, opened. With the rise of the distributor known as the "rack jobber," department stores all over the country dedicated a portion of the store just to record sales. During this time, entrepreneurs worldwide began to recognize the new opportunities of the music business, as nearly 200 record labels were created in the United States alone and retail record stores began to pop up in every town.

The music business had been formed. It had a delivery format (vinyl records), a delivery system (record stores), and a promotional system (radio and movies) in place. The opportunity for profits had not escaped many corporations, though, and by 1930, the long, slow road to industry consolidation had begun.

In 1929, Radio Corporation of America (RCA) acquired the largest manufacturer of phonographs and records, the Victor Talking Machine Company, to become RCA-Victor. In 1931, their British affiliate, the Gramophone Company, merged with the Columbia Graphophone Company to become EMI, a music industry powerhouse for years to come. RCA went on to sell its interest in EMI in 1935, but both companies were now in position to become major industry players in the future. The business was still in its infancy, however, and would have more than a decade to grow before it started gaining major traction with consumers.

MUSIC 1.0: THE ORIGINAL MUSIC BUSINESS

The music business as we know it today really started in the stage called Music 1.0, a period that lasted from the 1950s to the early 1980s. During this time, the music business experienced unprecedented yearly growth, except for a brief period around 1980, when it experienced a major recession. Year-to-year sales and profits surged upward until they caught the attention of Wall Street, an occurrence that turned out to be one of the industry's defining moments (more on that later). For historical purposes and to educate younger readers about how business was conducted during those times, here's an overview of the business structure of Music 1.0.

A Look Inside the Original Music Business

For almost 50 years, the way the music business worked remained the same. The artist was signed to a recording contract by the record label (usually after submitting his or her demo tape), which then assigned an A&R (Artist and Repertoire) person to be the liaison between the artist and the record company product manager for the record releases by the artist. In the beginning, the A&R person would also assign a producer, who was responsible for making the record, although this eventually became a mutual decision with the artist over the years. Many times, the producer would be on staff, and in other cases, the A&R person also served double duty as the producer.

The structure looked like this:

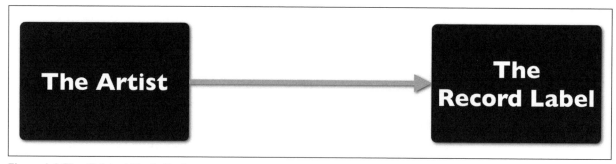

Figure 1-1: The Original Music Business

In the early days of the record business, the artist usually had minimal control over the end product, as that was the domain of the producer. As the business developed, and more and more artists demanded and received artistic control, the producer assigned to help the artist record was often an independent contractor from outside the label who was amenable to the musician's artistic wishes, as long as they fit the vision of the label. After some success (that is, hit records), many artists even bore responsibility for production as well.

After the song or album was recorded, the label pressed the vinyl record (and later, the cassette and CD) and distributed it to dedicated retail record stores either through the label's own distribution network or via an independent network of distributors, rack jobbers, one-stops, and wholesalers—which, under the right circumstances, placed the record in every record store, diner, car wash, department store, and anywhere else where floor space could be rented.

At that point, the structure looked like this:

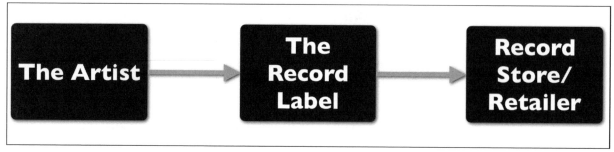

Figure 1-2: Music Product Flow

The record label was also responsible for the marketing of the record, which centered around radio airplay. If a record could get a sufficient amount of airplay, it would probably sell well (as long as the record was in the stores and available to buy at the same time it was being played on the radio).

The other thing is how people consumed content in those days, which was that people mostly listened to the radio. Then the Japanese came up with the transistor radio, which was portable. Suddenly portability meant that the consumer didn't have to sit in their living room in front of that radio. That was the start of something else from a distribution point of view. You can look at all the things that changed, but then you look at the transistor radio and think, "Gosh, the portability was so important."

—Rupert Perry

Airplay was crucial to the success of a record and resulted in large promotion departments within the record labels dedicated to getting radio airplay. Competition for airplay became so fierce that promotion departments began to resort to using gifts of cash, prostitutes, vacations, and anything that would influence a radio station's program director to place a song in rotation. This was known as "payola," a practice that eventually was outlawed and subsequently resulted in several scandals and investigations of the record and radio industries and the way they did business together.

PAYOLA BECOMES PLAYOLA

Not surprisingly, pay-to-play has come to the digital age as a new form of payola now attempts to influence what consumers listen to. Playlist promotion, or "playola," has become a big part of the promotional campaigns for many managers and labels. If a track is added to a popular playlist, its streams will spike and listeners will add it to their personal playlists, which sometimes adds a viral element that spreads to playlists on other networks as well.

As an example, a Spotify playlist created by tech entrepreneur Sean Parker has over 800,000 followers and was widely credited for breaking Lorde's "Royals." What's more, hot playlists are now watched by radio programmers to see both what's trending and what's not.

Prices for playlist promotion can be as little as $100, to a small blogger with a modest following, to as much as $10,000 for a six-week campaign for a major playlist owner.

The structure then looked like this:

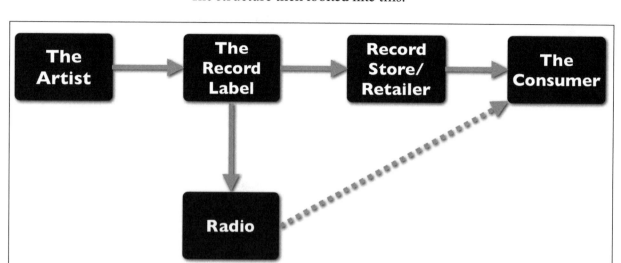

Figure 1-3: Full Music 1.0 Distribution Chain

In order to avoid being prosecuted for payola, record labels decreased the use of their in-house promotion departments and instead began to use independent promoters, on the theory that anything a third-party promoter offered to a program director essentially eliminated the label's legal responsibility. (The courts eventually found it to be illegal anyway.) Regardless, radio airplay was the key to a hit, and promotion was the key to radio airplay.

The structure for the Music 1.0 way of doing business finally evolved into this:

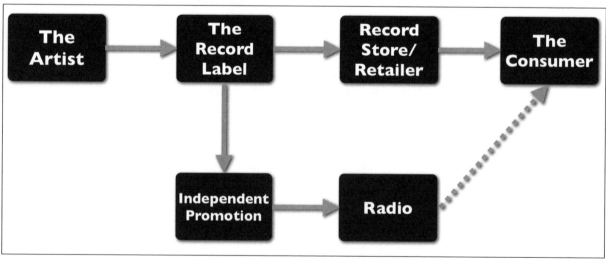

Figure 1-4: Music 1.0 Distribution Chain to Avoid Payola

With the exception of limited exposure to the consumer via fan clubs and in-store album signings, the artist was segregated from the consumer and distribution chain. The artist might have done some occasional promotion on radio, but his or her connection with the music consumer was limited. Luckily, interaction and communication with the fan wasn't needed much at this time, thanks to the overwhelming influence of radio, the 800-pound gorilla in the room of Music 1.0.

Music 1.0 gave in to lots of record-label foibles in addition to payola. In order to exaggerate chart position, labels would fudge sales by having record stores intentionally report that a record was selling even if it wasn't. This practice was later put to rest with the implementation of SoundScan technology, which would compute sales via the scanned bar code on each album or CD. Although it seems like a fair way to determine actual sales, SoundScan used a system that would weight a sale in each territory differently, causing a sale in a large city such as Chicago to have a greater determination on the chart position than a sale in Grand Rapids—a point that caused heated debate throughout the industry.

Another standard industry practice of the time used to game the system was to hire college students to go to what was deemed an important record store and buy a particular record to make it chart higher. This technique proved to be successful in that it was much more difficult to police than other methods previously used.

Another interesting practice of the era was the "shipped platinum" syndrome. To exaggerate sales, labels would ship huge numbers of records and then state that the record "shipped platinum" (meaning it sold enough to be certified as a platinum-selling record, with sales over one million units), insinuating that the demand was so great that the units shipped were presold. It usually wasn't reported, however, when the records were returned to the label in platinum numbers if the public turned a deaf ear to the product.

MUSIC 1.0

The record label is all-powerful.

The artist is isolated from fans.

Radio is the key to hits.

Artists are given multiple release opportunities for long-term development.

It's a singles world.

But the album makes more money.

MUSIC 1.5: THE SUITS TAKE OVER

The era of Music 1.5 produced the greatest level of business that the industry has seen or is ever likely to see.

When the CD was released in 1982, record companies got a boost to ever-greater profits in several ways. Because the technology was initially expensive, the labels increased the retail price on each CD while decreasing the royalty rate to the artist, supposedly because of the "technology expense" that was involved. While the retail price never decreased even after the technology was amortized (the retail price increased, in fact), artists eventually saw this royalty charge eliminated. *Breakage*, a 10 percent charge against royalties and a leftover from the days when vinyl records would break in transit (which became irrelevant in the new CD age), was another contract clause that was never removed from typical recording contracts during this period, giving the record labels an extra 10 percent piece of the sales pie.

Perhaps the biggest shot in the arm to record labels was the ability to resell their catalog to a public eager to switch to CDs and buy a copy of an album they already owned on vinyl. Catalog sales (sales of records from an artist before his or her most recent) increased profits because production costs were minimal (just the cost of pressing the CD), as were promotional costs. Consumers bought the new and better-sounding (to some) CD to supplement their newfound CD collections, thereby providing a financial windfall for the labels deep with catalog items.

Record companies now had a cash cow that shot profits through the financial stratosphere, which immediately gained the attention of Wall Street.

Always the poor stepchild of the entertainment industry, the music business was suddenly every investment banker's darling, with the remaining four of the six major labels that were still independently controlled eventually sold to multinational conglomerates during this period. Columbia Records was bought by Sony (eventually becoming Sony Music); Warner Bros. Records by magazine publishing colossus Time Inc. (becoming Time-Warner); Universal Music by the Japanese tech giant Matsushita (later purchased by Vivendi); and EMI by British electronics company Thorn Electrical Industries. Polygram was already owned by a conglomerate (the Dutch electronics company Philips), and BMG was owned by the German media giant Bertelsmann AG. Now, all six major labels were under conglomerate control.

> *The other big thing that happened was the compact disc. When it came along, there was a big up-surge in the growth of the business, and a lot of large corporations began to take notice. When CBS, who was the king of the business at the time, sold their record business to Sony—that was huge! It was a momentous happening because CBS decided they wanted to exit the music business, which they had been in for years.*
>
> —Rupert Perry

With conglomerate ownership came MBAs, accountants, and attorneys running the business—a major departure from the seat-of-the-pants, street-smart music men such as Mo Ostin, Ahmet Ertegan, Jac Holtzman, Berry Gordy, and Howie Stein, who could feel a hit in their bones. Where previously a label would nurture artists or groups through three, four, even five albums until they broke through with the public, the new corporate structure demanded instant results "this quarter." Artist development, so crucial to the careers of the stars and superstars that we consider legends today, died—slowly at first, then faster and faster as bottom-line results became the mantra.

The Rise of MTV
About this time, another unexpected boost came to the music industry in the form of a small cable television network startup called MTV. Suddenly, music was on television, and a new avenue of exposure increased sales yet again. MTV soon had the power to "make"

a hit, just like radio previously could, by the simple act of placing a music video in heavy rotation.

Although no one expected it at the time, the message behind The Buggles' song "Video Killed the Radio Star" (which was the first video ever played on MTV) actually came to pass. Image soon became much more important than musical ability. If you didn't look appealing, you weren't getting on MTV, and if you didn't get on MTV, your chances of having a hit diminished greatly. Quickly, the newfound corporate culture began to shift gears to find good-looking "musicians" to fill the bill. Artistry became just one component of a new act instead of *the* component, as image became foremost in the label mindset.

To an executive unfamiliar with the record business, art doesn't make sense. Business demands repeatable outcomes, and art is not a part of that equation. Craft was a big part of the corporate hit-making formula, though. First, find an artist similar to whoever is the most popular at the moment. Then get a successful songwriter to write the perfect generic (usually pop) song, add a producer with a proven track record, and then record it all in a studio where big hits have been previously made and with the musicians who have played on those hits. The actual "artist" matters little in this corporate scenario. He or she had better look great, though, because the music videos (put together by directors, choreographers, and stylists with recent hits on their résumés) must project the image that Madison Avenue deems necessary to sell product, since that's ultimately who's footing the bill.

The Farm Teams Disband

Unfortunately, the passage of the drunk-driving laws in 1983 negatively affected long-term artist development in a real way. Prior to 1972, the legal drinking age ranged from 18 to 21, depending upon the state, but the war in Vietnam brought about the "If I can fight for my country, I should be able to drink" argument (which we're seeing again today). By 1972, most states agreed that if you were old enough to vote and fight for your country, then it should be legal for you to partake in an alcoholic beverage, and the drinking age was lowered to 18 years old countrywide. This opened the floodgates to clubs far and wide to accommodate a whole new set of thirsty patrons, and the way to get them in the door was to provide live entertainment.

Clubs sprang up everywhere, and live music thrived. If you were a half-decent band, you could easily find somewhere to play almost every night of the week, and get paid for it too ("pay-to-play" didn't exist at the time).

This was great for the music business because it gave neophyte musicians a place to get it together both musically and performance-wise. Just like The Beatles did in Hamburg in 1962, a band could play five sets a night for seven nights a week and really hone their chops. Do that for a year or two, and you were ready to take the next step toward doing your own thing, if that's what you wanted to do.

Unfortunately, it was also easy to fall into the trap of just playing clubs forever because the money was so good, but those with ambition took their club days for what they were and moved on up. They had learned what they needed by constantly playing the hits in front of crowds.

Since the drinking age was raised nationwide to 21 in 1982, the excitement and diversity in music has steadily decreased. Music has become bland and homogenized, and there are longer periods between new musical trends. This is because of the large-scale reduction of the club scene due to the higher drinking age and the tougher DUI laws. A higher drinking age and more arrests meant fewer club patrons. Fewer club patrons meant goodbye to the many previously packed clubs that served as on-the-job training for up-and-coming musicians. To use a baseball analogy, the farm teams (the feeder system that supplies players to the major leagues) disbanded.

This musical support infrastructure is greatly diminished these days. A band that is considered to be working a lot today is lucky if it plays a show once a week. That means it will take a group a lot longer not only to become more comfortable in front of crowds, but also to become musically and vocally tight. The longer it takes a band to make progress, the more likely it will break up or change its direction, which means that perhaps the next great trend in music has shriveled on the vine.

Musicians need the constant feedback and attention that only an audience can provide. The more you play live, the better you get at it, which leads to more experimenting, which means the more likely you are to find your own voice.

MUSIC 1.5

Major labels now are owned by conglomerates.

Quarterly profits take precedence over art.

Many album songs are just filler.

MTV is created and plays a significant role in record sales.

The artist's image becomes more important than the music.

DUI laws kill the farm team.

MUSIC 2.0: ENTER THE DIGITAL AGE

The day the first MP3 music file was shared was the first day of Music 2.0 (sometime around 1994). Although no one knew it at the time, this became the disruption that would one day bring the music industry to its knees.

> *If we roll forward to the start of the Internet in 1993, people in the content industry didn't get just how monumental the change was. To have any form of content available through a computer was a totally new form of distribution, but the difference was that the record label had no control over it. Up until that point, any of the media distributors (film, television, or music) were always able to control the distribution, and when you did that, you could decide where it went, who got it, and what people paid for it. With the Internet, that went out the window fast.*
>
> —Rupert Perry

Until the MP3 arrived, a CD-quality digital file of a song was large in size (a little over 5 MB for every one minute of a stereo song) and took a lot of bandwidth to stream (1,411 kbps), which meant that it was just about impossible to play over the Internet given the severely limited bandwidth available at the time. The same file encoded with the MP3 format would be about a tenth of the file size if the bandwidth was between 128 kbps and 256 kbps, which would make the file easy to download even on the primitive dial-up network connections available during that period.

Using an MP3 codec is like letting the air out of a bicycle tire: the tire becomes small enough to fit into a tiny box, yet it's the same tire. The MP3 codec "let the air out" of a digital file, making it a lot smaller. Although the audio quality of the MP3 wasn't as good as what was on a CD, consumers had previously shown when they heartily adopted cassette tapes that audio quality wasn't a major issue in their purchasing and listening decisions.

P2P Makes Its Mark

Peer-to-peer (shortened to P2P) networking was the second new technology that changed the music business during this era. In a peer-to-peer network, each computer on the network can supply and receive files to every other computer on the network without using a central server, with bandwidth and processing distributed among all members of the network. In other words, files live on multiple interconnected users' computers, with each user able to download a file (or pieces of the same file from multiple computers) from anyone he or she is connected to (see Figure 1-5).

Napster was the first of the many massively popular peer-to-peer file-distribution systems, although it was not totally peer-to-peer

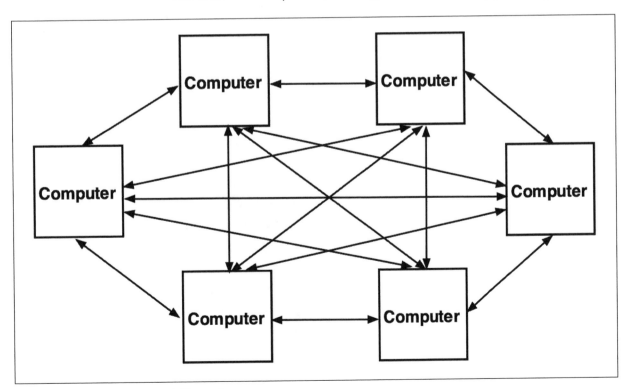

Figure 1-5: A Peer-to-Peer (P2P) Network

because it used central servers to maintain lists of connected systems and their files (a factor in their later legal undoing). Although there were already networks that facilitated the distribution of files across the Internet (such as IRC, Hotline, and UseNet), Napster specialized exclusively in music and, as a result of its enormous popularity, offered a huge selection of music to download.

Shortly after its inception, the company was presented with multiple legal challenges from artists (Metallica, Dr. Dre, Madonna), record labels (A&M), and the music industry itself (the RIAA) regarding copyright infringement, and it was eventually shut down in July of 2001. Napster use peaked in February 2001, with 26.4 million users worldwide, which seems laughably low today but was enormous at the time.

MP3.com, started in 1999, was another similar service, although it primarily featured independent music instead of signed acts. Sued by Universal Music Group for copyright violations, the company settled for an out-of-court payment of $200 million to UMG and was essentially put out of business. At its peak, MP3.com delivered more than 4 million MP3 audio files per day to over 800,000 unique users and had a customer base of 25 million registered users. The company was eventually purchased by Roxio and renamed Napster, then purchased again by big-box retailer Best Buy in 2011, and then merged with streaming music provider Rhapsody in June 2013. It now provides legal paid downloads and a subscription streaming service.

Although the original Napster and MP3.com were shut down by court order, they paved the way for decentralized, peer-to-peer file-distribution programs, such as Gnutella and Limewire (shut down in 2010 but restructured in a "Pirate Edition"), which were much harder to control. As a result, the RIAA aggressively prosecuted users who used those services, despite the outcry from the public and the industry.

After a short period of aggressive prosecutions, the RIAA backed off from taking legal action when it was determined that it was spending millions in legal fees only to recover paltry amounts in damages, not to mention the harm incurred to the industry's overall reputation as a result. More importantly, it was found that user prosecutions actually had little deterrent effect, and piracy numbers remained the same, although publicly the industry claimed otherwise.

Piracy Takes Another Form

Another major disruption of the traditional music business came as a result of the inexpensive CD burner, and its impact cannot be underestimated. In the days of vinyl, unauthorized manufacturing was almost unheard of because of the economics of a pirating operation. Pressing a vinyl record required large, costly, and specialized gear that was beyond the ability of even the most dedicated enthusiast. When the CD was introduced, the first CD recorders were found only in professional mastering studios because of their cost (about $250,000, with blank CDs costing $200 each). Economics kept the pirates and the casual traders at bay.

Of course, the audiotape cassette, from its very inception in 1964, was a thorn in the music industry's side. Using the compact, relatively inexpensive (around $1.00 for a blank tape), and easy-to-use cassettes, home tapers could record a hit song off the radio with ease. Generally providing mediocre audio quality, the cassette was the first example of quality being a minor consideration when compared with price.

When the CD burner began to come built in to just about every computer, and blank CDs fell below the $1.00 level, digital music rapidly became a runaway train speeding down a slippery mountain: you could try everything to stop it, but once it reached terminal velocity, there was no halting it. And so began the digital age of the record industry.

MUSIC 2.0

Digital music arrives.

Peer-to-peer music pirating arrives, too.

Digital music trading begins.

CD ripping/burning takes a bite out of sales.

The record labels are complacent.

MUSIC 2.5: DIGITAL MUSIC IS MONETIZED

Soon it became apparent that unless the music industry jumped on board with digital music, it would be left behind in an ocean of digits. Ironically, it was the computer industry that threw the music industry a lifeline. While different digital-music services presented alternatives to the labels for paid downloads, Apple Computer's iTunes proved to be the business model that worked. Basically a closed system, because iTunes initially required Apple's iPod digital music player (the platform choices were later expanded), iTunes was a winner with consumers for its ease of use (a trait Apple is known for) and the iPod's newfound place as a fashion accessory. Now the industry could finally monetize its digital offerings. But at $0.99 per track, there wasn't a lot left for profit (see Figure 1-6).

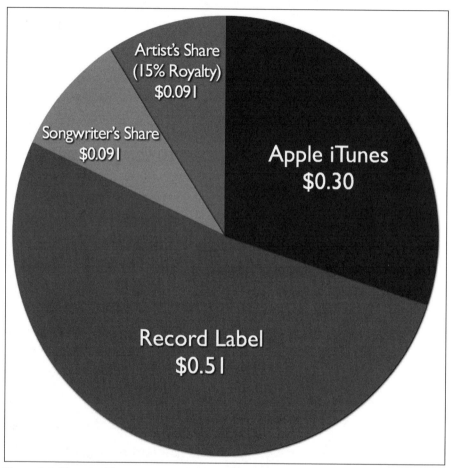

Figure 1-6: How the Money from an iTunes Song Is Distributed (in Cents)

Released in January 2001, iTunes was an instant success that was followed by frequent and significant upgrades. In late 2001, iPod support was implemented, which started the snowball down the hill for the industry as digital music began to become the rage. In 2003, the iTunes store was introduced, and both the consumer and Apple have never looked back. In the years since, movies, television shows, music videos, podcasts, applications, and video games have been added to the extensive iTunes Store's catalog. In April of 2009, the iTunes store went to a tiered pricing structure after much prodding by the major labels. Songs are now available for $0.69, $0.99, or $1.29. At the time this book was written, over 35 billion songs have been downloaded since the service first launched on April 28, 2003.

While iTunes is the monster of the digital-music industry, other worthy competitors have emerged. From Amazon MP3 to eMusic to Google Play, consumers can buy songs from numerous places online, though the popularity of the practice is dwindling. There are now even more places to listen to music when streaming services like Spotify, Pandora, and Deezer are taken into account. Of course, Apple has also entered the streaming ranks with Apple Music, as has YouTube Red, which threatens to shift the entire digital music paradigm once again. We'll go over these in more detail in Chapter 10, "The New Distribution."

Monetized digital music also brought about another big change with the return to a singles business that was similar to the '50s and early '60s. Rather than being forced to buy an album of ten songs in order to get the one he or she liked, the consumer could now buy only the songs that he or she wanted.

The entire economics of the music industry had been centered on the album format and the money it generated, so returning to the single-song purchase was a major blow to the financial model that had been in place for 40 years.

Overhead had been set up for sales that were in $10.00 increments (the approximate wholesale price of an album). That was suddenly cut to sales that were in increments of less than $1.00 (the sale of a download), and the labels' financial structures were shaken to their cores.

This was further exacerbated in the shift to streaming revenues, which operated on another smaller level altogether at fractions of a cent per stream.

Enter the 360 Deal

To make up for the lost revenue, the major labels needed income streams that went beyond the sale of the CD, and the logical place to get that was from the artist.

Since it's always been understood that 90 percent or more of an artist's income comes from touring, the record labels saw that as a potential income source and wanted a piece, and so they launched what came to be known as "360 deals." The term *360 deal* means that the record label shares in the income from all income streams available to an artist beyond just the music recordings, including consistent revenue generators like publishing, merchandise, and touring. The label would, in effect, become an artist's manager and share in everything he or she made.

You can see why a record label would want to share in all the income streams of an artist, but you have to wonder why an artist would want to let them. The argument goes that if the label's expertise is in selling music (which really isn't selling all that well), then what kind of management experience does it have?

For a while, even major artists like Robbie Williams and Nicki Minaj signed some form of a 360 deal with a major label (although Minaj has since renegotiated), but these deals are on the wane as artist representatives become more savvy and DIY resources become more widespread.

In the meantime, traditional artist management was becoming even more powerful because the manager was now required to make more decisions for the artist than ever before. With the influence of the record labels waning, it was now up to the manager to find new sources of income, to deal with potential sponsors, to handle social media, and to make deals with online digital distributors, among other things.

With much of the sales and marketing now in the hands of the artist, managers had incrementally larger responsibilities than in previous eras, and their guidance and impact became that much more valuable to the artist.

MUSIC 2.5 OVERVIEW

Digital music is monetized.

Sales change from album to singles (no more album filler).

Major labels try to impose 360 deals on artists.

Management becomes more important than ever.

MUSIC 3.0: THE DAWN OF ARTIST/FAN COMMUNICATION

The biggest change that came with Music 3.0 is that the structure of the business was reshaped. In M3.0, the middlemen could be cut out of the loop. The artist and the fan could keep in touch directly on any and every level they chose, from creation to promotion to marketing to sales. But merely staying in touch with a fan can be as fleeting as it sometimes is with friends or family. True fans, just like friends and family, want regular communication, and whether artists know it or not, so do they. The structure of M3.0 looked like this:

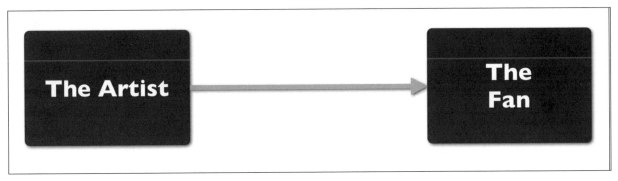

Figure 1-7: Music 3.0

Music 3.0 allowed the artists to promote and market directly to the fans. If they can reach the fans, they can make them aware of their products (music, event tickets, videos, and merchandise). If they can reach the fans, they can sell directly to them (although "offer them a product" might be a better way of putting it).

Most importantly, Music 3.0 allowed the artists to have conversations with the fans in order to help the artists with sales and marketing. What do the fans want? Just ask them. Do the fans want to be alerted when the artists come to town? Do the fans want remixed versions of songs? Would fans be interested in premium box sets? By the artists just asking, the fans will gladly let them know, and this is the essence of Music 3.0—communication between the fans and the artists.

Another factor in M3.0 is that the audience became niche oriented. From Swahili polka to Mandarin madrigal, if an artist searched long enough, he or she could find an audience. Although stratification of the audience meant more opportunities for more artists, it also meant that the possibility of a huge, multimillion-selling breakout hit diminished as fewer people were exposed to a single musical genre than ever before. Nearly gone were the days when a television appearance, heavy-rotation radio, or MTV airplay alone could propel an artist to platinum-level success.

MUSIC 3.0

The middleman can be eliminated.

Direct artist-to-fan communication pervades.

Direct marketing approaches can be offered to the fan.

Direct sales can be offered to the fan.

The audience is stratified.

MUSIC 3.5: YOUTUBE BECOMES THE NEW RADIO

As Music 3.0 progressed into 2012, music consumers gradually transitioned their music consumption to a new medium that somewhat replaced an old one. Although traditional terrestrial radio continues to be the principal way that all age groups discover new music (primarily thanks to the car radio), the crucial teen demographic not only prefers discovering music on YouTube, but actually listens to it there as well. According to Edison Research's annual Infinite Dial report, two-thirds of all Americans between the ages of 12 and 24 use YouTube as their major source of music consumption, and that number continues to grow.

It's a fact that YouTube has evolved into a major music destination site and has grown to become number one in music discovery online, as well as in music search, both of which are critical to the health of the industry. Music has become the number one content category on YouTube globally, partially because YouTube is available for free in web browsers and on most smart phones, and the music there is easily accessible and can be shared with friends simply via social media.

Part of YouTube's success in music came from the fact that the major labels were initially reluctant to authorize streaming services like Spotify and Pandora, so YouTube proved to be an easily available alternative. Plus, many streaming services weren't licensed to stream the songs of some of the major stars, like The Beatles, The Eagles, Pink Floyd, and Metallica, but you could find just about anything you wanted from any artist on YouTube via a user-generated upload.

While major labels continued to place a good deal of their faith and marketing money in traditional media like print and radio, indie artists like Psy, Gotye, Macklemore, and Baauer ("Harlem Shake") finally began to break out from their YouTube plays, using video views as the major marketing tool to propel themselves to the top of the charts.

This was the fruition of the promise that Music 3.0 held, where an unknown artist could actually have a hit without being signed to a major label, at least in the beginning. The fact is that all these artists eventually signed distribution deals with record labels in order to make their music more available to the public, but these were more license agreements than the traditional major recording contracts that used to be a requirement for a recording to hit the charts.

YouTube Exposure Becomes Universal

Perhaps the best thing about YouTube is that it's color blind when it comes to genres, providing an opportunity for exposure to some that would not have had a chance in a previous musical era.

Take the case of Ukrainian classical pianist Valentina Lisitsa, who began uploading her performance videos after her stage career stalled. Now, with more than 87 million views and 200,000 channel subscribers, not only has her career been revived, but it is flourishing. Then there's Gummibar, the brainchild of German producers Moritz Bad and Christian André Schneider, who have created one of the most successful acts of all time in terms of children's music, with channel views of over 3 billion!

Although it might seem like the public is focused on pop music, YouTube is proving to be surprisingly musically democratic, which again speaks to the changes brought about after Music 3.0.

Streaming Catches On

One of the byproducts of listening to music on YouTube is that the public became used to streaming, and with that comfort level came a gradual flourishing of streaming services, led by the proliferation of Pandora and Spotify's introduction in the United States. Music consumers began to see that having access to tens of millions of songs at any time was preferable to purchasing a few a month and clogging their hard drives.

The idea behind a streaming or "access" service is that you pay a set monthly fee to listen to as much music as you want during that time, with no limitations. The music is streamed, so you don't actually own it, but since it's available at any time, there's really no need to keep it on your computer, phone, or mobile device anyway.

Most of these services work on a "freemium" basis, where usage is either free with ads or capped after a certain number of hours per month. The difficulty is not getting consumers to adopt the streaming service in the first place, but getting them to upgrade to the paid tier. That, coupled with the fact that the majority of a streaming company's revenue is paid out as royalties to labels, publishers, and performance rights organizations, makes the future of some of the services (even some of the larger ones) somewhat tenuous.

That said, record labels have long dreamed of a paid subscription service that the majority of music consumers participate in because they like the idea of a more-or-less fixed monthly income stream as a result of their license agreement with the service.

The artists aren't as keen, however, since much of the money collected by the labels is not passed on in what they feel is an equitable fashion (see Chapter 9). Publishers are dubious as well, noting the high cost of administration versus the income generated (see Chapter 11). Regardless, although the number of registered subscribers is expanding, music subscription hasn't reached anything near critical mass yet.

During this period, many artists saw streaming in another way, since millions of streams at fractions of a cent each (we'll cover the subject more in Chapters 11 and 12) resulted in such meager payouts that they couldn't help but feel exploited. Which brings us to Music 4.0.

MUSIC 3.5

YouTube replaces radio for teens.

Music becomes the top content category for YouTube globally.

YouTube becomes the top place online for music discovery and search.

Indie artists break out big from YouTube views.

Streaming music picks up speed.

Artists complain about meager royalty payouts.

MUSIC 4.0: STREAMING BECOMES PROFITABLE

Music 4.0 was an era when a tipping point was reached, and streaming (or more accurately, the ability to "access" music) became profitable for the entire musical supply chain, from songwriters to artists to publishers to labels to the streaming services themselves. Let's look at how this happened.

Although the streaming market had been limited to Spotify, Pandora, Slacker, Rdio, Deezer, and a number of smaller services, they accounted for 41 million paying customers at the end of 2014, worth around $2 billion globally. A study by ABI Research predicts that figure will rise to 191 million customers worth a whopping $46 billion by the end of 2018, but this seems optimistic to say the least. That said, many feel that it's possible for streaming revenue to give the music industry its first healthy increase since it peaked in 1999.

That may seem like a pipe dream but for the fact that the major new entrant into the market is Apple Music, which has 850 million users worldwide, each with a credit card on file. Even prior to the introduction of Apple Music, iTunes users spent an average of only around $10 a year on music (according to Apple), down from a high of $72 in 2010. The real test will be how many of those 850 million users Apple can convert to customers paying $10 per month.

Other major players in the streaming music wars with significantly deep financial pockets include YouTube's new music subscription service and Amazon's Prime Music, which has yet to make the move into the mainstream. These services are all global, which means that they could reach far more potential consumers than ever before.

Couple that with the fact that consumers have already seen the light when it comes to streaming and are adopting it faster than anticipated. The first time a music fan runs out of room on a hard drive or storage device because it's filled to the brim with music files, the value of streaming music becomes very apparent. Once the consumer tries a service and realizes she has more than 20 million songs at her fingertips anytime and anywhere, she's sold.

What that means is that although each individual royalty stream might be small, there will be many more of them to make up the difference, much like music publishing experienced with the rise of the 200-channel cable television universe. Simply put, more users plus more streams plus more distributors equals more revenue, which every artist, musician, and songwriter (labels and publishers, too) should love. In Music 4.0, the "access" model revived the music business.

MUSIC 4.0

Streaming becomes the preferred method of consuming music.

New streaming services enter the space.

More revenue streams come from different sources.

The music industry's global revenue increases as a result.

MUSIC 4.1: THE BUSINESS MODEL CHANGES

In the Music 4.1 era, which we're entering now, both record labels and publishers discover how outdated their existing business models are and set out to change to something more nimble and fitting for the digital age.

Music is becoming more and more a digital product, which means that the old Music 1.5 thinking must be abandoned in order to thrive. As the older executives steeped in the CD begin to retire, new execs come on board with a distinctly fresher outlook that will enable their company's margins to increase, which means that profits also grow even if the revenue continues to shrink.

Catalog is the lifeblood of a music label, estimated to be 50 percent of its revenue but with 200 percent higher profit than new hits. The problem is that new music takes up 90 percent of the head count of a label, and that may lead to fewer new artist signings than ever before as the labels cut back on the less profitable parts of the business.

With new artists becoming ever more DIY, labels can afford to spend less on developing new music and wait for artists to become moderately successful before signing them, making them less of a risk. This would eliminate many of the staff positions, especially at the majors, further streamlining an already bloated entity.

What this all means is that the artist of today has to be more and more in control of her career and be more adept at marketing and promotion than ever before.

MUSIC 4.1

Record labels streamline their operations.

Labels sign fewer artists and provide smaller advances.

Artists need to be more hands-on and DIY than ever.

While remnants of the old Music 1.5 structure still exist (record labels, brick-and-mortar record stores, terrestrial radio, MTV, and so on) and can even be useful to the Music 4.1 artist, they will probably never again be the primary driving factor in the success of any artist. In a roundabout way, they never really were (the music is always the defining factor), although their influence was admittedly higher in the past.

It's said that a record label never signed an act because of its music; it signed the act for the number of fans it either already had or had the potential of developing. If you had lines around the block waiting to see you play, the music didn't matter to the label, because you had an audience that was willing to buy it.

So it is with Music 4.1, only now you can develop that audience in a more efficient way and actually make a living with a limited but rabid fan base (see the section "The 1,000 True Fans Theory" in Chapter 14).

The rest of this book is about how to make use of the benefits that Music 4.1 affords an artist.

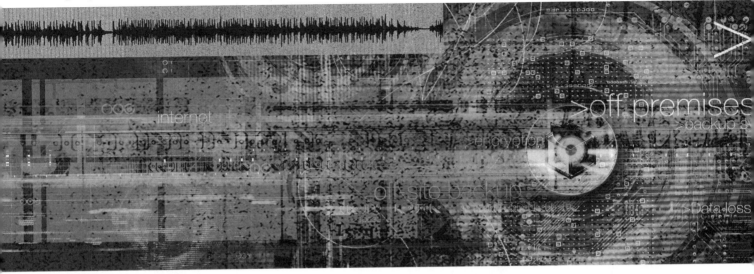

CHAPTER 2

How the Music World Has Changed

Just like everything else technological, the music business has changed considerably in the past few years, and it continues to change at a rapid pace. Although we've seen industry evolution before, never has there been one as dramatic as what started in M3.0. Although the phrase has been overused, the paradigm has truly shifted, and many of the traditional players in the industry have new, less prominent roles. Let's look at some of them.

WHO'S IN CONTROL?

Although it may not be readily apparent, Wall Street and Madison Avenue indirectly control what remains of the M2.5 music industry through their tremendous influence on the financial bottom lines of record labels, record stores, concert promotion, radio, and television.

If you're owned by a publicly traded conglomerate (as most major labels, major concert promoters, and radio and television stations are), then you're in the business of selling stock, not servicing the consumer.

What that means is that nothing matters more than quarterly earnings. To keep those earnings as high as possible, Wall Street turns to Madison Avenue to devise the best marketing strategies to sell to its customers. Madison Avenue (in the form of the major advertising agencies) can bring in the big ad dollars, but only under certain content conditions (such as programming that is tailored around the advertising), and the process repeats itself over and over.

The advertising industry (Madison Avenue), not the music industry, therefore indirectly drives the new music cycle in the United States, at least on radio and traditional media.

From M2.5 onward, it's all about passing focus-group tests, which have separated listeners into the distinct demographic groups that advertisers can tell stock analysts they have micromarketed their products to. As a result, radio, television, and live performances are no longer about aggregating and entertaining large audiences, but rather just a group of market niches. The bright side to this fact is that there's one heck of an opportunity opening up for folks who don't get hung up on trying to sell via traditional advertising.

Wall Street and Madison Avenue have tried to redefine what music means to people, but most music consumers have voted with their wallets by refusing to buy any new recordings on the scale that was previously expected (with the possible exception of Adele, who continues to be a singular phenomenon).

The view of the vast majority of consumers is that fewer new recordings are worth buying compared to those released a couple decades ago, and this has become the dilemma of the industry. You have to sell product to survive, but it's impossible to develop that product while trying to please your corporate masters. It might work when selling soap or clothing or any other consumer product, but a creative endeavor like music just doesn't work the same way. It's too personal, both to the artist and to the consumer, to be a mass-market product.

BEHIND-THE-SCENES CONTROL

**Wall Street and Madison Avenue
control the media.**

**Record labels need to keep stock price
and quarterly profits high.**

**Radio and television play only what appeals
to advertisers.**

**Consumers are divided into
demographic groups.**

Music becomes devalued.

WHERE DID THE RECORD STORES GO?

Sales of physical product, such as CDs, are way down in the music business (off by almost 80 percent since 2000, according to RIAA statistics), and a major reason for this is that consumers often can't find the product when they want to buy it. It used to be that almost every town had some kind of store where you could buy recorded music, but now even major shopping malls around the country are CD-barren wastelands.

Since 2003, 3,500 music retailers have closed, according to the Almighty Institute of Music Retail, an industry research group. Now, fewer than 2,500 dedicated retail music stores are left (although around 12,000 retail outlets sell prerecorded music of some type).

So where did the music retailers go? Like so much else in M1.0 through M2.0, music retailing was once a thriving business that had no shortage of customers, but several factors throughout the years delivered a knockout blow from which the retail part of the industry now finds it difficult to recover.

First came the closing of the large music retail chains, such as Tower (93 stores), the Wherehouse (320 stores), and Sam Goody (1,300 stores), all now defunct.

While initially good for business, these chains began to put price pressure on the small, independent retailers that had been the backbone of the industry. If you can buy it cheaper from the chain store, that's where you'll go, and so the buying public did.

But soon, the retail music chain stores got a taste of their own medicine. In the '90s, Best Buy, Target, and Walmart began to stock CDs as a loss leader in order to get customers in the door to buy their pricier merchandise. This combination of the music-buying experience along with traditional shopping proved hard to beat.

Soon, these three mega-retailers were responsible for more than half of all CD sales, and their leverage hit home with record labels and traditional record retailers alike.

The music retail chains, finding it impossible to compete with CDs priced at wholesale prices and below, soon closed, leaving only a dwindling number of independent stores. Ironically, all three mega-retailers have now decreased their in-store inventory to only Top 40 selections and are looking to trim that even more in the future.

Then came the rise of M2.5, and as digital music files (MP3s) penetrated the consciousness of the consumer, soon CD sales began to drop year after year. Digital piracy, online CD sales, CD copying via CD burners, paid digital downloads, and the lack of new music trends and blockbuster products caused the number of music retailers to fall to unprecedented low levels.

Even the highest-grossing record store in the country, Virgin Records in New York City's Times Square, closed in 2009—not because it was losing money, but because more money could potentially be generated from the rental of the real estate to another business. So even when a new blockbuster music product that everyone wants exists, you can't buy it if you can't find it.

Many of the indie record stores that are left have been forced to diversify in order to keep the doors open, concentrating more on hard-to-get box sets, books (yet another industry in flux), and music accessories and merchandise. While vinyl records have been a temporary boon to indie retailers, with sales in 2015 increasing by a whopping 30 percent (according to Nielsen), they still represent only about 9 percent of the business, totaling about 12 million units sold (not counting used sales). The used vinyl market, even though it's small, continues to thrive.

What does the future hold for the record store? No less than Sir Richard Branson, whose initial fortune came from his string of Virgin Megastores in the United Kingdom, predicts that there will be no record stores left anywhere in the world by the year 2020. That assessment may be a bit radical, but we can be pretty sure the number will continue on a downward spiral in the future.

REASONS FOR THE RECORD STORE DECLINE

Online purchasing.

Loss leaders from Best Buy, Walmart, and Target.

Digital pirating.

CD burners.

Fewer blockbuster releases.

The rise of the MP3.

WHY TRADITIONAL RADIO IS NO LONGER THE FACTOR IT ONCE WAS

Broadcast radio was once the lifeblood of the music industry. Even moderate airplay of a song could be enough to establish an artist, while heavy rotation of enough of his or her songs could almost guarantee the artist's long-term career success. Today, radio is just a shell of its former self, far less relevant in its impact on the success of an artist, thanks to limited and homogenized playlists and the rise of music discovery on YouTube and social media.

How has radio gone from Holy Grail to dirty coffee cup? Radio has undergone its own version of technological morphing, paralleling that of the music industry.

In the early days of radio, each station was locally owned and reflected the tastes of the community and region, including the music. Much of the great music from the '50s through the '70s came about as a result of these local tastes. From Philadelphia to Detroit to Memphis to Cleveland to Chicago to Houston to Los Angeles, each region had its own distinct sound.

Another factor in radio's rise was the relative freedom that disc jockeys enjoyed, being able to play just about any record they liked. In the late '60s and '70s, this freedom hit its apex on FM radio, as people tuned in specifically because they trusted the taste of the DJ. You could hear back-to-back a raga from Ravi Shankar, hard rock from Led Zeppelin, jazz from Miles Davis, and acoustic folk music from Richie Havens. With listeners flocking to the major FM stations in each region of the country, the DJ was your personal music guide, who could take you to new musical destinations if you just let him or her.

During this period, FM radio was considered a poor stepchild to AM because the proliferation of FM radio was just beginning, and its advertising revenues were still relatively low. As a result, large station ownership groups generally overlooked the format as a potential source of revenue.

But money always follows listeners, and soon FM radio was raking in big advertising dollars, which attracted major players from both Wall Street and Madison Avenue looking for a new income stream. Soon, local AM and FM stations were purchased by station groups, and then the station groups by conglomerates.

In an effort to maximize profits, radio "consultants" were hired to review the stations' playlists and make them more listener friendly. When this happened, the DJ lost all freedom of what to play as the playlists were tightened. The consultants even picked the time when the songs they chose could be played.

Since the same consultant was determining the playlists for the entire station group, stations using the same formats were playing the same songs virtually everywhere in the country, regardless of the region. Radio became homogenized and stale.

Worse still was the fact that what had always been a localized medium soon became anything but, with some stations turning to automated broadcasting with no live on-air personnel or even local news. Soon came the endless commercial spots from national advertisers, since few local advertisers could now afford the advertising spots.

For the listener, radio went from a point of endless music discovery, where listening all night could be considered a reasonable leisure activity, to a clump of audio goo designed to be as inoffensive as possible. In an effort to grow their profits, big corporations turned radio into a supplier of background music rather than the aural companion it used to be.

Prior to the influx of big-money ownership, radio couldn't afford demographic market research, and each station decided what to play by noting the calls they received from their listeners or by calling the local music stores to see what customers were buying. Although the possibility of overhyping a particular record existed, this information bore more of a relationship to what the people in the area were actually buying and listening to.

By the end of the M2.5 era, focus-group results took precedence over the preferences of listeners. As a result, there were more "turntable hits" than ever before, in which a recording received massive exposure but no one was willing to purchase it.

Advertisers want to control what's being played around their advertising dollars, and the need to please the advertiser (instead of the listener) is one of the reasons radio is where it is today. No advertiser is willing to take the risk of being associated with new music when, for the same money, they can be associated with a known quantity. Yet listeners have proven over and over that they are more than happy to embrace something new.

Arbitron ratings between stations continue to be important, but far less so than when there used to be competition between stations as opposed to station groups.

College Radio on the Brink

For many years, college radio had been the beacon of hope shining brightly across the wasteland that is commercial radio. As radio became more and more homogenized, thanks to group ownership and consultant-led playlists, the only place for many indie acts to break was the local college radio station.

Sadly, today's college radio faces extinction as more and more colleges either close their stations down, sell them off, or convert them to online only for a couple of reasons:

- **Fewer on-campus listeners.** Students just don't listen to radio as much anymore, opting to discover their music online. Ironically, studies by the stations themselves have found that most of a college radio's listenership is off campus. That being said, college broadcast courses will remain in place as university radio stations move online, but the traditional college broadcast radio station may soon become part of history.
- **Budgetary shortfalls.** Ever since the recession of 2007, college administrators everywhere have been faced with the prospect of making cuts, and frequently the first item to get the axe is the radio station, with its expensive upkeep, especially if it can be sold off at a profit.

Realistically, though, college radio had been infiltrated by big business more than a decade ago, after record labels discovered that it was the last bastion of open playlists. That being said, at least the consultants (who are largely responsible for homogenized radio) have been kept out of it, hence the continuing local flavor that each remaining station maintains.

Just like the music business, radio isn't what it once was and probably never will be again. In the end, it might not matter much if college radio ceases to exist, since in many ways it's been gone for a while—though not many have noticed.

BROADCAST RADIO'S DECLINE

Local control is lost.

Local stations are bought by station groups.

The programming consultant gains control.

Radio loses market share to Internet and satellite radio.

College radio dies a slow death.

WHY TELEVISION IS NO LONGER A FACTOR

It used to be that an appearance on television could give an artist a pretty good sales boost. During the heyday of *Saturday Night Live* in the 1970s and '80s, an act could count on at least 100,000 unit sales (usually more) in the week following an appearance, and, of course, MTV made acts into bona fide stars and superstars. For the most part, those days are over.

Today, an appearance on a late-night talk show like *The Late Show with Steven Colbert* will go largely unnoticed, since the targeted demographic is falling off to sleep and may not be interested in buying new music anyway. A new act might get some small amount of traction on Jimmy Fallon's or Jimmy Kimmel's show but probably won't sell many units because of it. Daytime TV can help sales, though. An appearance on Ellen DeGeneres's afternoon show can be sales gold, but the demographic is narrow (mostly women aged 25 to 45), so this type of appearance can't be used by every artist.

That said, the Disney Channel and Nickelodeon are the only major star-making venues on the television airwaves today, although they're limited by their demographic as well (kids between the ages of 6 and 14). An act appealing to prepubescents can truly move product, but the time window is small because the audience grows up, which usually makes for short careers. Disney and Nickelodeon sell cute, not art, and there's only room for a few acts.

In the end, television is much like the Internet, with so many vertical avenues that have sucked viewership from the major networks. If you have an eclectic viewing taste, there's probably a channel for you, but there's less and less space for music instead of more.

MTV and its sister stations are now more about lifestyle than music, and any music show on an outlying cable network has an already limited viewership. The fractured demographic and viewing habits mean that there are fewer exposure opportunities for the artist than ever.

What's happening is that the numbers for traditional broadcast television are dropping dramatically. In a 500-channel universe, viewers simply have a lot of choices, and a lot of the programming is simply not compelling enough.

—Media Consultant Larry Gerbrandt

MUSIC ON TELEVISION

Daytime television helps music sales more than nighttime.

Disney and Nickelodeon are the main outlets for star making.

Disney and Nickelodeon sell cute, not talent.

Most music shows have small audiences.

A television appearance no longer ensures a sales bump or great exposure.

THE TROUBLE WITH LABELS

The record label used to be the be-all, end-all of the music business. It was the gatekeeper, the taste maker, the banker, and the sales and publicity engine that the music world revolved around. While on the superstar level all that's still true in M4.1, a record label, especially a major label, holds less influence in many facets of the music industry than it did before.

Where Digital Music Has Failed

When the music industry was at its peak, all of its revenues and projected revenues were based on album sales. The retail price for a CD was anywhere from $10.00 to $18.00, which, although the margins were thin at many points of the supply chain, still provided enough of a return to drive industry revenue to new heights, thanks to the volume of CDs that were being sold. With sales of physical product in double-digit decline year over year, the industry held out hope that revenues of digital product might take the place of CDs.

According to the RIAA, even though digital revenue was up a full 23 percent from the year before in the United States for the first half of 2015, that still wasn't enough to offset the decrease in physical sales, which were down by about 85 percent from 2000 (see Figure 2-1).

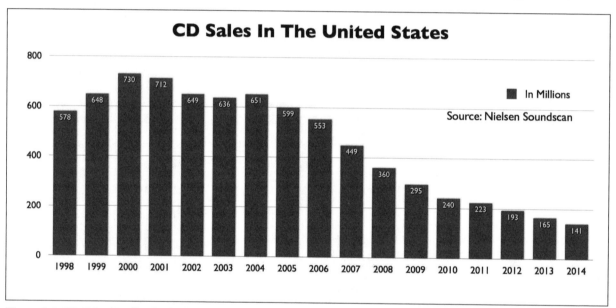

Figure 2-1: CD Sales Decline in the United States

This illustrates the big failing of digital music until now in that you can't take a product that sells for $10.00 to $18.00 and replace it with one that sells for $0.99, then change the game completely with digital streaming that pays in fractions of a cent, and still expect the industry to remain healthy. Plus, you can't sell fewer products than you did in the past and expect everyone in the business to keep smiling either.

A full 66 percent of record label revenues in the United States came from digital sales in 2014 (see Figure 2-2), yet total music sales were down 0.5 percent from the year before. Much of this has to do with purchasing habits changing from the album to the single to streams as we actually consume more music digitally.

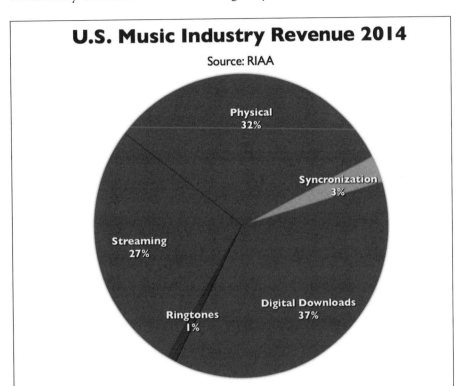

U.S. Music Industry Revenue 2014

Source: RIAA

Physical 32%

Syncronization 3%

Streaming 27%

Digital Downloads 37%

Ringtones 1%

Figure 2-2: US Music Industry Revenues, 2014.

The fact of the matter is that the album as a format is on the decline, with even digital album consumption falling in 2014 by 15 percent over 2013. So why has the album failed to catch on in a big way in the digital age?

- **It once was a visual experience.** During the vinyl record age, the album form had the advantage of that wonderful piece of cardboard known as the album jacket. The album jacket contained the cover art (still found on CDs but with less of an impact because of the smaller size), and most importantly, the liner notes on the back, which we'll get to in a second. But one thing that everyone either forgets or has never experienced is the fact that millions of albums were purchased completely on impulse because of the album artwork alone!

    It may be hard to believe, but it was quite common to come across an album cover that was so cool that you'd buy it without knowing a thing about the artist. Sometimes it would be a total loser, but you still had the liner notes to read, and occasionally that would still make it a worthwhile purchase.

- **It was an informational experience too.** Those too young to have experienced the golden age of vinyl don't know how much the liner notes meant to nearly everyone who bought an album. You could spend hours reading a well-written gatefold jacket, checking out every credit, wondering about where these exotic studios where the album was recorded were, and generally soaking up any info you could about the artist. Of course, this was in a time before the Internet, so the liner notes were sometimes the only place to find any info on the artist at all.

  To say the least, the visuals and information that came along with the music made buying an album a total experience that today's album doesn't come close to.

- **Too much filler.** Most vinyl albums are between 35 and 45 minutes long. This is out of necessity because of the physics of a record. Make it any longer and it starts to get noisy, the frequency response suffers, and it won't play as loudly. But 40 minutes or so turns out to be the perfect amount of time for listening. There's a time commitment you have to make, but it's well within reason, especially if you like the music.

  The average CD is capable of holding a bit more than 73 minutes of music. Unfortunately, artists began to think that it was a really good idea to include all the secondary material on the CD that they normally would've tossed from the vinyl version. Now, instead of having 40 minutes of great music, we'd get 55 minutes of mediocrity. Even if the artist had some great songs, they were frequently buried under another 50 minutes of filler. Now not only was the fan paying more money for the product, but he or she was paying more money for less quality. Something had to give.

When MP3s came on the scene, the music business was eventually pushed from an album-oriented business into the singles business that it now is. Ironically, popular music began as a singles business, whence it now returns.

It's the Music, Stupid

Overlooked in all this is the effect that the actual music had on consumer buying habits and currently has on their listening habits. If consumers can't relate to or identify with the music, they won't consume it. Some industry critics feel that the release of "safe music" guided by the hand of Madison Avenue (like the boy band One Direction or Justin Bieber) was as much a factor in the decline of music sales as anything else, and indeed, they may have a point.

The Death of Artist Development

For the most part, the music industry has been slow to develop a new generation of major artists capable of filling stadiums, and for too long it relied on so-called "heritage" artists like The Eagles and Madonna for large sales numbers.

True, there are always new stars who attain popularity quickly, but it's surprising how poorly many do when it comes to sustaining a career. The fact is that with fewer record labels and less artist development than ever before, the music industry may be fighting the artist discovery battle with one arm tied behind its back.

Artist development has always been the lifeblood of the industry, even as far back as M1.0. A good example of this is Geffen Records (now owned by the Universal Music Group). To build his label, David Geffen signed three of the biggest stars in the world at the time (1980): Donna Summer, Elton John, and John Lennon. Donna Summers's and Elton John's first albums for Geffen stiffed outright. Although John Lennon's was also headed for the dumper, he was unfortunately killed, which caused his entire catalog's sales to spike. It wasn't until the label signed new acts that it truly became successful, with Whitesnake and Guns N' Roses leading the way. As always, if you want to get rich in the music business, you've got to invest in the new.

The nature of artist development has changed through the years from being about patience to instant win or loss for the artist. In the music business's so-called glory days of the late '60s and '70s, it was not uncommon for a record label to stay with an artist for three, four, or even five albums (as was the case with megastars David Bowie, Fleetwood Mac, and Tom Petty) as the artist built an audience and eventually broke into the mainstream music consciousness. This is because the most successful labels, such as Warner Bros., Atlantic, and Elektra, were run by music visionaries instead of large corporations worried about their quarterly bottom lines.

As the conglomerates gradually took over the major labels, that patience grew less and less until it reached today's "the first record must be a hit or you're dropped" mentality. Luckily, M4.1 finally provides an alternative to this way of thinking within the corporate music industry.

The Death of A&R

The job of A&R isn't what it used to be, as the major record labels continue to feel that they can get by with fewer and fewer A&R executives. According to former Arista Records A&R man Rich Esra, one of the publishers of the *Music Business Registry*, a quarterly publication that tracks A&R hires and fires and provides their contact information, there were several reasons why A&R seems to be a part of the music business that's slowly dying:

1. The major labels are hiring fewer and fewer A&R executives because the volume of acts (and more importantly, the types of acts) being signed have dramatically decreased.

2. The A&R process used to be about the discovery, signing, and nurturing of the act. Today, A&R executives aren't looking for talent per se. They're looking for an artist who already has an audience and therefore an ongoing business.

    Today, acts need to be already "developed," or at least be developing in a business sense, for any label to have even the slightest amount of interest. The idea that today's A&R executives will discover an unknown act/artist and develop that artist is mostly an illusion. They currently have neither the desire nor the time—nor the money, for that matter.

3. This is why, from an A&R perspective, only the most generic, ubiquitous type of acts get any attention from labels today. There is only a certain type of artist that major labels are willing to sign.

We've all heard the stories about the meddling A&R guy who knows nothing yet demands that an artist change his or her music or direction for reasons known only to him, but the fact is that there were far more good A&R people employed than bad ones. Someone has to find the next generation of talent just to keep these companies alive, and without A&R, it's more likely than ever that the major labels will die along with the position.

The Piracy Argument Dissipates

For a long time at the beginning of the digital music age, illegally downloading songs was a way of life for many consumers. Now, streaming services have essentially rendered piracy moot, since it's far easier and more convenient to obtain music legally.

Exactly what effect piracy had on sales was always debatable, but the fact of the matter is that it certainly existed before digital downloads (especially in M1.5 and M2.0), going back as far as when recording devices first became commercially available.

While piracy's impact cannot be underestimated, it shouldn't be overestimated either. For many years, the music industry has used piracy as a convenient excuse to cover its many other ills and shortcomings.

> *What really people forget is that by the end of the '70s, the recorded music business was in deep, deep trouble. There was a recession and a couple of years of downward trends, and a lot of people thought, "This is the end of it." There was a lot of piracy, thanks to the cassette player and that issue of that "Record" button, and people just weren't buying vinyl records anymore. People making their own copies was a pretty big issue even in those days. People were copying music for free off the radio or from another cassette or record. We reckoned that we were losing at least 25 percent of our business to home taping. So when people talk about "free" today, there's nothing particularly new about it; it's just a different version of the same thing.*
> —Rupert Perry

While music industry sources such as the RIAA and IFPI often floated claims that nine out of every ten files that were downloaded at the beginning of the digital music age were illegal, it was always difficult to know what to make of these statistics. As difficult as it is to get precise numbers on real sales that don't get reported (like anything outside of SoundScan, such as direct downloads from artist's websites or directly from the act at a concert), what makes anyone think that the piracy numbers were or are now anything more than a number pulled out of thin air?

In fact, a study conducted at Carlos III University of Madrid in Spain, in collaboration with scientists at the IMDEA Networks Institute, the University of Oregon (USA), and the Technical University of Darmstadt (Germany), found that illegal file sharers tended to be either organizations, such as record labels, that put up fake or malware-infected files to discourage piracy (called "fake publishers"), or "top publishers" that earned a profit from advertising and subscription using pirated content as bait.

In the end, the study concluded that "since BitTorrent's popularity is tied to a small group of users who engage in illegal file-sharing for 'economic benefits,' if the same users lost interest or simply disappeared, BitTorrent's traffic would be 'drastically reduced.'"

A more recent study (2013), called "Copy Culture," by two researchers at Columbia University found that copying and online file sharing were actually mostly complementary to purchasing product. In other words, copying or sharing had no significant impact on music purchasing. The study also found that file sharers were heavy media consumers and purchased as many legal physical products and services as their non-file-sharing counterparts. Not only that, they also displayed a marginally higher willingness to pay.

The bottom line is that piracy isn't nearly the issue that it once was, mostly thanks to YouTube and the free tiers on streaming services. It undoubtedly still exists, and always will to some extent, but the major problems of the music industry now lie elsewhere.

THE TROUBLE WITH LABELS

Artist development severely diminished.

Only "safe artists" are signed.

More time passes between trends.

Album sales are in decline.

No replacement format for the CD.

Fewer A&R executives, with limited signing power.

Piracy problems have somewhat dissipated.

CHAPTER 3

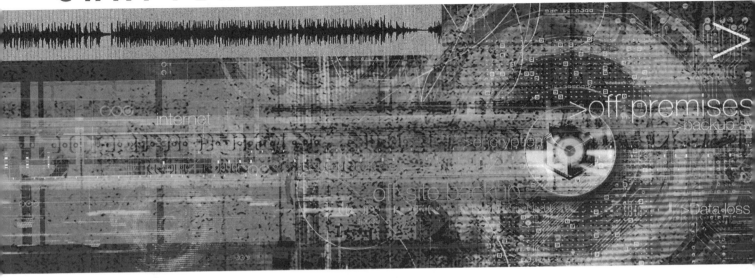

The New Music Industry

I f you've read the previous chapters, it's self-evident that the music industry is entering some uncharted waters. There are remnants of the old that will probably always survive, but what we're seeing is a reset from the old way of doing business to a new, still partially undiscovered method. This makes the new music industry both exciting and a little scary at the same time, but only if you've experienced the previous business version. Let's take a look at what the new music industry looks like.

THE MUSIC INDUSTRY IS NOT DYING

Despite the doom and gloom that you hear from many industry pundits, anyone who thinks the music business is really dying is absolutely wrong. It's evolving, morphing, transmuting, adjusting, adapting, reconfiguring, transitioning, and progressing; but it's not in any danger of dying.

Consider these figures:

- While it's absolutely true that CD sales are down 82 percent from 2000, that still means that 141 million were sold in 2015 in the United States alone, and that's only what we could count (direct sales on artist and band websites or distribution services are not included in that figure). Regardless, that's still a lot of physical music product being sold.

- The year 2015 also saw nearly 965 *million* digital single-song and album downloads purchased. Again, a huge amount.
- Internet radio service Pandora has 175 million registered users and 70 million active users a month.
- As of the beginning of 2015, more than 330,000 artists sell their music at CD Baby, and over 5 million of their CDs have been sold online to customers.
- The 2015 report by Nielsen reported almost 317 billion music streams, up nearly 100 percent from the previous year. This was before the introduction of Apple Music and YouTube Red.

There are still a lot of people out there listening to music, and many are still willing to part with their hard-earned money for the music they love.

For better or worse, more and more people make music than ever before, thanks to powerful yet inexpensive tools that go way beyond what an artist, producer, or engineer could have even dreamed about during the Music 1.0 era. The good part is that if you'd like to make your own music, it's easier than ever. The bad part is that there is more and more mediocre music available than at any other time, mostly because the built-in filters of the A&R departments of the record labels are extremely diminished in their clout or just bypassed completely.

Although consumers' listening habits have changed dramatically, there's proof everywhere that music lovers are still willing to pay for music they like. For example, British singer Adele sold over 30 million units of her album *21* between 2011 and 2015 (a figure that many industry observers believe will never be approached again) and is on a similar sales trajectory with her latest album, *25*. This shows that people are willing to pay for quality music; they just haven't seen or heard enough of it to get really excited with their pocketbooks in the numbers they used to. And there's lots of competition for those dollars and the listener's attention than ever before. If anything, music today has to be better than ever to compete.

Remember, the music industry dies only when people stop listening. See any evidence of that lately?

THE INDUSTRY IS NOT DYING

Huge numbers of CDs are still sold.

More people than ever before listen to music.

More people than ever before make music.

People are always willing to pay for quality music.

THE NEW RADIO

As outlined in Chapter 2, traditional radio went from being a cultural juggernaut to almost a media has-been in many ways, but new flavors of radio have significantly energized the medium to the point of rebirth. Let's look at some of the ways today's radio listeners consume its products.

Internet Radio

Radio is said to have gone through its own version of the music generations, with Radio 1.0 being the early, startup days of AM; Radio 1.5 being the age of the Top 40 formats of the '60s and '70s; Radio 2.0 being the rise of FM; Radio 2.5 being the rise of talk radio; and Radio 3.0 being the era of Internet Radio. You can say that we've entered Radio 3.5 as Internet radio has matured and now moves into the car (see Figure 3-1).

Radio 1.0	The startup days of AM
Radio 1.5	The age of the Top 40 format
Radio 2.0	The rise of FM radio
Radio 2.5	The rise of talk radio
Radio 3.0	The rise of Internet radio
Radio 3.5	Internet radio in the car

Figure 3-1: The Six Eras of Radio

Internet radio has risen in popularity quickly as a whole new set of online-only virtual stations have appeared along with Internet counterparts of many of the terrestrial stations as well. In fact, Internet radio has radically changed our listening habits, according to Edison Research/Triton Digital, leaders in media opinion and marketing research used by the radio industry. In their Infinite Dial 2014 report, they state:

- Approximately 124 million people a month listen to radio online.
- 47 percent of all radio listeners have listened to radio online.
- 75 percent of people ages 12 to 24 listen to online radio.
- They listen to Internet radio because of the control and variety it provides.
- Pandora is the clear leader in top-of-the-mind awareness, at 70 percent.
- 26 percent listen to Internet radio in the car via a cellphone.

Most independent Internet radio stations differ from their terrestrial cousins in that they utilize the vertical nature of the Internet to provide very specific, targeted programming to their listeners. But while terrestrial stations have a sales staff with a host of customers used to advertising, their independent Internet counterparts require a different business model to survive, as they are somewhat relegated to traditional Internet sales support, such as banner and contextual ads, paid search, and pay per click, if they don't use on-air advertising.

Pandora, iHeartRadio, iTunes Radio, Slacker, and similar services are successful because they solve the filter problem. You program your own music channel, and your choices are analyzed and some additional recommendations given. This is the antithesis of traditional broadcasting, where the programming choice is made for you via consultants, focus groups, advertiser requirements, or, in the good old days, by the DJ. It's also one of the reasons why these services will continue to gain support, as the various services try to outdo one another with better recommendations.

One of the biggest problems for Internet radio is the issue of performance fees, which broadcast radio does not pay (although this might change soon). Currently, an Internet radio station pays on a sliding scale, depending on the type of station and number of listeners, and they've just increased, indirectly jeopardizing one of the truly great resources available to new artists.

As the cost of doing business for Internet radio rises, many stations will have to resort to the advertiser-supported model of their terrestrial cousins to survive. This also brings with it the same problems that their terrestrial counterparts now endure, meaning outside pressure on the makeup of its playlist. The bottom line remains that the fans are out of the loop in advertising-supported entertainment, other than their passing interests in something like chart statistics.

In the end, technology doesn't change the lessons of broadcast history or the fact that there is always intense competition for advertising dollars. There is very little difference between electronic distribution and broadcasting once you peel away all the hype.

The Connected Car

The real revolution in radio is the connected car, and that journey is only just beginning. With WiFi, 4G (Fourth Generation), and LTE (Long Term Evolution) mobile data technologies becoming more and more available, any Internet radio station is capable of being streamed or cached. The current heavy-hitter apps—Pandora, Spotify, iTunes Music, and iHeartRadio—could change the driving experience forever.

How? Until the recent introduction of satellite radio, listening to radio in a car was a geographic experience, since you were limited to the local stations around you. With the connected car, this limitation is breached for good, as you can now access any station from any spot in the world. You can access any format, music genre, or personality that you desire.

Most auto manufacturers have already added Internet radio capabilities into their latest cars, with Ford, Mercedes, BMW, Chrysler, Chevrolet, Toyota, Buick, Lexus, Honda, and Hyundai leading the charge. Indeed, the race is clearly on to capture this huge audience, with the prize goal of 70 to 80 percent of in-car listeners for one lucky service.

Could the advance of Internet radio be the last nail in the coffin of local radio? Already suffering from corporate homogenization, local radio has been severely criticized in recent years for not attending to the needs of its immediate community. It's just not local enough anymore.

With local radio's listener base further fractured by yet more choices, online radio could either be a death blow or a new beginning, as corporations decide that radio is no longer a contributor to their bottom line and sell the stations back to the locals. It could be one situation where more diversity actually leads to greater listener selection.

Satellite Radio

Satellite broadcasting was once thought to be the next revolution in radio, and while it provides a superior listening experience to the consumer in many ways, it has run into many more snags than expected. The two original competing services, XM and Sirius, merged in the face of staggering startup costs and overhead to become Sirius XM. While the company's current subscriber base is a healthy 27 million listeners as of the writing of this book, program licensing costs with the NFL and MLB, and especially the $80-million-per-year deal with shock-jock Howard Stern, continue to be a huge impediment to profitability.

But despite these large cost burdens, Sirius XM provides programming unlike any found on terrestrial radio, with more than 165 digital channels coast to coast, including 72 commercial-free music channels. They also offer original music and talk channels created by the company's XM original programming unit and by leading brand-name content providers, such as Martha Stewart, Oprah, John Madden, Tom Petty, and Bob Dylan. Sirius XM is now available in the majority of new car models (cars being the main target of the service), and with new car sales showing a healthy increase, Sirius XM projects to add a million users a year to its subscriber base.

Some wonder whether Sirius XM can survive despite its die-hard following, since the eventual replacement of its satellites will require a large influx of cash that the marketplace seemingly can't support. This calls into question the subscription model for programming versus the age-old advertising model, which, as we've seen, eventually leads to controlled playlists. And while Sirius XM has solved the problem of endless radio commercials, it still hasn't solved the problem of many of their stations sounding just as much like the dreaded terrestrial ones, just without the ads.

What Is Radio's Future?

While we can easily see what radio is like today, it's much more difficult to look into a crystal ball at its future. But a study by Edison Research/Triton Digital called "The Infinite Dial 2014," which examined the media and technology habits of Americans, may give us some insight into what to expect. The first part of the study looked at the music discovery and consumption habits of this group and produced some significant findings:

- Broadcast radio has over 242 million listeners per week, with an average listen time of 2 1/2 hours every day.
- Radio reaches 90 percent of every age group from 12 years old on up.
- Online radio reaches 120 million listeners a month (more than a third of the population).
- 75 percent of all listeners use AM/FM radio to keep up to date with new music.
- Surprisingly, AM/FM radio continues to be the medium most often used by 12- to 24-year-olds for keeping up with current music, with 35 percent of all listeners reporting that they "frequently" find out about new music by listening to the radio.

Providing that none of this data is skewed (no guarantee there), radio is currently listened to more, and has a greater influence, than most people believe. While it may be true that local radio is on a serious decline, and Internet may be its future, good old-fashioned terrestrial radio has some life left in it yet.

THE NEW RADIO

Internet radio has energized the medium.

The connected car is the next evolution.

Local radio is on the brink of death as a result.

**Satellite radio is holding its own,
but its prospects look shaky.**

People still discover music via the radio.

THE NEW TELEVISION

As with just about all media, television is in the middle of a huge transition. Where cable television dominated for the last 30 years with one of the most desirable subscription models of any business, it's showing signs of deterioration as more and more video is being consumed online. Indeed, some of that content may be restricted in the future in an effort to stop the cannibalization of the broadcast audience and to keep the connected viewers from "cutting the cord" by dropping their cable service and viewing strictly online.

The Effect of YouTube

In many ways, YouTube can be considered the new television. Consider the following numbers for 2014:

YouTube has over 1 billion active viewers each month.

- 7 billion hours of video are watched each month on YouTube, or almost an hour for every person on earth.
- 300 hours of video are uploaded every minute.
- YouTube is the number-two search engine, behind Google (although it's owned by Google); it's bigger than Bing, Yahoo, Ask, and AOL combined.
- YouTube is part of 28 percent of all Google searches.
- The average YouTube user views 186 videos a month.
- 90 percent of Internet traffic is video.
- People now consume more music by watching it than by any other means; 57 percent have watched music videos on computers from sites such as YouTube in the last three months.

As far as music is concerned, YouTube has become the top music discovery site online, with music accounting for 38 percent of the site's visits every month—by far its largest category. As a matter of fact, the IFPI "Digital Music Report 2015" states that 9 of 10 of the most watched videos are music related, but 27 percent of YouTube users listen to music without even watching the video!

What's more, YouTube has become a major source of income for record labels, as half of the 25 billion views each month that contain music generate $167 million to $650 million in advertising revenue, depending on the source. As we enter into M4.1, YouTube has morphed from strictly a major music delivery platform to one that makes money as well.

YouTube Gets Challenged

In M3.5 through M4.0, YouTube was the undisputed champion of online music video distribution, but the platform recently received its first real challenge from the social media king of the hill—Facebook.

In an attempt to replace YouTube as the go-to video platform, Facebook made posting native video an attractive option by giving those posts priority in friends and follower newsfeeds without the poster spending any money to promote the post. Posts that don't feature video require paid promotion to reach more than the 2 to 3 percent that would organically find it. This applies only to video that's been uploaded directly to Facebook and not the link or embed from YouTube or another service, which is treated like a normal post.

Although Facebook Video provides greater no-cost exposure for music, as of the writing of this book, Facebook had no way to monetize these videos, and no Content ID–like system to protect the video's copyright. (We'll cover Content ID in Chapter 13.) This has made record labels wary of using the service, despite its promotional potential.

The Broadcast Alternatives

Traditional over-the-air or cable television is taking a hit from alternative forms of television consumption, such as Netflix and Hulu. With DVD sales declining even more quickly than CD sales, there's now a 61 percent chance that any given legal movie stream or download comes from Netflix, thanks to its inclusion in newer televisions and set-top boxes. In fact, Netflix subscribers can stream videos to practically every popular device currently available, including iOS devices, Android devices, Roku boxes, Apple TVs, Xbox 360s, and more. And with a huge library of movies and television shows, it has quickly become the service of choice of many consumers.

With 9 million monthly users who access over 260 million content streams, Hulu is already big, but it has become much more influential in recent years thanks to original content good enough to earn a host of Emmy nominations in 2014. Hulu boasts 627 advertisers and 250 content partners as of the writing of this book, which represents meteoric growth over the last three years. When the site launched, it had only two content partners and a dozen advertisers.

What does the change in television have to do with music? Where once upon a time, a performance on television could ensure a boost in sales and some new fans, that's not the case any longer, as television has become just as fragmented and stratified as music. Indeed, a performance on a late-night television show is for fans only (if that), resulting in few new fans and a negligible sales bump. With the new on-demand nature of television instead of the "television by appointment" of the past, a television appearance or show underscore can no longer be counted on to be fresh and up to date.

The Connected TV

With most major consumer electronics manufacturers now offering some sort of connected TV, watching online videos is no longer relegated to the computer. What is a connected television? It's a TV that connects directly to the Internet, like a computer, allowing the viewer to access content from YouTube, Hulu, Netflix, Amazon, or any other video distributor so it can be watched on a big 55-inch screen instead of a 15-inch laptop.

But the connected TV means much more—potentially. It now lends itself to true interactivity, allowing the viewer to discover information on the characters, actors, and back story, and even to socially connect with friends and other viewers in real time. Until now, you'd need a computer or tablet (known in the tech industry as "the second screen") to be able to do at least some of that.

The connected TV is also a new means for marketing and sales, allowing consumers to buy products they see onscreen, to respond instantly to discount offers, and even to browse the Internet while watching a program. Tablet computers also open up new avenues of viewership as the screens are optimized for video. In the future, many kids may prefer iPads to televisions in their rooms. They're more personal.

While sales of connected televisions to date have been plagued by customer unfamiliarity, connection confusion, and customer support, they're clearly the wave of the future. They open a wide range of creative, marketing, and sales opportunities to the M4.1 musician.

THE NEW TELEVISION

The future television viewer will be increasingly connected.

The "second screen" becomes part of the viewing experience.

YouTube is the new television in many ways.

YouTube is now a major music consumption and discovery site.

Facebook is challenging YouTube for online video dominance.

Television performances no longer add fans or sell product.

THE NEW PLAYERS

Control of the music industry has slowly drifted from the power days of the record label executive to the new power base of today—management and the promoter. That said, a new generation of record label entrepreneurs could someday change that balance.

Management

Managers of talent have always been powerful (especially with a big-selling act in the stable) and have, for the most part, stayed behind the scenes. After all, it's the acts that should get the most attention. But as the music industry transitions into Music 4.1, managers are more powerful, and more needed, than ever.

The reason is that the fortunes of the manager are directly tied to the act. If the act makes money, so does the manager. If the act tanks, the manager starves. As a result, the manager has to truly believe in the act and represent it with a passion. The manager's singular vision must be to make the act successful. Any other member of the artist's or group's team, from producer to attorney to record label to publicist and so on, will not have his or her fortunes tied so directly to the artist's success, and, as a result, his or her passion can't be expected to ever be as high.

With most service contractors that an artist employs, you can never be sure where their loyalty actually lies. Is it with the record label, distributor or promoter, or the artist? With a manager, the answer to that question should never be in doubt.

Why has the manager's role become more profound in M4.1? Because as the choices for the artist have expanded, so has the manager's influence. In M1.0 through M2.5, the manager's main focus was on dealing with the record label and getting the act booked. The label was the 800-pound gorilla in the room, and the manager was the keeper. With the record label's influence now decreased to that of a chimpanzee, the manager has ascended to become the giant in the act's life. As we'll see in later chapters, there are far more possibilities for every aspect of the act, and that means far more decisions are required.

An interesting trend is that management is now adapting to M4.1, bringing multiple talents in-house for instant access and attention by the artist. These talents include concert promotion, Internet promotion, dedicated social networking, the handling of street teams, and where it's legal, even acting as a booking agent.

Not every artist is able to connect with forward-thinking management of this type—or even any kind of organized management—but that's okay. Personal management is ineffective unless the manager is passionate about the artist, since passion can overcome inexperience.

Passion is something that you can't buy or contract—the manager has to truly believe in you or you're wasting your time. As the act gets bigger, it's easier for a less powerful manager to plug into a larger management company and "four-wall," or get the best of both worlds: the power of the larger management company with the attention of the smaller.

The Promoter

The second most powerful entity in M4.1 is the promoter. Regardless of whether he or she is booking a coffee house on a community-college campus or a 10,000-seat arena, the promoter is needed to keep the act doing what it should do best: playing in front of people.

Promoters have always been important because, despite what you might think, most artists have always derived the majority of their income from touring rather than from record sales. In M4.1, promoters are an even more crucial link in the chain than before.

No longer do acts tour to promote their records, as they once did in M1.0 to M2.5. Since M3.0, the record promotes the tour and is often relegated to being an additional piece of swag for the onsite vendors to sell. In M4.1, it's more important than ever that the artist's tour be successful, and the promoter's influence has risen appreciably as a result.

Promoters used to rely on SoundScan numbers to determine the ticket-selling potential of the act. These days, they could care less where a record sits on the charts, because ticket sales are the only figures that matter. In the promoter's M4.1 world, success begets success. If you sell tickets in one region or venue, a promoter in another is more likely to work with you than if your current hit is sitting at the No. 1 chart spot.

Thanks to changing tastes and leaner economic times, promoters' general approach to talent has changed. Back in the M1.0 to M2.5 days, the promoter was willing to lose money on an act on its way up in the clubs in order to reap the rewards in the arena later.

Unfortunately, there's little of that these days because there are fewer indie and regional promoters than ever before, having been rolled up in numerous industry consolidations into what has become the Live Nation and AEG behemoths. As a result, most of the middle- and upper-tier promoters are large corporations with deep pockets (sound familiar?), which leaves the smaller indie promoter unable to roll the dice on an act for fear of losing money. While a promoter might have taken a chance in the past in the hopes of gaining some loyalty from the artist, this scenario has become less and less likely.

That being said, today's promoter is more willing to think outside the box. Paperless tickets (which are hated by some and declared the future by others), multitiered pricing, coupons, and promotional tie-ins to other entertainment, such as restaurants, are all things that a promoter is now willing to try.

Promoters still hold the keys to a successful career for an artist. Financially successful recorded music is very much a reflection of people's experiences in enjoying live music. The more they experience it, the more they are likely to buy it. The promoter is an integral part of that success.

The New Record Label

Record labels both large and small are transforming before our very eyes in order to adapt to the new music-buying audience. Where once the record label was the gatekeeper to talent and a filter that separated the worthy from the worthless for the masses, today's label is in many ways struggling to find its way in the M4.1 world.

While major labels are excellent at exposing and exploiting mainstream-oriented acts, they're no longer in the business of much else. And as outlined before, talent development and A&R have largely fallen by the wayside. The problem is that it's a numbers game, and the numbers are no longer on the side of the majors. If only one out of ten acts makes money and only makes one-tenth of what it made during the good old days, that's not much of a value proposition.

The M4.1 indie record label is no different from the record label of the '50s in spirit. It's built by people who love music and who are more concerned with exposing talent than making money. Their overhead is low, the execs don't draw hefty salaries (or any salary at all in many cases), and they're willing to keep putting out releases by artists they love regardless of the sales figures.

Their marketing consists mostly of social media and online promotion because that's all they can afford and that's all their audience responds to. And they're willing to try different approaches. Labels like Kill/Hurt, Not For Fun, Bridgetown Records, and Burger Records print limited runs of cassettes and vinyl, two formats long ago given up for dead (although vinyl has had quite a resurgence), and they not only stay alive but manage to grow.

The major labels of tomorrow are the indie labels that are a mere blip on the industry's radar screen today. Those labels wedded to the past will be engulfed by it.

THE NEW PLAYERS

Managers have more power and influence than ever.

Management has brought many traditional artist services in-house.

To a promoter, only ticket sales, not chart position, matter.

Promoters are less willing to take a chance on a new act.

Record company influence has decreased.

New indie labels are more concerned about music than money.

And they're willing to think outside the box.

THE NEW AUDIENCE

Today's audience is a combination of a stratified vortex of special tastes and ultra-targeted desires, yet it still has a profound fancy for all things Top 40–oriented. Regardless of whether your taste lies in electronic Bantu music or alien space music, if it's out there, you can find it. But finding the music that moves you is both the key and the dilemma.

> *I see more and more niche markets finding more coherent audiences. You can be into Hungarian Death Metal or Central Canadian Bluegrass and easily find songs of that particular genre, then in your spare time you can read blogs pertaining to only that subject.*
> —Bruce Houghton

One of the main attributes of the new M4.1 audience is how it likes to receive and play the music it loves. More and more of the current audience chooses to listen to its music in a digital streaming format from YouTube, Pandora, Spotify, or any number of alternative sources.

With more than 92 percent growth in streaming and a total of 135 billion streams in the first half of 2015 alone, digital music has become a major distribution method, as 65 percent of all music purchased in the United States is now in a digital form (according to the RIAA). Digital music has indeed caused listening and buying habits to change.

The new digital demographic has become a consumer of the single song not only when streaming but when purchasing as well, opting for buying only one or two known and liked songs as compared to the 10 or 12 normally found on an album.

While full-length albums were the cash cow of the industry through M2.5, the music buyer from M3.0 onward has returned to the habits of the '50s, when the single was the main point of interest. The M4.1 consumer still wants to discover new music and is willing to sample songs from any of the music distribution or discovery sites, but he or she is no longer compelled or required to purchase an album that has only one or two good songs on it. As a result, CD sales have fallen every year since 2002.

The new audience also has many more entertainment choices than ever before, and it's only natural that music is going to suffer for it, just as network television has suffered in the face of the expanded cable universe. Social media, video games, YouTube, and a host of other on- and offline activities now occupy the time that used to be reserved for listening to music.

The tastes of the new audience are different from their predecessors as well. A shorter attention span and proficiency in multitasking have taken their toll on the album. In the late '60s and the '70s (M1.0 and M1.5), an album release would be an event, usually followed by a listen, front to back, without a break; that rarely happens today. The current audience wants to taste a little from everywhere rather than take a big gulp of just one drink.

THE NEW AUDIENCE

Singles are more important than the album.

Album filler material is rejected by the music consumer.

The audience has a shorter music attention span.

Ultra-targeted demographics have developed.

Stratified tastes have arisen.

Music buyers have more entertainment choices than ever.

ENTER MUSIC 4.1

Music 4.1 is the natural evolution of the music business. The public has solidly voted in favor of streaming as their consumption method of choice, and today's artist has to deal with the consequences.

No longer can the artist rely on music sales as a way of supporting a career (although sales are far from dead now and won't disappear for quite a while). For all but the luckiest 1 percent, artists can no longer depend on the record company for large advances and tour and promotional support. Today's artist must be self-sufficient on many levels to survive, but luckily, there are more tools available for this than ever before.

Today's artist must also look at the business of music in a different light, as fractions of a cent instead of dollars dictate the nature of a successful deal. As you'll see in the coming chapters, the revenue pie may finally be growing, and those penny fractions might soon add up to some real money.

The good thing is that M4.1 now allows the artist to take into account the current deficiencies of the business entities that were prevalent in previous music generations and provides the ability to bypass them completely in the course of building an audience and career, until those entities can be used to the artist's advantage.

In M4.1, the artist has the ability to directly engage the fan with no one in between, and the fan has the ability to engage back. Assuming that the artist creates music that can capture an audience in the first place (however small it might be), the opportunity to build an audience is more available than ever before, providing that the artist has the skills to take advantage of social media. Let's take a closer look at Music 4.1 and the best way to develop those skills.

CHAPTER 4

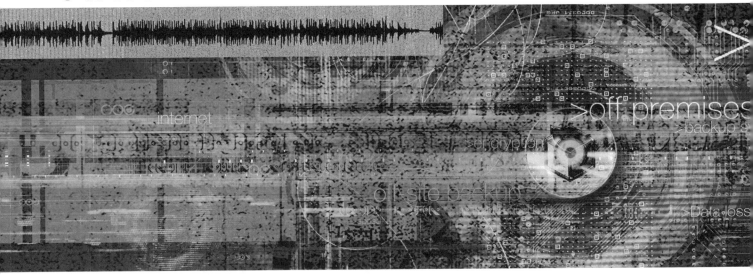

The New Masters of the Domain

To understand Music 4.1, you have to understand its major influencers. M4.1 (and beyond) has been partially shaped by the following people and the concepts they bring, so it's important to grasp the significance of their contributions. They set the guidelines for the future of music and the way the artist interacts with it.

There are also a number of important sales and market concepts in this chapter. Some are interesting from a historical perspective because they apply more to physical sales, so they won't necessarily work today (although they may be effective with merch), while others are totally in sync with the strategies of today's artist.

SETH GODIN'S TRIBES

Seth Godin has been one of the most influential voices in marketing for some time now. He has written 17 bestselling books on marketing, and his marketing blog (sethgodin.typepad.com) is one of the most read on the Internet. His most significant contribution in terms of M4.1 comes from his book *Tribes: We Need You to Lead Us. Tribes* illustrates a concept that is at the core of M4.1, which is that an artist's fan base is his "tribe," and the artist is the tribal leader.

A tribe, in the context of M4.1, is a group of people who are passionate about the music of an artist (although it could be about an entire genre or subgenre of music, too). The artist is the most passionate (because she's the creator) and is therefore the leader of the tribe. What the tribe craves most is communication and direction from the leader, which is the key component of the concept.

A tribe can have a large number of members or be very small, but it must have at least three members to exist. It's different from a typical fan base, special-interest group, or community in terms of its intense passion. A fan base usually has one thing, such as a person or product (or both when it comes to music), that draws people to the group, while a special-interest group is built around a shared interest or value, such as C++ programming or voluntourism. A community involves a special-interest group that has some form of group communication, such as a newsletter or a phone call, to keep the members informed. Thanks to email, blogs, chat, and Twitter, these groups become a tribe when its members gain the ability to interact with each another and a leader comes forward.

Some leaders create the tribe, while some tribes find their leader. The leader sets the direction and facilitates a way for tribe members to communicate and share with each other.

How is a tribe different from a brand? A brand is a promise of quality and consistency. No matter where in the world you go for a McDonald's hamburger, you know what to expect. No matter what product you purchase from Apple, you can expect sleek, high-tech design and an easy-to-understand user interface. Brand management is protecting the image of the brand and carefully selecting how to best exploit it.

Tribal management looks at its brand in a different light.

Whether the tribe revolves around a brand, a person, a service, or music, people want to interact with other people, not with a company or the "brand" itself. For example, if someone in the Killers' Brandon Flowers's tribe hears from Island Records in company-speak rather than from Brandon directly, that satisfies no one and defeats the principle of the tribe.

Now, if a real person who happens to work for Island interacts with the tribe, or if Brandon's assistant communicates with the tribe on behalf of Brandon, that can work. The tribe wants a story to tell and something to discuss, but only if it comes from another tribe member.

The idea in M4.1 is to feed and grow the tribe and not the brand. You don't look for a customer to sell music to; you look to provide music that the tribe will want. The M4.1 artist should be aware that people will form a tribe with or without him or her (if he or she is popular enough already), but the artist can be a part of the tribe and make it better.

Here's how a tribe works in M4.1. Let's assume that you're a big fan of singer/songwriter Ingrid Michaelson. As a member of her tribe, what you want most (besides her music) is communication directly from Ingrid herself. If she's touring near where you live, you want an email from her asking you to come to the show. If she's planning to record a cover song on her next album, you want her to ask you for suggestions (see the two-way communication?). If she's coming out with a limited box set, you'd love to hear from her about the chance to buy it before anyone else can. Maybe Ingrid is trying to raise some money to record her next album and asks you to pre-purchase a copy. If you're a big fan, you might buy five just to make sure that the album comes out in a timely fashion.

But being the leader of a tribe takes a lot of work and some expertise. Many artists justifiably prefer to spend their time making music, or maybe they want to lead but just can't get their arms around the tech side of the job. Some artists are afraid to interact with fans in such an electronically intimate way. That's why an external tribal management source is so important. This is what a record company should be doing in M4.1: either helping to manage or directly managing the tribes of their artists.

While we're illustrating a tribe in the context of music, remember that brands, products, services, and even experiences can all have tribes. For instance, Disney, Virgin, and Apple Computer are brands that have their own tribes, while services such as Greenpeace and Wikipedia do, too. Products like Kleenex, Sharpie pens, and Harry Potter have tribes, while leaders like Al Gore, Nelson Mandela, and Malala Yousafzai have founded tribes that have a much larger impact than the individuals themselves.

Perhaps the best illustration of the ultimate leader of a tribe is an example that we'll get to in a little bit—Trent Reznor of Nine Inch Nails.

A TRIBE

A group of people passionate about the music, the artist, or both.

The artist is the leader.

Members crave interaction with the leader and with each other.

RADIOHEAD'S GRAND EXPERIMENT

On October 1, 2007, the highly respected British alternative-rock band Radiohead announced that its seventh album, *In Rainbows*, would be released in ten days.

Normally, an album-release announcement wouldn't be anything special; it's been happening somewhere almost every day for the past 70 years or so. But *In Rainbows* was different because it was going to be available only as a digital download and because the band would allow its customers to pay *whatever amount they liked* to download it.

It's still unknown whether this strategy was part of a grand master plan or was a simple salute to the band's fan base, but the move paid off handsomely as a public-relations coup, with press from all over the world running with the story and the album and band receiving much notice within the music industry.

In the ten days running up to the album's release, Radiohead reportedly received 1.2 million prepays for the album (the band's management never released the official figures). Little did they know at the time that this would be a much-heralded and -studied test case.

With a website offer that stated "It's up to you" in the payment box, the *In Rainbows* experiment yielded some interesting statistics. According to the Internet marketing-research company comScore, 62 percent of the album's buyers in their focus group did not pay a single cent for the album—they downloaded it for nothing! Four percent of the band's fans paid between $12.00 and $20.00 (about the retail cost of a CD), while 12 percent paid between $8.00 and $12.00, which comScore determined to make up 52 percent of the band's profits.

In the end, those who paid forked over an average of $6.00, with the buyers from the United States paying about $8.05 per purchase and those from the United Kingdom paying about $4.64.

According to comScore senior analyst Andrew Lipsman, Radiohead made a profit, whether they intended to or not. "If [Radiohead] is getting $6.00 on average, and it's basically going straight into their pockets and their costs are minimal, it could be economically viable," Lipsman told *E! Online*. The band needed to make about $1.50 per download to break even, he estimated, so at $6.00 per buyer, the group seems to have made out pretty well.

But having the fans decide how much to pay accomplished something else that was perhaps more important. By giving *In Rainbows* away, Radiohead actually strengthened the sales of the CD when it was released later that year. Going directly to No. 1 on both the US *Billboard* 200 and the UK Album Chart, the disc box set (including a second disc and a hardcover book of artwork) went on to sell more than 3 million units worldwide.

By allowing the customer to set the price, Radiohead exercised what was then a new business theory called "The Economics of Free" (or EoF). EoF encourages content owners to give some of their products away for free, because if done correctly, you can increase your market size greatly, as seen in the case of *In Rainbows*.

Shortly after the success of *In Rainbows*, both Franz Ferdinand and Arctic Monkeys unofficially leaked their initial releases for the same reason, and with great results.

You can't just start giving away your precious content without thought, though. It has to be the center of a larger marketing plan. In terms of M4.1, an EoF campaign means that you, the artist, have two types of products: infinite products and scarce products.

- Infinite products would be your music, especially in digital form. Physical products, such as CDs, don't fit in here because it actually costs you money to produce them (the CDs, not the music on them). Digital music is easy to find on a streaming site, and just as easy to give away.
- Scarce products are tickets to live shows, access to musicians, signed merchandise, backstage passes, private concerts, custom CDs, CD box sets, time spent with you, writing a song for a fan willing to pay for it, and anything else that has a limited supply (see Figure 4-1).

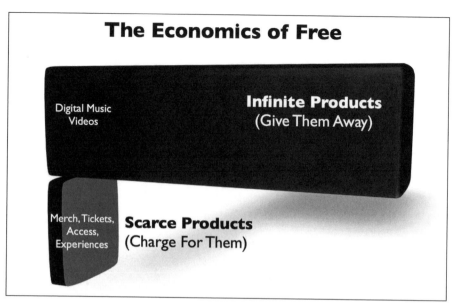

Figure 4-1: The Economics of Free

To take advantage of the Economics of Free, the artist must do the following:

1. **Set the infinite products (or just some of them) free.** Put them on a torrent site, Facebook, YouTube, Spotify, and anywhere you can. The more you get it out there, the greater the visibility. This makes the scarce products more valuable.

2. **Because of the free infinite products, you can now charge more for the scarce products.** Before number 1 is implemented, access to the artist or backstage passes might not be worth anything, but now they are. Before number 1, maybe no one wanted your CDs or vinyl albums, but now they're valuable as collectors' items, as are the box sets.

Setting your infinite products (your music) free expands your core audience (your tribe) by making your music your marketing tool. As your core audience expands, the demand for your scarce products grows. In M4.1, the artists who stick to the belief that their songs are their product will be relegated to a small audience forever.

The EoF theory is perfectly illustrated by Trent Reznor and NIN, the next example in this chapter. Radiohead and *In Rainbows* took the EoF concept one step further by giving it away for free but asking their fans if they'd like to pay for it, and many did. It's interesting that the band did not return to the pay-what-you-want method on the next album,

King of Limbs, instead employing a multitiered pay product offering, which we'll look at next.

It should be noted that there haven't been any successful examples of asking fans to "pay what you want" since. One of the reasons is that many artists (including Radiohead's Thom Yorke) felt that the *In Rainbows* experiment actually hastened the public's desire for free music, stripping its value along the way.

That may be true, but it's also true that the tide had already begun to turn to digital music instead of CDs when that album was released. It wouldn't be long before people would become so used to getting as much music as they wanted for free that even a group as popular as Radiohead couldn't give away many CDs. The times have changed, and the strategies must change as well.

ECONOMICS OF FREE

Give away infinite products (digital music).

Sell scarce products (CDs, merch, tickets).

Giving a product away can increase audience size.

Giving away infinite products makes scarce products more valuable.

You can now charge more for scarce products.

THE WISDOM OF TRENT

Taking the Radiohead pay-what-you-want experiment one step further, and totally taking advantage of his relationship with his tribe, was Trent Reznor and his Nine Inch Nails project *Ghosts I–IV*. After splitting from Universal Records' Interscope imprint in 2007, Trent decided to take advantage of his passionate fan base and the new online consumerism with his first post-major-label release.

Having an innate feel for dealing with his tribe even before the theory was articulated in Seth Godin's book, Reznor modeled his first release after the Radiohead experiment but with two important exceptions: he would give away some of the new album *Ghosts I–IV* for free, and he would provide products of the same release at different price points ranging from $5.00 to $2,500.

Here's how *Ghosts I–IV* was offered:

FREE DOWNLOAD includes:
- The first nine tracks of the album
- DRM-free MP3s encoded at 320kbps
- A 40-page PDF book covering the album
- A digital extras pack with wallpapers, icons, and other graphics.

$5 DOWNLOAD includes:
- 320kbps-encoded MP3 files
- FLAC lossless files
- Apple Lossless files
- A 40-page PDF book covering the album
- A digital extras pack with wallpapers, icons, and other graphics.

$10 TWO-CD SET includes:
- Two CDs in a 6-panel digipak with 16-page booklet
- 320kbps-encoded MP3 files
- FLAC lossless files
- Apple Lossless files
- A 40-page PDF book covering the album
- A digital extras pack with wallpapers, icons, and other graphics.

$75 DELUXE EDITION includes:
- A large fabric slipcase containing two embossed, fabric-bound, hardcover books

Book 1 includes
- *Ghosts I–IV* on 2 audio CDs
- A data DVD that can be read by Mac and Windows computers containing multitrack sessions for all 36 tracks in .wav file format, allowing easy remix
- A Blu-ray disc containing the stereo mixes of *Ghosts* in 96kHz/24-bit audio plus an exclusive slide show that plays with the music

Book 2 contains
- 48 pages of photographs by Philip Graybill and Rob Sheridan
- 320kbps-encoded MP3 files
- FLAC lossless files
- Apple Lossless files
- A 40-page PDF book covering the album
- A digital extras pack with wallpapers, icons, and other graphics.

The release was a smashing success, so much so that the NIN servers were knocked offline with the massive interest in the project. A $300 limited-edition package completely sold out of its 2,500-unit run, and Reznor sold nearly 800,000 total units within the first week. A grand total of $0 was spent on the marketing of the record, since Reznor announced it only on his blog. Even more impressive was the fact that *Ghosts* was an instrumental album!

By year end, *Ghosts* became the best-selling album on Amazon's MP3 Store and was nominated for two Grammy Awards.

In an attempt to move beyond the industry's old pricing model of one product, one price, this is a perfect example of giving something of value for free (in this case, a free nine-song download) in order to make the music easily accessible to fans and as a sample for potential fans. The massive publicity it generated, plus the multiple price points, meant that there was something for every economic and interest level.

It also proved that fans are willing to support artists they really care about even if their music is given away for free.

Ghosts was licensed under a Creative Commons Attribution Non-Commercial Share Alike license that allows noncommercial redistribution. Creative Commons provides easy and effective ways to publish your content without abandoning all rights to its use—free distribution might be allowed, for instance, but only as long as the author is attributed and the distribution is noncommercial. For more information, go to creativecommons.net.

Besides the sales, Reznor gained something else equally valuable with each transaction: email addresses. This allowed him to expand his fan base by reaching out to them personally, an act seen as unusually generous by most casual fans.

While Reznor was very successful as a DIY act, he and NIN returned to the major label fold in 2012, signing with Columbia Records, which proves that the responsibilities of DIY can overwhelm even artists who are particularly good at it and who have built their own DIY infrastructure. That said, the practical knowledge obtained by being successful as an independent provides a level of oversight not available without that experience.

JOSH FREESE'S MULTITIERED HUMOR

Another artist who has used multitiered product offerings with great success is Josh Freese, who uses the tactic with an interesting and amusing twist. Freese, the Los Angeles–based drummer for Devo, Perfect Circle, and others (including Guns N' Roses), doesn't have the high visibility of an artist like Reznor but makes up for it with a huge dose of humor, which becomes a marketing tool in itself.

Here are some of the package offerings for his *My New Friends* EP (taken from his website at joshfreese.com).

$5—Digital Download

$12—CD of *My New Friends*

$50—CD of *My New Friends*, CD/DVD of *Since 1972* CD
- A thank you call from Josh for purchasing his record

$125—Limited Edition Box Set
- 1 of 100 Box sets of all 3 of Josh's CDs
- Thank you phone call
- Set of Signed Drumsticks
- Copy of Josh's 5th grade report card
- 1 of Josh's boarding passes from a past flight
- Bumper Sticker "I ♥ Josh Freese's New Friends"

$350—The Lunch Date

- Take Josh to lunch at P. F. Chang's in Long Beach
- 5 copies of both "My New Friends" and "Since 1972" (Pass 'em out to friends. A perfect way to tell someone "I love you" or "You are very special to me")
- Copy of Josh's 5th grade report card
- Bumper Sticker "I ♥ Josh Freese's New Friends"
- Signed drumhead
- Signed sticks
- Signed photo (can't promise what the photo will be . . . but it will be signed)

$7,500 Limited to 1—Evoke Spirits with Tommy Lee, Danny Lohner and Josh

- Engage in light "'80s hair metal/pinup girl gossip" w/ Tommy, Josh and Lohner while a "C-List Porn Star" applies "corpse paint" to your astonished face. Next you'll be escorted to the opulent gardens of Castle Renhold'r, where the four of you will be Throwing Bones under the midnight moon in a blasphemous attempt to evoke the spirit/entity of YOUR CHOICE! (BYOB)
- 10 Copies of "My New Friends"
- Get a diddy written about you for next record (not necessarily a full on song but definitely a "diddy")
- $50 gift certificate to P. F. Chang's
- "Since 1972" CD
- "The Notorious One Man Orgy" CD
- Copy of Josh's 5th grade report card
- Bumper Sticker "I ♥ Josh Freese's New Friends"

- Signed drumhead
- Signed sticks

$10,000 Limited to 1

- 100 Copies of "My New Friends"
- Take home Josh's now infamous Volvo 940 Station Wagon (Perfect for hauling drums, plenty of room for getting busy in spacious back-seating area. Good for trips to Good Will or disposing bodies.)
- Make Josh's next record for him
- Josh joins your band for 2 days (quick book some studio time!)
- "Motorboat" Sarah for a minute or so (Josh's wife's friend...couples welcome, discreet parking available)
- Oh yeah . . . $100 gift certificate to PF Chang's and a bumper sticker that says something funny on it

$75,000 Same As It Ever Was

- Josh joins your band for a month (or becomes your personal assistant)
- Take home one of Josh's drumsets
- Josh writes and records a 5 song EP entirely about YOU
- Take Shrooms and cruise Hollywood in Danny from TOOL's Lamborgini
- 500 copies of "My New Friends" (start your own online CD store . . . specializing in just this one CD)
- Go get matching outfits at Tommy Bahama's and make everybody very sad

One of the things to note is the similarity of sales package tiers to crowdfunding tiers (which we'll cover in depth in Chapter 9), the difference being that a sales tier offers a currently available product while crowdfunding offers one available in the future if the funding goal is reached. In either case, the success relies on having enough tiers to satisfy the majority of fans' price comfort levels.

The bottom line is that multitiered offerings work, and the more exclusive they are, the more you can charge for them. Sometimes the offering itself (especially if it involves being in close proximity to the artist) is more interesting than the music itself.

THE WISDOM OF MULTITIERED OFFERINGS

Offer multitiered product prices, from free to very expensive.

Sales package tiers are similar to crowdfunding tiers.

Make the music easily accessible to fans and potential fans.

Harvest email addresses from free offerings.

Fans find exclusive offerings interesting.

Sometimes an offering that involves close proximity to the artist is more interesting than the music itself.

Have the leader directly communicate with the tribe.

Expand the fan base by personally reaching out.

CHRIS ANDERSON'S LONG TAIL

The "Long Tail" is a concept first put forward in an article by Chris Anderson in the October 2004 issue of *Wired* magazine that basically puts the old 80:20 rule on its ear.

For those of you who aren't into sales, the longstanding 80:20 rule refers to the concept that you usually get 80 percent of your business from 20 percent of your customers, or, in the case of the music industry, 80 percent of the sales come from 20 percent of available albums (in other words, the current and recent hits).

Because of limited shelf space and the fact that hits are the products that sell quickly, most retail stores carry the current hits but only a limited number of catalog albums. This becomes a self-fulfilling prophecy, since if only the hits (the 20 percent) are available, there's little possibility that much of the other 80 percent will sell because they're not available.

The Long Tail turns the 80:20 rule around by stating that most of your sales will come from that other 80 percent of products *if they're made available and are easy to purchase* (the key phrase). A customer may buy the hit, but then buy another two pieces from the artist's catalog (or even from another artist's catalog) while he or she is at it.

This concept was originally able to be implemented only in a few brick-and-mortar megastores, such as the Amoeba Music stores in California or the now-defunct Tower Records chain, but that all changed with online stores like Amazon and iTunes and with the movie site Netflix. Now an artist's entire catalog is more than likely available online and subject to the Long Tail rules as a result.

As Chris Anderson points out in his book *The Long Tail* (derived from the original *Wired* magazine article), half the products that Netflix rents are ones that a retailer would never have the space to carry. Over half of Amazon's book sales are unavailable at the retailer Barnes and Noble. Most of what you can buy on iTunes is not available in any record store.

It turns out that when customers are given a huge number of choices in every genre possible, they start looking down the "tail" to find what else might be interesting to them, and sales increase accordingly. As a result, where the attention used to be focused on the Top 40, now there's much more attention given to other titles in the catalog (the Long Tail), and because they're immediately available, consumption goes up.

A word of caution: the Long Tail doesn't work if *all* of your products are considered Long Tail. You must have the hits as well to offset the catalog. Likewise, it doesn't work if only hits are available. The Long Tail needs the balance to operate effectively.

So how does this affect music in M4.1? Anderson offers the following three Long Tail rules:

Rule 1: Make Everything Available

Members of an artist's core audience want as much of the artist's music as they can get. Rehearsals, outtakes, different versions—they want it all and they want it now. While it was impractical to make everything available in the past, that's no longer the case online. Put it on every music site or limit it to your personal website; just make it available to your fan base.

Rule 2: Cut the Price in Half, Then Lower It

Many of the items that a tribe most adores are the ones that an artist spends the least time and money on, such as rough mixes, rehearsal and live recordings and videos, and original song demos. If it doesn't oppose the artist's artistic integrity, make it available to the tribe. Since the production costs are low, the prices can be low too. For older catalog items (especially those in a digital format), prices can be lowered if a service such as Kunaki (kunaki.com) is used for CD pressing. Kunaki will press and drop-ship CDs on demand for as low as $1.00 each.

Rule 3: Help Me Find It

It does no one any good if the customer can't find the product to buy. The Long Tail works only when the catalog items are easy to find. You must do everything in your power to make the experience of finding your catalog products as easy as possible.

Rebuttals from economists and bloggers have claimed that the Long Tail theory is full of holes, and it's true that generally it hasn't lived up to its original promise in terms of vastly increasing catalog sales. In fact, one study by Nielsen SoundScan of the tracks sold in the iTunes store in 2011 found that 94 percent of the tracks sold had sales of fewer than 100 units, and an astonishing 32 percent sold exactly one copy. On the other end of the scale, 102 tracks sold more than a million each, which accounted for 15 percent of the sales.

If you look at those figures, you're bound to think that the Long Tail is a joke. While it might not be as effective as originally outlined by Anderson, I believe that the premise is basically sound and that the underperformance has been one of poor execution in most cases.

Customers will buy or consume your older products (this goes for digital products like videos as well) if they are available and *easy to find*, and they'll consume more of these products if they're less expensive than the newer products, but all three of these principles must be in play in order for the Long Tail strategy to be effective. When you look at iTunes, or any digital music service for that matter, you can't exactly say all of the points are followed.

Follow the three rules of the Long Tail on your website, store, and merch table. You'll be surprised how effective it can be.

THE LONG TAIL

More of your sales come from older products (catalog) than from newer.

It doesn't work unless you have hits to balance the catalog.

Customers can't buy older products if they're not available.

They'll buy more of these products if they're cheaper than newer products.

Make everything available as a product.

Sometimes the most valuable products are the ones that the artist spends the least to produce.

Make all products easy to find.

IRVING AZOFF'S STEEL FIST

The most powerful man currently in the music business is Irving Azoff. Actually, he's been one of the most powerful men in the business for decades, but what he currently represents is a model for M4.1 and beyond because of the large scale he operates on.

With the innate ability to drive a hard bargain, Azoff rose to prominence in the early '80s as the head of Frontline Management, which represented musical heavyweights The Eagles, Steely Dan, Heart, Stevie Nicks, and Jackson Browne, among others. Azoff soon became the head of then-major label MCA Records (which later became what we now know as Universal Music Group), and then later owned his own Giant Records (a Warner Bros. imprint) before selling out and returning to managing a few selected clients, such as The Eagles and Christina Aguilera. In 2005, his reconstituted Frontline became the most powerful management company in the history of the music industry as a result of Azoff's buying some 60 smaller management companies.

As a former label head, Azoff understood the dilemma of the record labels. Realizing that he could do business without them, he went directly to the most powerful retailer on the planet, Walmart, to distribute The Eagles' first album since 1979, the double CD *Long Road Out of Eden*, released in 2007.

Azoff recognized the power of the chain's 6,500 stores, their ability to reach their 140 million visitors a week, and the promotional value of Walmart's weekly circular seen by 85 million potential customers. Even though it was priced at only $11.88 (extremely low for a double-CD set), the set reportedly netted the band nearly $50 million, far more than it ever could have had the band been signed to a record label. Thus, Azoff sent the first warning shot across the bow of the old industry guard.

Then, realizing how the concert-promotion business was tightly controlled and that artists make most of their money from touring, he merged with the giant Ticketmaster, and then again with their major competitor Live Nation, becoming executive chairman in the process. This meant that Azoff was then able to manage talent, book concerts, issue tickets, and sell artist-related merchandise under one roof.

Azoff bailed as executive chairman of Live Nation at the end of 2012, only to merge his Azoff Music Management Group with Madison Square Garden Company (MSG) in September 2013.

What makes this venture interesting is that the company has four divisions: artist management, music publishing, television production and live event branding, and digital branding. Couple that with the many venues owned by MSG that could host concerts for the company's artists, and you have a look at what the new world record major label possibly looks like, even though they're not calling it a label (we'll look at this more closely in Chapter 15).

Now, this is great if you're already a legacy artist, because now presumably you'll receive a larger part of each ticket sale, but what does it have to do with an up-and-coming artist in M4.1? It shows that the new music industry is a business of talent (as compared with distribution in the old model), and he who controls the talent, and the means to best utilize it, wins. As for the talent, the most essential part of an artist's team is the manager.

The major labels have less and less to offer an M4.1 artist. They sell music, but that's not where the business is today. The real business lies with everything else that an artist brings to the table. The labels now offer 360 deals to new acts, but that mostly benefits them and not the artist. If they can't do the one thing that they're supposed to do well, which is sell music (as the sales figures show), how can you expect them to sell your merch or get you gigs?

M4.1 is the music business requiring a new record label strategy different from what worked in the past. Irving Azoff sees it, and so should you.

THE NEW M4.1 REALITY

A record label is no longer necessary for success.

Management is more important than ever.

Talent, not distribution, is king.

Distribution is easily available for any artist.

The record label of the future looks more like a management company.

SANCTUARY'S BLUEPRINT

In 1979, Rod Smallwood and Andy Taylor discovered and then managed the legendary metal band Iron Maiden. They subsequently named their management company after the band's song "Sanctuary" and expanded their roster to include similar bands of the genre.

Soon afterward, Sanctuary Management had a brilliant idea. As managers of "heritage acts," which had long-term appeal and large fan bases but no record deals, the company decided to independently finance CD releases for the bands themselves. After all, the audience was already grown and had an appetite for new product. They'd buy anything the bands would put out, so why not release it themselves if a major label wouldn't? The bands were going to tour anyway, so they might as well have a product to sell.

Little did they know at the time, but this was the beginning of the new business model where the tour sells the recording instead of the recording selling the tour, as it did in M1.0 to 2.0.

In the past, if an act would get hot as a result of local radio play, they would then tour in that location to take advantage of the energized interest. The record sold the tour by virtue of the airplay it received. The record was selling the tour. If the record flopped, there would be no tour.

But in the new Sanctuary model, since the act had a strong-enough fan base to support a tour anyway, why not have some product to back it up? With these new economics of self-financing the release, the act could now make more money than ever on fewer units sold. Plus, by that time, it was cheaper than ever to create a release (since most musicians had studios at home that were more powerful than anything The Beatles had during their heyday). The stage was set for taking advantage of both the technology and the consumer environment.

For a time, Sanctuary Records and its artists succeeded wildly, to the point that the company expanded into a full-fledged record label (and a subsidiary of Universal Music) with traditional M2.0 staff and infrastructure. Soon afterward, however, it collapsed under the weight of that traditional system. The company had ventured beyond its original concept and comfort level and eventually paid for it. Sanctuary essentially ceased to exist as a record label at the end of 2007, although its assets have since been sold to BMG.

Sanctuary started the trend of an artist self-releasing a record during M2.0, way ahead of the curve and way ahead of what's commonplace today. Without knowing it at the time, the company paved the way for artists living in our current music generation, where self-production, self-promotion, and self-distribution are not only common, but the norm.

THE SANCTUARY MODEL

The tour sells the recording, not the other way around.

The CD or music product becomes just another piece of merchandise.

The artist markets and sells directly to his fan base.

Self-releasing can be more profitable than having a label.

The artist can make more money on fewer sales.

JUSTIN BIEBER—THE SOCIALLY MADE STAR

To many, Justin Bieber is just another example of a short-on-substance teen idol, but if you forget about the artist and look at how he was discovered and how his career was built, you'll find the perfect example of how social media can work in a big way in M3.0 and beyond.

Justin Bieber was the first artist made by YouTube. He was discovered there, and has prospered there almost more than any other artist except Lady Gaga. In fact, Bieber's song "Baby" has had more than 1.2 billion views alone, and all of his official videos together equal nearly 6 billion total views as of the writing of this book.

His career began when he was captured on a cellphone video as he was busking outside the Avon Theatre in Stratford, Ontario (population 32,000), hoping to get noticed, a moment that has since been shared some 8 million times on YouTube. In just a little over 9 months, Bieber went from playing to 40 people at an outdoor water park in Poughkeepsie to headlining sold-out arena shows, all while moving over 13 million albums worldwide over 14 months, opening his first movie on 3,000-plus screens with box-office earnings that topped $98 million, and inspiring hundreds of licensed merchandise items.

More than that, Bieber is one of the first artists to use social media to achieve superstardom, using all forms of social media to capitalize on his success with over 68 million Twitter followers and 73 million Facebook fans. In fact, he is number 1 in the top 100 Twitters and accounts for about 3 percent of all Twitter traffic as of the writing of this book in fall 2015.

Bieber is not the only current superstar to fully take advantage social media, though; Shakira has more than 100 million Facebook fans, Eminem has more than 90 million, and Rihanna, Taylor Swift, and Katy Perry each have more than 70 million, according to Fanpagelist.com. Katy Perry has more than 70 million Twitter followers, while Taylor Swift, Lady Gaga, and Rihanna each have more than 50 million Twitter followers, according to Twittaholic. All of these stars have more than 100 million YouTube views, with several near or over a billion.

It's a fact that the superstar of today cannot reach that level of success without a large social media presence. While Twitter and Facebook strengthen the connection with the fan, YouTube acts not only as the major music delivery system, but now plays a huge part in music discovery as well. Even though superstars have the resources to better craft a message and media campaign than a new act just starting out, social media is essential to artists at all levels in order to prosper.

SOCIAL MEDIA: THE CRUCIAL COMPONENT

Social media engagement strengthens the connection with the fan.

Engagement is the key social media element.

YouTube is still the major music delivery system.

YouTube is a major music and artist discovery portal.

AMANDA PALMER—THE SOCIAL CELEBRITY

If you're in the music business, there's a good chance you've heard of Amanda Palmer, although there's an even better chance that you've not heard her music. Palmer represents a conundrum in social media, where she's become a huge presence, thanks to her extremely effective social media and crowdfunding campaigns. But that hasn't helped to spread her music much beyond a small yet avid following.

Palmer rose to a low level of prominence as half of the duo Dresden Dolls before going solo in 2008. Her cult following grew from there, thanks to her extremely hands-on relationship with her fans. In an interview with *Techdirt* in 2012, she gave her secret:

> I've been tending this bamboo forest of fans for years and years, ever since leaving Roadrunner Records in 2009. Every person I talk to at a signing, every exchange I have online (sometimes dozens a day), every random music video or art gallery link sent to me by a fan that I curiously follow, every strange bed I've crashed on . . . all of that real human connecting has led to this moment, where I came back around, asking for direct help with a record. Asking EVERYBODY . . . And they help because . . . they KNOW me.

Palmer's notoriety again grew thanks to reports of big merch sales through Twitter campaigns (like $19,000 worth of T-shirts in less than a day), to where it reached a peak with a massively successful Kickstarter campaign in 2012, when she raised $1.2 million (the goal was $100,000) from nearly 25 thousand fans in 31 days for the marketing of an album/art book/gallery tour. This was followed shortly thereafter by a riveting TED talk where she described her fan-first business model.

Considering the exposure that Palmer has garnered from the mainstream media thanks to these events, her music still hasn't gained much traction, and she remains very much a niche artist, though one with a fanatical following. Only three of her videos have barely cracked 1 million views, she has just over a million Twitter followers, and she has received around 350,000 Facebook Likes.

While these are really great numbers for an indie artist, Palmer hasn't managed to transcend that narrow category despite vast and generally positive exposure and a supercharged fan base.

Amanda Palmer proves that no matter what your social media connections are, star and superstar success still depends on your music. In order to gain a mass audience, it must connect with the masses.

THERE'S MORE TO MUSIC THAN SOCIAL MEDIA

Social prominence won't automatically cause people to like your music.

But it can cause people to notice you.

Caring deeply about your fans builds an avid fan base.

An avid fan base is essential for crowdfunding.

PSY—THE VIRAL STAR

South Korean pop star Psy broke on the world scene in 2012 with the catchy electronic K-Pop (Korean pop) song "Gangnam Style," complete with an irresistible dance, that chalked up over a half-billion YouTube views in its first five weeks. The video went on to record over 2.4 *billion* views. (Yes, that's *billion* with a *B*.) What's more, his follow up, "Gentleman," eventually cleared a half-billion views as well. His entire channel has over 4 billion views, which is the sixth highest of any on YouTube according to statsheep.com. And if you keep up with the social media side of things, "Gangnam Style" has over 9.7 million thumbs up, and "Gentleman" over 3.3 million.

No one could have predicted that a pudgy Asian singer in his mid-30s would have near that kind of massive worldwide success simply because of a clever YouTube video, but that's exactly what happened.

As the viewership of the song began to snowball, Psy made the wise decision to connect with Justin Bieber's manager Scooter Braun, which then led to high-profile personal appearances and television commercials all over the world as well as distribution for his music with Universal Republic.

Psy already had some measure of success in Korea, with a number of hit albums and awards to his credit, as well as being the scion of a wealthy family with a large stake in the Korean semiconductor industry. It was this basic infrastructure that provided the means for "Gangnam Style" to initially take off, along with the persistent rumors that many of the initial YouTube views were bought in order to trigger the YouTube algorithm to sense virality.

Interestingly, it's estimated that Psy only made a bit over $10 million from YouTube, even with the record-setting view count. And despite going to No. 1 in 30 countries, the song sold just 9.7 million units. This was good for only third place, behind Carly Rae Jepsen's song of the summer "Call Me Maybe" and Gotye's "Somebody That I Used To Know," which were both products of massive radio airplay. Perhaps the most profit that Psy (and his family) made came from the 30 percent rise in stock value of their DI Corporation brought about by the success of "Gangnam Style."

We've seen viral YouTube hits both before and since Psy—like OK Go's "Here It Goes Again," Baauer's "Harlem Shake," and Macklemore and Ryan Lewis's "Thrift Shop"—but few have been able to re-create a high level of commercial success unless they secure the help of a sophisticated management team and the distribution of a major label. Virality is one thing; exploiting it is another.

One of the problems with a short burst of success is the ability to sustain it. Most successful careers are built over time, converting one fan at a time at one show at a time. Instant success tends to come and go quickly as the next success story replaces the previous. When it comes to music careers, long and slow usually beats the short and fast.

THE GLOBAL NATURE OF YOUTUBE

YouTube virality can make a hit almost overnight.

Global stars can now be made more easily than ever.

But you still need an infrastructure to get to the next level.

Instant success doesn't necessarily create a career.

MACKLEMORE AND RYAN LEWIS— TURNING THE RECORD LABEL PARADIGM AROUND

When Ben Haggerty (stage name Macklemore) and producer/partner Ryan Lewis were readying the self-release of their 2012 album *The Heist* in their small, 500-square-foot distribution office, the only thing they knew for sure was that they were determined to stay independent.

After some moderate success with several singles and a 2009 album called *The Unplanned Mixtape*, there were several major label deals on the table, yet Haggerty and Lewis felt that retaining their independence was important enough to forgo the huge publicity push that could only come with the help of a major.

When the album rose to No. 1 on iTunes, with 78,000 copies sold the first week, the Seattle-based duo was so hot that the majors upped their offers.

Of most interest was the offer from the management team at Sony Music subsidiary Epic Records, who came with a unique proposal. Since the duo had come this far without a label, they knew that the chances of signing were limited. As an alternative, they suggested that Sony do the radio publicity for free in exchange for the band signing with them for the next album. Haggerty and Lewis rejected Epic's offer, but the proposal got them thinking outside the box.

Haggerty and Lewis were distributed by the Alternative Distribution Alliance (ADA), an independent-label service company that handles physical distribution and is a subsidiary of Warner Music Group. ADA was already working radio for free in an effort to boost sales. The duo, still determined to stay independent, went to Warner Bros. with their own version of the Epic proposal: Could they use the publicity resources of Warner Bros. in exchange for a small percentage of *The Heist* only?

After initially rejecting the offer, Warner Bros. accepted and, thanks to their massive publicity efforts, pushed three singles to No. 1 and the album to No. 2 on the *Billboard* charts. Macklemore became a major worldwide star as a result, yet the duo remain totally independent.

While many DIY artists have met with small to moderate success, Macklemore and Ryan Lewis have proven that it's truly possible to become a superstar without signing a traditional record deal. You still need the infrastructure of a major label for that to happen, but it's now also true that other types of deals with major labels are now possible to get that help in Music 4.1.

DIY VS. RECORD LABEL

DIY provides freedom.

Major labels still have the publicity machine that can't easily be copied.

Publicity is required for superstardom.

It's possible to gain access to that infrastructure without signing a traditional record deal.

JACK & JACK SHIFT THE RELEASE SCHEDULE

The mantra of the M4.1 artist could be "More and more often," meaning that frequent releases of single songs work better for today's socially connected audiences than the previous paradigm used by the album-oriented artist. One of the best examples of this is Jack & Jack, the pop duo from Omaha, Nebraska.

Jack Johnson and Jack Gilinsky were childhood friends who began releasing six-second comedy skits on the video network Vine that included nothing more than lip-synching videos, song parodies, and their take on British slang. After their "Nerd Vandals" video went viral, the duo amassed a huge following that swelled to more than 5 million by 2015.

Jack & Jack parlayed their popularity into two mobile game apps and then into a music career with the help of some high school musician friends. Their first official single, "Distance," was self-released via

TuneCore and rose to No. 7 on the iTunes US hip hop charts. That was followed by 11 more singles and three music videos, all in 2014.

The duo continued their success in 2015, releasing five more videos and an EP, *Calibraska*, that rose to No. 1 on the iTunes US album charts almost as soon as it was released. The group remains solidly independent, with *Calibraska* being distributed by digital aggregator DistroKid.

All told, Jack & Jack have sold more than 1 million songs on iTunes, and many of their songs have topped both the iTunes and *Billboard* Digital Songs lists, all while staying independent.

Although we'll discuss this more in the next chapter, Jack & Jack proved the case that a constant stream of content is more conducive to building an audience than the album mentality of the past. New content keeps you fresh in the mind of your fans and provides more opportunities to expand those numbers.

A CONSTANT STREAM OF CONTENT

Provides more opportunities to grow your fan base.

Keeps you fresh in the minds of your fans.

Works well with varied types of content.

Works best for an indie artist.

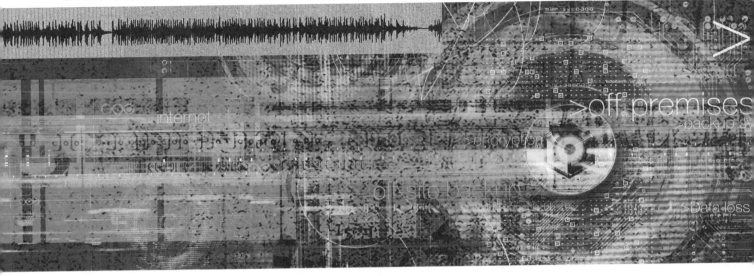

C H A P T E R   5

The New Marketing—Part I

An artist in Music 4.1 requires an entirely new marketing plan than in prior periods because the techniques commonly used in the past won't work anymore, at least with the degree of success that they once did. Traditional media, like radio, isn't as much of a music-marketing factor as it once was; nor is television, unless you're an artist whose image counts more than your music.

YOUR MUSIC IS YOUR MARKETING

The major marketing tool for the M4.1 artist is the music itself. It's no longer the major product that the artist has to sell, although it still is a product, so it has to be used differently and thought of differently as a result.

Perhaps recorded music was never the product we were led to believe it was. In the M1.0 and M1.5 days of vinyl records and CDs, the round plastic piece (the container that held the music) was the product. Although the songwriter always made money when a song was played on the radio, the artist never did (although artists might soon get their due, depending on the status of impending Performance Rights Act legislation). Even when it was sold, the artist made only a small percentage of CD and vinyl sales (10 to 15 percent of wholesale, on average).

In order for the artist to make any money from the recording, the costs involved in the production of the music product and the manufacturing of the container that transported the music (physical material costs, artwork, and so on) first had to be recouped. The fact of the matter was that the artist made most of his or her money on concert tickets and merchandise sales while touring, not in record sales.

While this has been the system that artists and labels have worked under for years, if you look at music in terms of the advertising world, you see it in a different light.

If you're selling a soap product, for instance, the production cost for a commercial to broadcast on television or the radio is trivial. It's the total ad buy (the total radio or television time that's purchased) where most of the money is spent. Even then, it's considered part of the marketing budget of the product, which might be about 3 percent of total sales.

In M4.1, if you consider the music production costs as part of the marketing budget in the same way as a national product, it takes on a whole new meaning.

Since the music is considered the major marketing tool for an artist, it could be considered a free product, a giveaway, an enticement. Put it on a streaming service's free tier, give it away on your website, place it on the torrents, let your fans freely distribute it. It's all okay.

Because most people under age 25 already feel that music should be free and have lived in a culture where that's mostly so, don't fight it. Go with the flow! Just as it was during the past 60 years, the real money in the music business is made elsewhere anyway.

Furthermore, just because you're giving it away doesn't mean that you can't charge for it, either at the same time or at some time in the future. There are numerous cases in which sales actually decreased for an artist's iTunes tracks when the free tracks were eliminated.

One such musician is Corey Smith. After six years, Corey has built his gross revenue to about $9 million, and free music was the basic building block of his ever-increasing fan base. You can buy his tracks on iTunes (he's sold more than 1.2 million singles and 250,000 albums so far), but when his management experimented by taking the free tracks down from his website, his iTunes sales went down as well. The free music Corey offered allowed potential fans to try him out. If they emailed and asked for a song that wasn't available for free, he just emailed it back to them. He was tending his fan base!

Corey's albums made such an impact that they eventually began to rank high on various *Billboard* music charts, getting as high as No. 2 on the Heatseekers chart and No. 5 on the US folk chart.

Another example of reaping the rewards of giving it away for free is the electronic artist Moby, who's "Shot in the Back of the Head" became the bestselling iTunes track after he gave it away for free on his website for two months.

Of course, eventually you can charge for your music with enhanced products, such as box sets, compilations, special editions, and other value-added offerings. To build a buzz, however, the initial releases for an artist (except for the already-established star) must be free and easily available, which is much easier to do these days thanks to the free tiers of streaming services.

YOUR MUSIC IS YOUR MARKETING

Music is your main marketing tool.

Give it away for free, but charge for it, too.

Most of your income comes from elsewhere anyway.

Value-added products are your best revenue source.

Embrace the free streaming tiers.

THE NEW RELEASE SCHEDULE

M4.1 requires new thinking regarding song releases. If we go back to the '50s, vinyl singles had a notoriously fast manufacturing turn-around time, despite the labor-intensive process required to make a vinyl record.

At that time, it was not uncommon to have a single (the small, 7-inch "45" with a song on each side) on the streets within days of recording (and sometimes even writing) the song! Of course, the quick turnaround was helped by the fact that the song was usually recorded in a few hours, since there was little or no overdubbing, so it was possible to record a song on Monday and have it on the radio on Wednesday of the same week.

When the emphasis on releases turned from singles to albums, the length of time between releases increased accordingly, which was natural considering that more songs were being recorded.

During the M1.0 days, there was a limit to how many songs could be recorded for an album because of the limitations of the vinyl itself. Twenty-three minutes per side was the goal to get the loudest and highest-fidelity record. Any longer and the noise floor of the record increased as the volume decreased. As a result, artists were confined to about 45 to 50 minutes per album. Consumers didn't seem to mind, because they still felt they were getting value if they liked the songs. In fact, many hit vinyl records regularly clocked in at between 35 and 40 minutes of music.

The time limitation lifted with the introduction of the CD in M1.5. When first released, the CD had a maximum playing time of 74 minutes (the number rumored to be chosen by the chairman of Sony at the time because it could fit Beethoven's entire Ninth Symphony), which was later increased to a full 80 minutes. No longer saddled with the vinyl album's built-in time limitation, artists were able to stretch out and add more and longer songs to each album release. This soon proved to be a double-edged sword, since it now took longer to finish recording each release because of the inclusion of all those extra songs.

Having more songs on an album doesn't necessarily make a better record though, and longer albums sometimes backfired on the artist's popularity. While 40 to 45 minutes was a time bite easily digestible for a listener, 60 to 70 was not. The extra songs were not only generally unappreciated but, even worse, thought of as mere filler. The consumer began to think (sometimes rightfully so) that the songs were there just for the sake of being there, and they began to feel ripped off. Why pay for songs that you'll never listen to? Because you had to!

Over the years, the time between record releases gradually lengthened to the point that a superstar act might take several years. While this might have worked in M1.5 and 2.0, that strategy would never work in M3.0 and beyond, as the fans have an insatiable appetite for product. What's worse, the fan base can actually dissipate if the product does not come at regular intervals—the shorter the better.

And with CD sales way down, the album format itself seems to be going the way of the vinyl single of the '50s and '60s. Consumers in M4.1 listen only to the songs they want to hear, and therefore, they consume mostly singles. Which brings about a new philosophy regarding recordings and how they are released.

In M4.1, artists record fewer songs but have more frequent releases. It's better to release a song or two every 6, 8, or 12 weeks than to wait a year for one release of ten songs. This benefits the artist in the following ways:

- The artist keeps his or her fans happy with a constant supply of new music. New music keeps the fans interested and keeps the buzz and dialog going.
- The artist gains increased exposure for every song. In a ten-song album release, it's easy for a fan, reviewer, or radio programmer to focus on just one or two songs while the others fall in priority. When releases are a single song at a time, each song gets equal attention and has the ability to live and die on its own merits.
- Each song is its own marketing event, which means it can be promoted directly to fans and on social media. Therefore, 10 songs released individually are 10 separate events, each with its own promotional cycle. An album just gets one.
- All the songs can still be compiled into an album after having been individually released. At the end of the year, or at the end of the artist's creative cycle, the songs are then compiled into an album that can be released in any format. The advantage is that the album has much more advanced exposure and publicity thanks to numerous single releases. Plus, it can be treated as an additional marketing event, which is also to the artist's advantage.

Make no mistake, the album format is not dead in M4.1 (although sales of even digital albums are decreasing at about the same rate as the CD), but the emphasis has shifted to the individual song.

THE NEW RELEASE SCHEDULE

Release a song or two every 6 to 12 weeks.

Frequent new music keeps the fans happy.

Exposure for all songs is increased.

Singles can be compiled into an album later.

Singles act as advanced publicity
for the album.

Each release can be treated
as a separate marketing event.

Artists get multiple events to promote.

TEN MUSIC MARKETING IDEAS

It's easier to sell your music if you add extra value to it. Here are ten ways to think outside the box when it comes to distributing your music. Thanks to Bruce Houghton for numbers 7 through 10.

1. **Develop a package:** This could mean anything from a CD and vinyl album to a high-resolution digital download and album with alternative mixes to a boxed set of CDs, or anything in between (see Trent Reznor's Ghosts I–IV or Josh Freese's offerings in Chapter 4 for ideas). The idea is to go beyond just the typical CD and digital offerings.

2. **Sequential numbering:** Limiting the availability of physical products and numbering them (for example, number 7 of 500) gives it the feeling of exclusivity. The product becomes a special edition and a must-have for the true fan.

3. **Tie it to merchandise:** Bundles are where the artist or band combines multiple products at a special price that's lower than whatever the individual prices together might have been. They've proven to be a very effective way to sell both music and merch. Typical bundles include a CD with a T-shirt, a brand new CD with one from the catalog, a CD with links to the songs on a streaming site like SoundCloud or Spotify, a CD with digital downloads—the combinations are limitless.

4. **Release a "double-sided" digital single:** Rhino Records' digital releases celebrating 60 years of the 45 RPM single set a fine example for this format. For between $1.49 and $1.99, Rhino provided the original hit song, its B side (the flip side of the vinyl record), and the

original artwork. You can do the same by providing two songs for price of one—an A and a B side—or even tying two songs together in the same stream.

5. **Release on an old alternative format:** A number of artists, like Jack White and Radiohead, have released a vinyl-only physical product to great success. Cheap Trick did it on the old 8-track format from the '60s, and some bands have even recently released their latest albums on cassette tape. Releasing on an older format can be good as a publicity tool (as long as everyone else isn't doing it), and who knows, maybe you can start a trend?

6. **Release on a new alternative format:** A new alternative format is always a good way for an album to gain some traction. Trent Reznor met with great viral success by planting unmarked memory sticks in bathrooms at NIN's concerts, and Sony released the 25th anniversary of Michael Jackson's *Thriller* in that format. Performance artist Charlotte Jarvis and the Kruetzer Quartet teamed with scientist Dr. Nick Goldman to imprint their music on DNA molecules suspended in soap bubbles, which is an impractical delivery format but garnered them lots of publicity. And don't forget alternative packages like Shidlas' *Saliami Postmodern* CD (see Figure 5-1), which can work great as well.

Figure 5-1: Shidlas "Salami" CD

7. **Three sides:** Offer a song in an early studio version, the final mix, and then captured live.

8. **Radical mixes:** Offer two or three very different mixes of the same song, perhaps even done by the fans.

9. **Two sides of [your city]:** Two different bands each contribute a track to a series chronicling your local scene.

10. **"Artist X" introduces _____:** Add a track by your favorite new artist/band along with one of yours. This is similar to a gig tradeout with another band, which many bands use as a way to play in new venues. The idea is that the band you feature will feature you on their release as well.

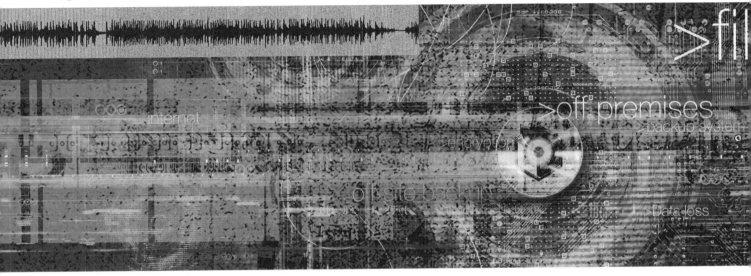

CHAPTER 6

The New Marketing—Part 2

here once an artist's major marketing thrust was directed at the traditional media of radio, television, and print, today it focuses more online to reach current and potential fans. While social networks tend to wax and wane in popularity, there are other aspects of an artist's online presence that can't be ignored. That said, it's not the social network or the online presence that's important. Those are only mechanisms to reach the most crucial element to an artist's success—the fans themselves.

THE NEW IMPORTANCE OF THE FAN

As pointed out elsewhere in the book, prior to Music 3.0, the fan was treated differently. The artist wasn't able to easily come in contact with fans and, for the most part, didn't want to. Except for special releases and perks to the fan club, the fan was treated mostly as a consumer and kept at arm's length.

M3.0 changed all that with Seth Godin's tribal concept, and now fan communication is a direct and integral part of an act's success. It's possible for an act to become hot for a while, but if the tribe of fans is not created and constantly enriched, any success will be short lived.

Not only can the artist directly interact with the fan, but he or she must interact in order to maintain the tribe!

That being said, fans know when they're being hyped, exploited, or taken lightly, and receiving anything less than total respect can prove disastrous to the fan base/tribe. Fans don't want to be marketed to, but they want to be informed of things that might interest them.

Fans want to know that the artist is listening to them. They don't need direct communication (although that's the best), but they want acknowledgement that they're being heard. Fans don't want to be talked at, but they want to be spoken to. They want to hear from the artist but not hyped or sold to, as that cheapens the experience. They don't want ad copy; they want it from the heart.

Going back to the email that Trent Reznor sent his fans:

Hello everyone.

I'd like to thank everyone for a very successful year so far in the world of Nine Inch Nails. I'm enjoying my couple of weeks off between legs of our Lights In The Sky tour and got to thinking . . . "wouldn't it be fun to send out a survey to everyone that's shown interest in NIN?" Well, that's not exactly how it went, but regardless—here it is. As we've moved from the familiar world of record labels and BS into the unknown world of doing everything yourself, we've realized it would benefit us and our ability to interact with you if we knew more about what you want, what you like, what you look like naked, etc. I know it's a pain in the ass but we'd truly appreciate it if you'd take a minute and help us out. As an incentive, everyone who completes the survey will be able to download a video of live performance from this most recent tour (and I know what's going through your little minds right now: "I'll just grab this off a torrent site and not have to fill out the survey!!!" and guess what? You will be able to do just that and BEAT THE SYSTEM!!!! NIN=pwn3d!!!)

BUT

What if we were to select some of those that DO complete the survey and provide them with something really cool? I'm not saying we'll ever get around to it, but if we did maybe something like signed stuff, flying someone to a show somewhere in the world, a magic amulet that makes you invisible, a date with Jeordie White (condoms sup-

plied of course), you know—something cool. See, you'd miss that opportunity AND be a cheater.

Do the right thing—help us out. You'll feel better.

Thank you and I've had too much caffeine this morning,

Trent

Reznor treats his fans with respect, bidding them "hello everyone" and thanking them at the end. He tells you a little bit about himself with, "I've had too much caffeine this morning." He engages his fans to interact and help him, but most of all, you get the feeling that he's talking directly to you.

A fan who's treated well might not always stay a fan (though he or she probably will), but while a fan, he or she will remain loyal and an uber-consumer of anything the artist has to offer.

THE NEW IMPORTANCE OF THE FAN

**Communication with the fans
is now integral to an artist's success.**

**Fans know when they're being hyped,
exploited, or taken lightly.**

**Fans want to know
that the artist is listening to them.**

Fans want to be treated with respect.

Fans want to be informed, not marketed to.

THE NEW ARTIST ONLINE STRATEGY

The biggest difficulty artists, bands, musicians, producers, songwriters, publishers, and even record labels have when it comes to social media is that they don't have an online focus.

They may have a website but rely on Facebook for most of their traffic. Maybe it's a Tumblr or Wordpress blog that gets the most attention, with a Facebook page getting some consideration depending on the whim of the day. Even worse, maybe they have a website, Facebook page, blog, Twitter account, mailing list, Instagram account, and more, and all get random attention.

The problem is, until you have a single focal point online, you don't really have a strategy. That's where your website comes in as your primary online element.

A Typical Artist Website

A website should be unique and individual in design, and that means it should obviously reflect the brand and music of the artist. That said, if we were to look at the ideal artist website, we would find the following common elements:

- **The Bio or About page.** This provides a brief background of the artist. Three or four paragraphs is enough, as a longer bio can go in the Press section.
- **The Contact page.** This provides information about how to contact you, your agent, or your management.
- **The Subscribe section.** A place on each page where a fan can subscribe to the artist mailing list.
- **The Press page.** This not only contains press clippings of the artist, but also critical elements for the press to make it easier to write an article about the artist. Among the items to include are high- and low-resolution graphics of the artist and the artist's logo; an extensive biography; links to interviews; PDFs of adverts, flyers, and posters; web-ready graphics and banners; press releases; and links to music and videos.
- **The Booking Info page.** This can contain contact information for bookings, but also is a good place to include statistics that help influence promoters, like average gig attendance, markets and venues previously played, a photo gallery from gigs, quotes from fans and other promoters, a typical set list (if you're a cover band), and a stage plot.
- **Social Media Connections.** Add links and buttons for Facebook, Twitter, YouTube, and any other social network where you have a presence.

The Steps to a Successful Online Strategy

Here are the six basic steps for designing a modern online strategy:

1. **Make your website your main online focal point.** Make sure that

all your important information is curated there and is easy for a site visitor to find.

2. **Create accounts on the "Big 3" social networks (Facebook, Twitter, and YouTube).** You can't be everywhere at once. Even if you could, it would take so much time that you'd never have any time to make music, which is what you want to avoid. That said, in order to get the most out of social media promotion, you need the following:

   - A Facebook page. Regardless of how you feel about Facebook, you still need a presence on it if for no other reason than its easy proximity to lots of potential new fans. If you're just starting out, you might want to start with a personal page instead of a fan site, though. It can be embarrassing to have a fan page with only a few followers, and a personal page is a way to gain some momentum before you make the leap.
   - A Twitter account. The people who dismiss Twitter simply don't know how to use it for promotion. It's extremely powerful for attracting new fans and keeping your current ones instantly informed.
   - A YouTube channel. Videos are such a major part of any musician's, artist's, or band's online presence that you really need your own channel to exploit them successfully.
   - A look at other networks. There are many other significant social networks, and some of them might deserve your attention. There comes a point when the amount of time invested versus the potential outcome just doesn't balance out, which is why you should probably stay with the previous three networks until you reach a level of comfort before you take on another one. The only exception to that would be if a big portion of your audience is on a particular network other than the "Big 3" (like Instagram or Pinterest, for example); then you might want to substitute that network for Twitter.

3. **Use a social media broadcast app for all your updates.** An app like Hootsuite or Buffer is one of the keys to streamlining the process that saves time and makes what you do online more efficient.

4. **Develop your social media sites so they all feed viewers into your main site.** The key is to make sure that any viewer on any site is

aware that you have a website and knows that it's the main repository of information about you.

5. **Be sure that email list subscribers from all sites go to same email service.** Having different mailing list services won't do you much good if you have to create a separate newsletter blast for each one.

6. **Get third-party help when you get overwhelmed.** At some point, social-media management gets too complex for the artist to maintain, and third-party help is needed. This is usually a good thing because it means you've progressed to a point that things are so massive that you can't keep up. Furthermore, a company that specializes in social-media management can keep you current with new tools and techniques that you might not be aware of. Even when outside help arrives, remember that you're still the one who drives the bus. Be sure to take part in all strategy discussions, but leave the actual facilitation to the company you've hired.

For more information about artist online strategy and promotion, check out *Social Media Promotion for Musicians*.

YOUR MOST IMPORTANT TOOL— YOUR EMAIL LIST

By far one of the most, if not *the* most, important marketing tools that an artist has is his or her email list. It's the direct link to the artist's most rabid fans and one of the primary drivers of commerce in the artist's online arsenal.

Your email list is a major component for marketing to your fan base. It's widely overlooked, since most artists believe that their Facebook friends and Twitter followers are enough, but your email list allows you to reach out and personally connect with fans and control your message while you're doing it.

A well-thought-out email blast allows you to do the following:

• Engage your fans individually
• Design the communication without the constraints of a social network
• Add a call to action

Your email list makes it easier to inform, market to, and sell to your fans in a manner true fans (superfans, uberfans, tribe members—whatever you want to call them) enjoy, if you do it well. That said, execution is always key in the success of any venture, so here are some aspects of your email list to be aware of.

Mail List Services

Having an easy way to sign up for the list is essential, but having a way for the artist to maintain and control the list is just as important. Most artists just starting out rely on their own email client, such as Outlook or Mac Mail, to manage their lists, but these have built-in limitations that you'll soon outgrow.

For one thing, you must manually clean the list of bounces and drop-offs, which is time consuming. Another major problem is that ISPs (Internet Service Providers) limit the number of emails that can be sent in a batch in order to eliminate spamming. This can mean that if your email list exceeds as few as 100 people, the email blast will get rejected by your ISP, and you'll have to divide it into many smaller email groups.

A way around that is to use an email service provider (ESP) such as iContact, Constant Contact, MailChimp, or any of the other similar services to maintain your list. For a small monthly fee (as little as $10.00 depending upon the mailing-list size), your email list can undergo a significant change for the better in the following ways:

- No limit on the number of subscribers in the email blast
- The list is automatically cleaned of bounces or invalid addresses
- Easily handles subscribers and opt-outs
- Extensive analytics reveal who opens the email, how many of them click through, how many forward it, and how long they view
- Many professional email templates to choose from

Right now it's that combination of having a great email list and a great website that's constantly updated and gives the fans a reason to come back. In terms of growing an email list, I'm a big fan of the tools that Topspin and Bandcamp have. I'm a big fan of anything that encourages viral growth.

—Bruce Houghton

Most email services have essentially the same feature set and prices, so the main difference between them is a user interface that suits the list owner—you. Most services offer a free tryout period, although some may limit the number of emails or addresses during this period.

Six Keys to Building Your Mailing List

Building an email list seems like an easy thing to do, but there's a lot more to it than you'd think. Here are the six keys to building a successful list:

1. **Offer a high comfort level.** People don't like to give their email address out unless they're getting something in return. In other words, they use their email information as a form of currency. If they don't trust your site or they're unsure what you'll do with their address, it's really difficult to get them to register. If the site, offer, post, or page is unprofessional and feels like it may disappear any day, chances are they won't sign up.

2. **Make the sign-up form easy to find.** Make the registration prominent on not only your website and social media, but every marketing piece that you have. Most email services provide HTML widgets that both look good and work seamlessly without any programming on your part.

3. **Make it easy to register.** That means don't ask for too much information. It's easy to get their first name and their email address and maybe their city, but beyond that, many potential users begin to feel uncomfortable. Remember, you can always ask them for more information later, after they sign up.

4. **Give them an incentive to subscribe.** They need a contest, access to exclusive material, or a promise of receiving something later as a reason to register. Remember, they're buying something with their email currency. They're thinking, "What's in it for me?"

5. **Cross-promote.** Promote your list through your social networks, including Twitter, Instagram, Facebook, your blog, and even something as simple as on gig flyers or business cards. Every address is valuable, so don't let any opportunities for another registration fall by the wayside.

6. **Use reminders.** Remind people about your email list in your videos, blog posts, podcasts, CD covers, and any other kind of content you produce. You don't have to be blatant about it; just make sure that the info is always present.

Designing Your Email Blast

There's no doubt that email is an important part of an artist's social strategy, but sometimes a poorly-thought-out email blast can be worse than none at all. Here are some important questions to ask yourself that will guide you in designing your email. These are questions you should know the answers to way before you hit the Send button.

- What's the purpose of this email? To inform? To sell? To entertain?
- Why should my subscribers care about what I'm sending?
- Why did the subscriber sign up to receive my emails in the first place? Does this email live up to that expectation?
- Did I include a call to action?
- Is my most important message above the fold (the point before the reader has to scroll down)?
- Did I check the grammar, spelling, and all the links?
- Have I run a test send?

While the first three points involve the conceptual part of the email, the second three are important design considerations. Keeping your most important message above the fold gives you the best chance of capturing readers' attention before they delete the mail and move on.

The last point, doing a test send or two to yourself, is the best way to prevent an embarrassing oversight or glitch (like the links not working or a spelling or grammar mistake) from happening. Do it even if you're 100 percent sure you're ready to go. You'll be surprised how often you'll find that you're not.

Best Email Practices

When it comes to emailing, there are good and bad ways to do it. Here are what you might consider "best practices" as revealed by Jed Carlson, founder and CEO of ReverbNation, in his "Email 101 for Artists, Labels, and Venues" article on Music Think Tank.

1. **Always respect a person's desire to unsubscribe from your list.** Immediately unsubscribe them or allow them to do it themselves if your mailing list isn't what they expected. Not only is it a good idea for keeping a good relationship with your fans, but, thanks to the CAN-SPAM Act of 2003, it's also the law.
2. **Always talk to them without swearing.** It may be part of your

"persona" as a band, but some people don't like that language. Many ISPs don't like it either, and your message will go directly to the junk box if it contains anything they deem "too colorful." You wouldn't talk to your grandma that way, would you?

3. **Always avoid "scam" words in the subject line.** Words such as *free* and *help* will land your message in the junk box the majority of the time.

4. **Always target fans with messages that are relevant to them.** If you have a show in Seattle, don't message your fans in Miami. Keep your powder dry for a message to them later about something else.

5. **Always give them the basics about the information you are conveying.** Reporters call this the "who, what, why, when, where, how" model. If you have a show coming up, do your fans (and yourself) the service of providing dates, times, locations, ticket links, and lineup of the show. Over 75 percent of artists miss this essential piece when they email. If you want someone to respond and come to your show, for goodness' sake, go so far as to give them driving directions if you can. Each ticket sold is money in your pocket.

6. **Always link them to some place to find out more info about the band.** This could be ReverbNation or a homepage or blog, but *always* give them a way to find out more.

Don't overlook the obvious. Your email list is your most important tool in Music 4.1 for reaching your fans, but you need a specialized application to use it to its utmost.

More Is Less

In M4.1, "more is less" should be one of your main mantras. There's a limit to what fans can absorb, and exceeding that limit can alienate them. Too much communication can be counterproductive. Once a week is a good amount, although once a month can work, too. More is okay if there's a real purpose, like a special event to talk about.

Mailing list blasts have a definite point where it's too much. We like to limit those to a couple of times a month, or once a week at most if you're really doing something special or have unique content. If it's just announcing tour dates or trying to sell something, you shouldn't do it more than once a week, but we find once or twice a month works best. If it's unique content, that could be cool to blast weekly.

On the other hand, if you're Twittering, the more the merrier because that's the kind of minutia that people are into. That platform is great for 3, to 10, to even 20 times a day.

—Jacob Tell of Oniracom

Just as 15 songs on a release are not necessarily better than 8, even if they're all great, there is a tipping point for email blasts at which fans go from feeling informed to being intruded upon. It's just overload at that point and actually dilutes the effectiveness of your message and your marketing. The leader of the tribe must have a feel for where that point is and be sure never to cross it.

YOUR EMAIL LIST

Email is the most important marketing tool you have.

Professional email list-management services offer significant extra benefits.

Make your list sign-up easy to find and easy to do.

Think through your email blast before you send it.

Always observe best practices.

Fewer emails is always better.

THE EIGHT RULES OF FAN COMMUNICATION

1. **Talk to your fans, not at them.** Don't try to sell them, but keep them informed. Anything that reads like ad copy might be counterproductive. Always treat them with respect, and never talk down to them.
2. **Engage in communication.** Communication is a two-way street. Fans want to know that they're being listened to. You don't have to answer every email, but you have to acknowledge that you heard it. The more questions you ask, polls you supply, and advice you seek, the more your fans will feel connected to you.
3. **Keep your promises.** If you say you're going to do something, do it in a timely fashion. Don't let your fans wait. If you promise you're going to email a link and post a song, sooner is always better.
4. **Stay engaged.** Even if you're only sending something simple, such as

a link, take the time to engage the fan. Tell him or her about upcoming gigs, events, or releases. Take a poll. Ask for advice. This is a great opportunity for communication, so take advantage of it. Some of the things that you ask might be:

- Where do you live?
- Are there any venues nearby where you'd like to see us play?
- Do you prefer studio recordings or live performances?
- Would you like to obtain copies of our live performances?
- If we offered high-quality recordings of our shows, would you be interested?
- Would you prefer personal updates or unreleased music from our newsletter?
- Would you be interested in purchasing merch from us, and if so, what kind?
- Are you interested in seeing behind-the-scenes footage of our tour or recording sessions?

5. **Offer preorders.** If you have a release coming out soon, take preorders as soon as you announce it, even if it's free. It's best to get people to act while their interests are high, and it gives the fans something to look forward to. To motivate fans for a preorder, it sometimes helps to include exclusive content or merchandise.

6. **Appearance means a lot.** Style counts when talking to fans. Make sure everything looks good and is readable. Spelling or grammar mistakes reflect badly on you. Try to keep it simple but stylish, but if you or your team doesn't have the design chops to make it look good, then it's better to just keep things simple and readable.

7. **Cater to uberfans.** All the members of your tribe are passionate, but some are more passionate than others. Fans have different needs and wants, and it's to everyone's benefit if you can cater to them all. Try always to include a premium or deluxe tier for every offering, such as a free T-shirt, a backstage pass, a free ticket to an upcoming show, some signed artwork, some extra songs—anything to satiate the uberfan's interest.

8. **Give them a choice.** Give fans numerous ways to opt in, since not everyone wants to receive information in the same way. Ask if they would rather receive info by email, SMS, or even snail mail. Ask if they'd like to receive info on upcoming shows, song releases, video content, or contests. And ask how often they'd like be contacted.

ANOTHER USEFUL ONLINE TOOL—
YOUR BLOG

A blog is an excellent way to both communicate with your fans and have them communicate with you and with each other. It's easier than ever to create a blog these days with Blogger, Wordpress, or Tumblr (which is less sophisticated and in a slightly different "microblog" category), which are priced the way most artists like—free. Blog features are also built into most site-building websites, like Section 101, Weebly, and Wix, so you don't even need to go to an outside app.

You can design a fancy blog site if you want, but it's really not necessary. A generic one will do just fine as long as the look is somewhat consistent with your website and marketing materials to maintain your brand. If you can't do that, or if it will take too long to design, just make it plain vanilla. Since a blog is such a valuable tool, simply having one far outweighs how it looks.

Make sure that you update it regularly with photos, videos, and journal entries of your band's latest antics. Daily updates are best, but any interval can work as long as you consistently stick to it. For instance, it's best if your fans always know that you post at 11 a.m. every Wednesday, but you'd better make sure that you don't miss a day or post at a different time because that can lead to reader attrition.

You can also link with other musicians' blogs and sites, have fans subscribe, add a list of blogs that you like or suggest, and add widgets from other promotion sources. If you add keywords to your posts, they will be searchable through Google, and you can even set up Google AdSense to generate some additional revenue through ads on your blog or RSS feed.

A blog can do wonders for your communication with fans and for general visibility, and all it takes is a little time on a regular basis.

Other Music Blogs

By using the general music blogs and the blogs relating to both your genre of music and similar-sounding artists, you can develop a very effective marketing strategy. Especially when you're first starting out, any review or mention that you get on a popular blog is an important step to spreading virally across the web.

Everybody knows to set up a Facebook page and a YouTube Channel. Beyond that, regardless if you're offering your music for free or not, you want to utilize the rest of the Web that doesn't cost you anything, meaning all the social media stuff like personal profile pages, bookmarking and tagging, and an official Twitter channel. It's figuring out a way to broadcast to your fans and affinity groups, which are groups of people that like the type of music that you play. For example, if I sound a lot like John Mayer, then I want to reach out to John Mayer fans. You can do all that at no cost by simply putting the time in.

—Gregory Markel

So how do you get attention from a blogger? Unlike traditional media, where it's difficult to make a magazine or newspaper editor aware of you, most bloggers are typically not inundated with press releases and attention. Even the ones with large readerships are pretty much open to stories or communication because of how difficult it is to fill blog space every day.

The best way to establish a relationship with influential music blogs that discuss music similar to your own is to post frequently so the blogger gets to know you, then begin a relationship with the blogger via email, and finally send your music and ask for a review. Only do this after the blogger is very comfortable with you and either replies to your comments or answers your emails.

That still doesn't guarantee that you'll get a review, since the music still has to fit the tastes and mood of the blogger.

Here's some great info on finding the right blogs, from the DIY section of Bruce Houghton's ever-informative music blog Hypebot.com:

Most bloggers are true music fans who want to discover great new music and share it with the world . . . or at least their 37 friends who read them faithfully. If 10 percent of those 37 readers come to one of your shows, that's 3 or 4 fans that you didn't have yesterday telling their own 37 friends about you.

Bloggers are also more approachable than most print journalists, who often can only write about what editors assign them. And bloggers have influence. Fans respect writers that are passionate about music and prove it by writing for love instead of a paycheck. One study from NYC's Stern School of Business even showed that blogs more than some social networks helped to sell new music.

How to know which blogs to target? Two words: niche and location. Using a blog-specific search engine such as Google Blog Search or Technorati, type in "music + Chicago," or better yet a use specific genre, such as "heavy metal + Chicago." Think fans of Arcade Fire would like your band too? Try "Arcade Fire + [your city]." Try all kinds of combinations, including that obscure band that you think copied your style. If they wrote about them; why wouldn't they write about you? You can do the same thing nationally by simply searching under genres or similar artists.

Michael Terpin's Social Radius specializes in PR via blogs, and he suggests the following:

Quite frankly, if you're trying to "court" a blogger who covers your space, the best thing to do is to first start reading them. The nice things about blogs is they all have RSS feeds, and most of them link their most important posts to their Twitter account, which is mobile and a lot easier to deal with than a large RSS aggregator. You can follow all these bloggers on Twitter, and it'll be on your iPhone, Blackberry or anything that has a Twitter client, and they'll sort of recognize you as you become a Twitter follower and are watching what they say. You can comment on some of their posts, and all of a sudden, you have a bit of a relationship, so that when you come out, you don't come across as a salesman who's trying to spam 50 sites with the same information. It's better to come out and say, "Hey, I read your site frequently and here's what I'm doing."

BLOGS

Blogs are great for direct communication with fans.

A fancy design isn't necessary.

Post on a regular schedule.

Marketing through existing music blogs is an effective strategy.

Establish a relationship with the blogger before asking for a review.

CHAPTER 7

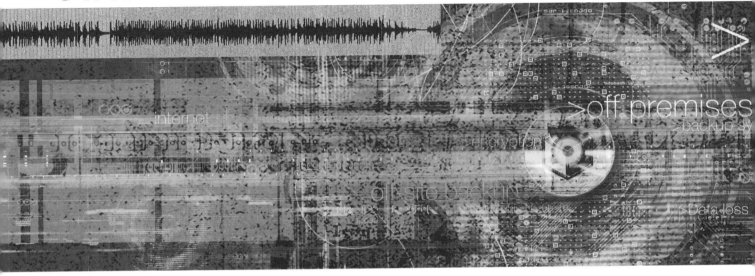

Marketing with Social Media

One of the most powerful methods of marketing in M4.1 is using social media, which means social networks (Facebook), microblogs (Twitter), video portals (YouTube), and photo/video platforms (Instagram). While Facebook and Twitter are primarily used for communicating with fans, their importance as marketing platforms should not be underestimated, and as noted several times before in this book, YouTube has become the primary means of music discovery and distribution today. Before we look at these networks more closely, let's look at a former online giant that's quickly moving toward irrelevance.

THE DEATH OF MYSPACE

MySpace has been on a downward spiral since being purchased by media giant NewsCorp in 2005, mostly for not acknowledging what it was and focusing on what it wasn't instead.

At its core, MySpace was an entertainment site centered on music. It didn't perform that function well enough to maintain its audience, though, and instead of improving its core value, it chose to try to be more of a general social network. That failed miserably, with Facebook coming from nowhere to dwarf MySpace's huge initial lead in both visitors and revenue.

While Facebook has become the dominant network of the social world, it's still not an obvious successor for music, since it still lacks many of the core assets that MySpace offers, despite some of the available music apps, such as BandPage and ReverbNation. The fact is that mixing a social network with a music network hasn't worked so far (e.g., iTunes Ping, Apple Connect in its new Apple Music service), and it remains to be seen if it will work in the future.

That said, MySpace still has more than 24 million visitors per month as of the writing of this book, but that has decreased from a peak of nearly 50 million in January of 2014 (according to research site Statista). After several years of rumors regarding its imminent closure, MySpace was sold at a fire-sale price to Specific Media in July of 2011, with singer Justin Timberlake as one of the investors.

In June of 2013, MySpace shut down the "Classic MySpace" in favor of a new updated version and, in doing so, created a scenario warned about elsewhere in this book by deleting years of user and follower data from every loyal member who stuck with the service. This created an uproar as everyone on the platform (even Timberlake) now started from the same place—zero.

With that, "New MySpace" also introduced several new features aimed directly at artists, like a new user interface, a mobile app, integration with social networks, and more.

MySpace has essentially put all of the best tools from these other platforms together in one place, and they're more artist and user friendly today than they were in the past and probably more useful, in terms of suite of features, than other social platforms. You can post status updates on MySpace and then share them on Facebook and Twitter. You can upload and host a video on MySpace and then build some nice-looking galleries. You can create video, music and picture compilations, which is great when you're trying to tell a story with a multimedia campaign. You can have pictures from the tour, video from backstage and the music video all in one "mix," which you can't do on any other platform. Every artist also has their own radio station, so you can curate your own music to show who you are as an artist. You can have a video that floats with the user as she moves around MySpace. There's also a lot of analytics, which are important for your strategy.

—Dae Bogen

Even with the new ownership and platform overhaul, there's little to indicate that the network will be able to reconstitute its once formidable user base. Despite its new features, the company has been ineffective at communicating its new abilities to artists, which, along with the stigma of the MySpace of the past, may have caused its slow growth.

MySpace held such promise and delivered little of it. It's another example of a multinational company getting involved in the music business only to slowly run itself into the ground. History repeats itself again.

MARKETING WITH FACEBOOK

In a few short years, Facebook has transplanted MySpace not only as the most formidable social network in the world, but also as an indispensable one for musical artists. According to Facebook's own stats (as of the time of this writing), the social network has more than 1.49 billion active users; 968 million of them log in to the service every day and spend an average of 20 minutes. The average user has 245 friends (teens have 300), is connected to 80 community pages, groups, and events, and creates 90 pieces of the more than 30 billion pieces of content (web links, news stories, blog posts, notes, videos, photo albums, etc.) shared each month. Plus, it's truly international, with 83 percent of active Facebook users living outside the United States, and entrepreneurs and developers from over 190 countries building for the platform. And it's still growing!

With Facebook's huge influence on almost any social happening, every artist should have his or her own page for promotional purposes. With numerous artist apps, such as BandPage (Bandpage.com) and My Band (facebook.com/rn.mybandapp), and utilities from artist platforms like ReverbNation, it's easier than ever to design a custom page that perfectly fits the artist's needs. That said, it still comes down to regular posts for effective promotion, and many of the same rules that apply to Twitter also apply to Facebook.

Eight Rules of Facebook Engagement

The research site Buddy Media Platform provides a number of interesting points in a white paper called "Strategies for Effective Facebook Wall Posts: A Statistical Review." In the study, they determined the Five Rules of Facebook engagement:

1. **Keep your posts short and sweet.** Posts of 80 characters or fewer have 27 percent higher engagement rates.
2. **Think twice before using URL shorteners.** Engagement rates are three times higher using full-length URLs.
3. **Post when people are listening.** The highest traffic occurs mid-week between 1 and 3 p.m.
4. **Some days are better than others.** Engagement rates are 18 percent higher on Thursday and Friday than on the other days of the week, but Saturday and especially Sunday are good, too. This can vary by industry, though.
5. **Avoid the noise of Monday.** There's too much going on after the weekend.

You can add a few more to this list that exactly parallel the email and Twitter advice:

6. **Keep your posts relevant.** You're trying to promote your brand, so stay on topic.
7. **Don't post unnecessarily.** Too many posts can cause your fans to tune you out. It's been discovered that engagement decreases after two posts a day.
8. **Keep the interaction high.** Ask your fans for their opinions and advice. It will not only keep them involved, but you'll immediately feel the pulse of the tribe.

If you're posting to keep in touch with your friends or to let them know what you're doing, then the above data is of no consequence to you. If you're posting strategically to promote your brand, then follow the eight points for better fan engagement.

Best Time of Day for Facebook Posts

While you might be writing the best, most engaging posts, they do you no good if no one reads them, so the question then becomes, "When is the best time of day to post to Facebook so my readership will be high?"

A study from the social media company Vitrue, "Managing Your Facebook Community: Findings on Conversation Volume by Day of Week, Hour and Minute," which looked closely at the viewing habits of Facebook channels of selected companies and brands, found some clues:

- The best times to post are 11 a.m., 3 p.m., and 8 p.m. ET.
- Of those times, the absolute best is 3 p.m. ET on weekdays.
- Wednesday at 3 p.m. is the best time of the week to post.
- Fans are less active on Sunday.
- Posts on the weekend can be more effective than during the week.
- Posts that occur in the morning tend to perform almost 40 percent better in terms of user engagement than those posted in the afternoon.
- Posts at the top of the hour (:00 to :15 minutes) get more comments than other parts of the hour, with posts at the bottom of the hour (:30) getting the least.
- 65 percent of users only access Facebook in the evening.

Understanding the "Like" Button

It's important to understand just what a "Like" means and not make too much or too little of it.

First of all, a Like is an endorsement by the fan. It has touched a nerve or a similar opinion or emotion, and it's an expression of that. It doesn't necessarily mean that you're especially clever, only that your post refers to something he or she wants to associate with.

It's important to step back and look for a pattern of Likes or comments and then analyze them to see if there's a common thread. It's the best way to take the pulse of your tribe.

It's also important not to get too hung up on Likes, especially if you feel that you're not getting enough. According to the analytics firm Locowise, you can expect less than 1 percent of your total followers to post a Like (sometimes way less), since only an average of 2.6 percent see your posts in the first place. These real-life examples shed some light on how fans use the Like button:

> The Black Keys have 4.4 million fans, and their average post gets around 2,000 Likes (0.045%), with an occasional spike to around 30,000 (0.68%).
>
> Justin Bieber has 73 million fans and gets between 75,000 and 150,000 likes per post (which is 0.1 to 0.2%).
>
> Mumford and Sons has 5.4 million fans and only occasionally get as many as 30,000 likes (0.55%), with most posts getting about half that.

It's important not to buy into the thinking that if someone doesn't register a Like, then they're not actually reading the post, which is not the case at all. In fact, many of us see and react to posts without ever registering a Like.

The reason an artist should continue to post without worrying about getting Likes is the same reason advertising works—it's all about the impressions. The more impressions, or views, the more likely the viewer will take some action, such as listening to some music, going to a show, or buying a T-shirt.

As long as the information you post is valuable to the reader in some way, it's worth doing, because you're reaching him or her in some way. In other words, it's nice to be "Liked," but it's not necessarily a sign of a successful post.

Facebook Ads

One of the most useful marketing tools for an artist is Facebook ads, which can boost Likes, comments, awareness, and even sales. The beauty of Facebook ads is that you don't have to pay a lot, as you can set the price that you want to pay each day and the ad campaign duration. You can also target the ad's exact audience, from either all your followers, the friends of all your followers, people in a geographic location like a country, town, or zip code; or even followers of a certain kind of music.

You're also able to promote a link to an outside website, a Facebook post, a video, or a photo, and you can select whether you want to display the ad in the newsfeed of your targeted audience (which is the most effective) or in the ad box on the right side of the page.

Although you can promote any post by selecting "Boost Post," a much more precise way is to use the Facebook Ads Manager and Power Editor (see Figure 7-1). This subject can take up an entire book by itself, but you can check out *Social Media Promotion for Musicians* for more details.

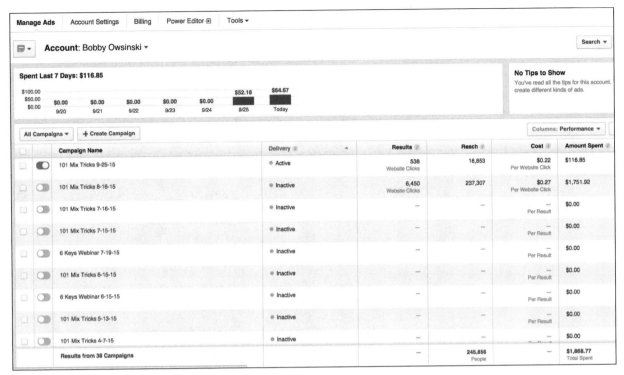

Figure 7-1: The Facebook Ads Manager

Now Facebook has added a new twist in that no one will get to see your post unless you pay, and now we have a problem. We've been saying for years that it's all about great content and engagement and keeping things interesting, and Facebook has come along and said, "Actually, no. If you pay us, we'll promote something that's not interesting to get you more eyeballs." This is detrimental because it's diluting the whole point of Facebook in the first place. That's why I find Facebook to be a necessary evil. There's still a huge number of active users so you need a strategy for it, but both the platform and the strategy are rapidly changing.

—Ariel Hyatt

MARKETING WITH FACEBOOK

Design a custom artist page using one of the many tools.

Keep your posts short.

Make sure to include a link back to your website or blog in posts.

The best times to post are 11 a.m., 3 p.m., and 8 p.m. ET.

The number of Likes gives you a feel for the pulse of the fan base.

Less than 1 percent of your fan base will register a Like because most won't see your post.

A post can be effective without receiving a Like.

Facebook ads boost Likes, comments, and awareness.

MARKETING WITH YOUTUBE

YouTube has become much more than just a site for watching amusing videos. It's now a major distribution point for music, and its value as a taste maker is now unparalleled. Why is the service so influential? Here are some staggering facts from YouTube's press section:

- Over 7 billion hours of video are viewed every month.
- As much as 300 hours of video footage is uploaded to the site every minute, or over a decade of content every day!
- YouTube has more than 1 billion monthly users, or more than the entire population of Europe.
- More video is uploaded every 60 days than the three major US television networks produced in 60 years.
- Two billion video views per week are monetized, and that number is rapidly increasing.
- YouTube is localized in 75 countries across 61 languages.
- Seventy percent of YouTube traffic comes from outside the United States.

- More than half the videos on YouTube have been rated or commented on by users.
- The most searched-for topic on YouTube is "Music."
- Music videos account for 38 percent of all YouTube views.

When it comes to music, YouTube has now become a major platform for music discovery. In fact, it's now the single most widely used website for music discovery and distribution, not to mention the second-largest search engine, according to a survey by Nielsen Music and Midem. According to the study,

- People now consume more music online by watching it than by any other means.
- Age makes a bigger difference in consumers' music-video-watching preferences than gender. The younger the consumer, the more likely he or she is to have consumed music videos.

That's why it's so important to an artist's development to create a YouTube channel and start uploading videos. If you want someone to discover you, you have more of a chance here than almost anywhere else online.

Essential YouTube SEO

YouTube can be used as an effective marketing tool, but you must observe the SEO (Search Engine Optimization) techniques outlined here and later in this book. Before you go live on a video, make sure you do the following:

1. **Name your video something descriptive.** "Untitled_bandvideo12. mov" is not descriptive at all, so your video will never get added by the search engines, and your fans won't find it. "Emerald at the Lone Star Club video 1/9/16" is much better.
2. **Make sure your description contains the same phrase as your title.** For example, "This video features Emerald at the Lone Star Club on January 9, 2016." A title like "Here's our band at the Lone Star Club" wouldn't be as effective because it omits the keyword "Emerald."
3. **Make sure you fill out the description.** The more detail contained in the video description, the better. That means you should include

a brief summary of what the video is about, who's in the video (including band members and actors), and the names of the director, producers (video and recording), songwriters, and everyone else involved. If someone does a search for any of these people, having them listed in the description can make your video show up in the search results.

4. **Always include a link.** Make sure to include a link to your website or social media profile in the description. Make sure it includes the full "http://" at the front so the link will be active.

5. **Use the proper tags.** Not only should the artist's name be included, but also any similar artists, the type of music, and even the mood of the song will help the video be found during a search.

6. **Include the name of the original artist when doing a cover song.** Cover songs are a good way to get an artist noticed on YouTube, but the song selection, performance, title, and proper tagging play a big part in its popularity.

If I had to give some advice, I'd say song choice is number one. Choose songs that are relevant today by using the Billboard charts as a guide. Select a song that's on the top of the charts today, then post a really good cover, then make sure the video title is appropriate by posting the original artist's name, the song name, then your name. Make sure it's tagged with the original artist's name, the song name, as well as the record label name and anything else about it. If it's a love song or a pop song, put that descriptive tag in. Sometimes people just search for love songs, so they'll come across your video that way. Finally, make sure the video description is complete.

—Dae Bogan (on choosing a cover song)

7. **There are other ways of using YouTube promotionally.** You can:
   - Find people making creative videos on YouTube and offer them some original music to pair with their videos.
   - Run a contest to see who comes up with the best music video for one of your songs.
   - Run a contest to see who can do the best mash-up of your existing videos.

Also, the more text you put in the body of your description, the more likely it will be found by a search engine. A hundred words works well, but so could 500.

These are just other ways to get not only your current fans involved, but also potential new fans as well.

The Half-Life of a Viral Video

Video distributor TubeMogul's *Insider's Report* states that a typical YouTube video gets 50 percent of its total views in the first 6 days. After 20 days, it's already received 75 percent of the total views that it will ever see.

You may think that if your video doesn't receive many plays in the first week, it may never get any, but that's just not true. This study obviously applies to the DIY "novelty" videos, and not ones that are meant to extend your brand. Many videos gradually gain an audience and continue to build over time, especially after a mention on a blog or social network. If you maintain a good video SEO practice and your video is aimed at building your brand, you'll quickly prove this study wrong.

Making Money from YouTube

YouTube has gone from a distribution-only platform to one that actually can be a revenue generator for artists and record labels alike. An act can make some revenue from Google's AdSense program simply by selecting the "monetize" button on each video, but a more favorable income split comes from joining YouTube's Partner Program, which is open only to the most prolific content creators.

To be frank, the income generated through YouTube is not going to make most artists wealthy, as it ranges from around $2.50 to $9.00 per thousand views before a 55/45 split with YouTube (55 percent for the artist or label) kicks in. The exact number is difficult to determine because so much depends on the type of advertisement (pre-roll, post-roll, in-movie banners, etc.), how long it's watched, and the amount paid by the advertiser. That said, a general accepted average of what to expect from a million video views is around $1,750, or $0.00175 per view after the split with YouTube.

Many content creators subscribe to a multichannel network (MCN) like Full Screen or Maker Studios because they promise more aggregate views based on the fact that their channels get more eyeballs than a normal individual channel. You pay for that privilege, however; the multichannel network may take anywhere from 10 to 30 percent of your portion of the split with YouTube, although that might be worthwhile if it ultimately means more views and therefore more money generated.

Larger MCNs have dedicated ad sales teams that can pair an advertiser with your channel, hopefully at a higher ad rate, so you may make more money as a result.

That said, some money is better than no money, and in today's Music 4.1 world, every revenue stream, no matter how small, counts. The YouTube payouts may not be as high as artists and labels would like, but they're a vast improvement over nothing at all.

Real-Time Streaming Video

While YouTube has been a force in the music community for quite some time now, streaming video from services such as UStream, Concert Window, and Livestream is a trend that is just starting to explode.

Artists can use real-time streaming to offer live performances, jam sessions, studio sessions, or acoustic "unplugged"-style performances from the comfort of their own homes.

It's also possible to directly engage fans through a real-time question-and-answer session, or even allow fans to request songs during a performance. To be sure, live streaming will become much more important to the artist of the future as the services become more widespread.

YouTube Measurement Tools

YouTube has upgraded its analytics continually over the years to the point where there's plenty of information about your channel and individual videos available to access how they're being received. Here's what can be found under YouTube's Analytics tab:

- An overview showing channel performance, engagement, demographics, and top ten videos
- Real-time information about what was watched in the last 60 minutes to 48 hours
- A daily, weekly, and monthly look at the number of views for each video, along with total minutes and average minutes watched and where and when they were watched
- Filter by city, country, or globally

- Demographics, traffic sources, the type of devices used to watch, retention rates, subscribers
- Likes, dislikes, comments, and sharing
- Annotation and card performance

The basic built-in analytics make it easy to spot trends for both your videos and your channel, but it's important not to depend on only one source of metrics. Most professional online marketers use multiple services to get a better picture of exactly how well a network is performing, because none of them (not even YouTube) measures the same way.

Clicky (clicky.com) and StatCounter (statcounter.com) are two other measurement tools that offer a free tier capable of supplying additional information that you may find useful, and dozens of other services supply similar information for a subscription fee. Using a third-party measurement service along with YouTube's analytics will ultimately provide a better picture of the success of your channel and videos.

MARKETING WITH YOUTUBE

People now consume more music by watching it than by any other means.

You should create a dedicated YouTube channel.

Keep video titles descriptive.

Take extra care with the tags (be sure to include the mood of the song).

Having more text in the description is better.

Make sure to include a link back to your website or blog in the description.

YouTube views can now be a revenue source.

Live streaming will become more important in the future.

Keep track of your video progress through YouTube Analytics and an outside source.

MARKETING WITH TWITTER

Twitter's importance in the social media value chain has dropped as its user numbers have plateaued. Once one of the prime platforms for artists everywhere, the service has fallen on some disfavor, usually because it's not understood just how helpful a tool it can be. It's amazing how much you can say in 140 characters, and unlike email blasts, your fans usually don't feel intruded upon receiving multiple tweets a day.

The secret to successful twittering is to tweet only about relevant topics of interest to your fans. Keep the tweets informative and not so intimately personal that you lose people. Here's an example:

"Playing at the Lone Star in Memphis tonite. 9:30 p.m. sharp. Meet and greet afterward in the bar. Great place. Come and join us."

This is an effective tweet because it provides some real information for the fans, although only on a local basis. A tweet that's a bit more global yet informative might look something like this:

"Great gig at the Lone Star tonite. You people ROK! Two girls jumped on stage and Jimmy boogied with them. Video at http://bit. ly/7GFjDq."

See how much info can be communicated in just 140 characters? Notice how it made people interested to go to the website to check out the video? Most of all, notice the link to the video for more information and content?

Here's an example of a tweet that doesn't work because it's a bit too personal to be effective, unless your name is Prince or Bono:

"Just had bacon and eggs and potatoes for breakfast. The bacon was greasy and the potatoes were burnt. The coffee was good though."

This isn't a compelling use of the medium because it's mostly irrelevant information to the person reading the tweet. A way to take that same idea and make it work might look like this:

"Just had breakfast after a great gig at the Lone Star last night. Met Sally B and Adrian there and they were at the gig. Thanks a lot guys!"

This gives a shout-out to some fans and talks about the gig. The fans love it because they were acknowledged, and it makes other fans hope that you'll acknowledge them as well, all in exactly 140 characters.

The beauty of Twitter is that you don't have be "Friended" by somebody. You can follow anybody you want (thousands of people if you want) and they can follow you unless you're blocking your profile. And if you're following each other, that constitutes a friend relationship and that means you can direct message them. It becomes a very sophisticated way to search and have conversations with a wide array of thought leaders. It's a very sophisticated crowd now, but it's starting to expand to the masses. It's not real big in music promotion yet, but it will be.

—Michael Terpin

The Secret of the Hashtag

One of the most egregious errors for an artist using Twitter is overlooking the use of hashtags (the # symbol before a keyword). Using a hashtag is like including a keyword in your tweet. It's an unofficial feature of Twitter but now widely accepted and supported, and it's an easy way for people to search for and find a particular topic.

Here's how it works, using some of my own tweets:

"The Secret To The Merch Table. Want to sell more merch at gigs? Here's how. http://bit.ly/7GFjDq #merch #bands"

This is a simple tweet regarding a post from my Music 3.0 blog (music3point0.blogspot.com), complete with a shortened URL link. At the end are the hashtags #merch and #bands. How were they selected? First of all, "merch" appears in the tweet, but it was researched first at search.twitter.com to see whether it had many previous searches. On the site, I searched for "#merch" and determined that there was enough search traffic to make it worth using. And since the post was aimed at bands, and "bands" was a topic that they'd be most interested in, I used #bands as well after another search found that "#bands" was also a popular search term.

Here's another way the hashtags could have been used in this tweet:

"The Secret to The #Merch Table. Want to sell more merch at #gigs? Here's how. http://bit.ly/7GFjDq"

In this case, the hashtags are embedded directly into the tweet text. This method works, but it's sometimes too difficult to read, so the practice can quickly turn into a negative for less sophisticated users. Leaving room at the end of the tweet, especially for the hashtags, usually gets a better response.

Here's another example of a tweet from my Big Picture production blog (bobbyowsinski.blogspot.com):

"15 Steps To A Better Mix. A blueprint for better mixing. bit.ly/vj-gIUQ #recording #musicians"

As in the previous example, a quick search revealed that #recording had more traffic than #mixing (there was also some confusion with a food processor) and that many other tweets that contained #recording contained #musicians as well, so it was a good match to include.

Using hashtags is a key way to help people find you, but don't forget to include a link to take them to your blog or website as well, since that's the real goal.

The Best Time to Tweet

If you're using Twitter for promotion, then the timing of your tweets is critical. Tweets generally have a shelf life of less than an hour, so if you do it when most people are busy and not paying attention, then you have little hope of engaging them.

According to a study by Dan Zarrella, a social media researcher who analyzed millions of tweets and revealed the results in a webinar titled "The Science of Timing," the later you tweet in the day, the better. The reason is that from 2 p.m. to 5 p.m. EST, your followers are more likely to see your tweet because there are fewer things demanding their attention. In fact, 4 p.m. was deemed to be the best tweet time of the day.

Zarrella also found that the weekends are great for tweet attention as people are more relaxed and aren't conflicted by work. He also found that tweeting the same link multiple times a day is an effective strategy, and unlike excessive emails, followers don't seem to mind.

It was also discovered that 92 percent of all retweets and 97 percent of all replies happen within the first hour of the tweet lifetime. After that, it's as good as gone.

Twitter Tools

There are a number of websites that can provide keyword search, trending, and measurement information that will be useful in maximizing Twitter as a promotional tool. Keep in mind that these were accurate as of the writing of this book, but websites frequently disappear, change names, or change focus without much warning.

1. Search.twitter.com is more of an all-purpose Twitter search site. If you're looking for any keywords used as hashtags, be sure to place the hash mark in front of your search term (such as *#keyword*). If you select "advanced search," you can make your search even more granular.
2. Twellow (twellow.com) is a Twitter yellow pages directory. If you search for a keyword, you'll get the profiles of users who have that keyword in their profiles based on who has the most tweets.
3. Tweetstats (tweetstats.com) is a good way to look not only at your personal stats, but also at the latest trends on Twitter.
4. Twitter Counter (twittercounter.com) is an excellent way to keep track of your total follower count over time as well as see some future predictions.
5. Klout (klout.com) is unique in that it measures your online influence in terms of Likes, retweets, mentions, and comments. The idea is to measure the size of your true Twitter audience instead of just your follower count. Klout also measures your other social activity besides Twitter as well.
6. Tweepi (tweepi.com) allows you to easily manage your Twitter account and unfollow anyone who's not following you back.
7. TweetDeck (tweetdeck.twitter.com) allows you to organize your followers, keep an eye on the really interesting ones in separate groups, and schedule tweets.
8. TweetChat (tweetchat.com) allows you to isolate the conversation based on the hashtag.
9. Hashtags.org is a good way to research hashtags and their alternatives.

Remember to insert the hashtag (#) before your keyword when doing a keyword search. Also, a quick look at both the searches and trends before you select a keyword can make a difference in your Twitter traffic and ultimate attraction to new followers.

MARKETING WITH TWITTER

Start tweeting, but make sure you have something to say.

Always use hashtags to reach a greater audience.

Research the traffic a hashtag has before using it.

Make sure to include a link back to your website or blog.

The best time to tweet during the day is from 2 to 5 p.m.

A tweet's lifetime is short, with most retweets or replies happening within the first hour.

Check multiple measurement tools to evaluate your progress.

GOOGLE+

Google+, or G+, was launched with much fanfare in 2011 and, for a while, looked as if it might even overtake Facebook in terms of users as it peaked around 540 million in 2013. The problem was that the user numbers were somewhat deceptive because anyone with a Gmail or YouTube account was automatically signed in to G+, but that didn't mean they were actually using the platform.

Today, G+ is still available, but some of its best features are being spun off as their own separate platforms. At the beginning of 2015, Google separated out its popular Photos feature, and then followed that up later in the year with Hangouts. Although Google+ still exists, it looks as if Google is slowly winding it down, proving that even a product by one of the most powerful and dominant Internet companies in the world is never a sure thing.

Hangouts

Hangouts is a video chat feature that allows up to ten people in a group to come together for an online video conference. This can be expanded by using Hangouts On Air, an extension of the feature that broadcasts your chat on YouTube for your fans to see. That means that the chat can be broadcast to literally thousands of people at a time if they have the correct URL to link to.

A Hangout is easy to set up, looks and sounds good, and is perfect for today's artist to visually keep in touch with the fan base either with an impromptu concert, an intimate look backstage, or a virtual meet-and-greet. Plus, a number of third-party services, like WebinarJam, use Hangouts as a basic platform and add even more features for conducting true webinars.

Hangouts allows you to share your screen, so others on the call can see the windows on your desktop; to create annotations, allowing you to draw on the screen; and to play director and feature one of the people on the call. It's truly a "killer app" that musicians, artists, and bands should learn to take full advantage of.

For more detailed information about using social media for marketing, check out my book *Social Media Promotion for Musicians*.

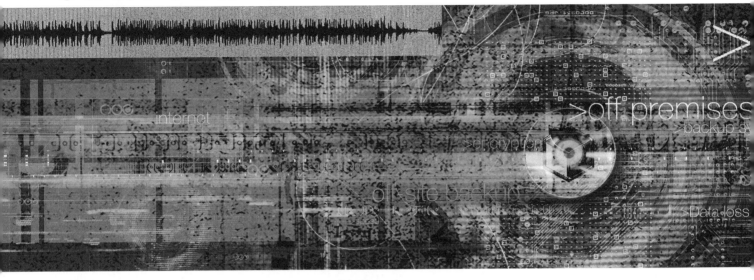

CHAPTER 8

Social Media Management

So many areas of social media require attention that it can get a bit overwhelming at times, and that's when you need a social media management strategy.

A common mistake that artists who manage their own social media assets make is to have too many focal points (such as YouTube, their website, their blog, Twitter, and ReverbNation, for example) all residing in different places and requiring separate updates. You can imagine how tough it is to keep every one of those sites updated regularly! Worse is the fact that it's confusing for the fan, who just wants a single place to visit.

Yet another problem is that you may be collecting email addresses from each site, and they may all be going on different email list providers.

The solution is to use one site (usually your website) as your main focal site and have it feed daily updates and info to all the other sites via RSS or social media broadcast tools, such as Hootsuite (hootsuite. com), Buffer (bufferapp.com), SocialOomph (socialoomph.com), or Social Flow (socialflow.com). This means that you only need to update a single site, and all the others get updated automatically.

The second component of this management strategy is to have all your satellite sites (blog, Facebook, and so on) designed in such a way as to feed your social media viewers into your website (see Figure 8-1). At a bare minimum, the email registration of each satellite site should feed into the same list as your main site.

Figure 8-1: Your Website Is the Center of Your Online Universe

At some point, social media management gets too complex for an artist to maintain, and third-party help is needed. This is usually a good thing, since it means you've progressed to a point where the job is large enough to require specialized assistance. Furthermore, a company that specializes in social media management can keep you current with new tools and techniques that you might not be aware of.

Even when outside help arrives, remember that you are still the one who drives the bus. Be sure to take part in all strategy discussions, but leave the actual facilitation to the company you've hired.

SOCIAL MEDIA MANAGEMENT

Keep a single site as your main focal point.

Feed all your updates from your main site via RSS or social media broadcast app.

Develop your satellite sites so they all feed visitors into your main site.

Email list subscribers from all sites should go to same email list provider.

Get third-party help when you get overwhelmed.

Keep driving the bus!

MEASURING YOUR SOCIAL MEDIA EXPOSURE

How many people have you reached with your message? How many could you have reached? In social media, some measurements are about as reliable as a print magazine's circulation (which was never all that accurate), but knowing your potential audience does have value because it represents your potential sales lead pool.

Unfortunately, as of the writing of this book, some of these metrics have to be accounted for manually, so you'll have to balance the level of effort to track the metrics versus the value you'll receive from them to determine their importance to your overall strategy.

A good example of unreliability in social measurement is when isolating unique users for each of your metrics. You want to avoid counting the same person twice in the list below, but realistically, it's difficult to do.

These measurements highlight the number of people you've attracted to your brand through social media. To mitigate the potential for duplication of users, track growth rate as a percentage of the aggregate totals. This is where you will find the real diamonds.

- **Twitter:** Look at your number of followers and the number of followers for those who retweeted your message to determine the monthly potential reach. You should track these separately and then compare the month-over-month growth rate of each of these metrics so you can determine where you're seeing the most growth. A great free tool to use for Twitter measurement is TweetReach.

- **Facebook:** Track the weekly post reach and number of engagements along with page Like trends. Facebook Insights provides value here, as does Klout.
- **YouTube:** Measure the number of views for videos tied to a promotion or specific period of time, as well as the total number of channel subscribers. Check the number of comments and thumbs up.
- **Blog:** Measure the number of visitors who viewed the posts tied to a promotion for a specific period of time. Check the views over a period of time. If it's falling month over month, it's time to either adjust your posting habits or post content.
- **Email:** Take a look at how many people are on the distribution list and how many actually opened the email, and then look at the number of people who actually took action (click-throughs, forwards, general responses).

Social Media Measurement Tools

Measuring just how successful an artist's promotional campaign is (the artist's buzz) and all the data that surround an artist is a top priority in Music 4.1. Precise analytics were impossible in M1.0 and 1.5 and somewhat available in M2.0, but have been much more widely available and easier than ever to use since M3.0. With so many new avenues available for music discovery and promotion, knowing where the buzz is coming from and how to use it is more important than ever.

Here are six tools to help track your buzz:

Google Alerts (google.com/alerts)—sweeps the Web and delivers buzz to your inbox.

Mention (mention.net)—newer and more comprehensive than Google Alerts, Mention looks at all of social media and sends an email whenever you're mentioned.

Twitter Search (search.twitter.com)—track your buzz on this popular microblogging service.

StatCounter (statcounter.com)—statistics about who visits your site and blog.

Musicmetric (musicmetric.com)—provides social network tracking, P2P network analysis, radio and sales data, and fan demographics.

Klout (klout.com)—measures your mentions, likes, comments, and followers to determine your reach and influence.

Advanced Social Media Analytical Tools

As social media becomes more sophisticated, so do the measurement-tool requirements to determine both your impact and branding possibilities. Three updated methods of analyzing social media data are increasingly being used by some of the more advanced (and expensive) measurement services:

- **Sentiment analysis** is a process that tries to determine the attitude of a writer or commenter with respect to the topic he or she is writing about. If you actually read a blog or posting, you can tell the writer's sentiment immediately, but this analysis method tries to define and measure it as a point of data.
- **Cluster analysis** tries to analyze how certain words are gathering (or "clustering") relative to a search topic. It finds the words that are mostly likely to be associated with your search word, which may provide unexpected insight into what's being said about you and even predict sales before they happen.
- **Semantic analysis** is another measurement tool that strives to understand what words mean in context to one another. Once again, it's something that we do for ourselves as we read, but this tool puts a number to it.

All of these tools are trying to measure what we can immediately see for ourselves empirically by just wading into the social media pool. They put a number to something that we can feel.

New measurement platforms such as Sysomos and Radian6 (now a part of SalesForce Marketing Cloud) use these tools to provide a more precise look at how you or your brand integrates with the social world.

If you need data for a meeting, to sway an investor, or to appease a boss, these tools are important. If you're a marketer on a very high level, you might find the data immediately useful. If you're a band or artist just trying to make the next merch sale, land the next gig, or make it through the next day of social media management, you'll find them interesting at best and parlor tricks at worst. These tools may be cutting-edge today, but you never know if they'll be an essential part of your marketing toolbox tomorrow. Stay tuned.

THE IMPORTANCE OF MEASUREMENT

Know where the buzz is coming from.

Know what's working and what's not.

Know who your fans are.

Know where your fans are from.

Know what your fans like.

WHAT IS A BRAND?

For an artist, a brand means a consistency of persona and usually a consistency of sound. Regardless of what genre of music the artist delves into, the feel is the same, and you're able to identify the artist by the sound.

Madonna changed directions many times during her career, but her brand remained consistent. Her persona remained the same even as she changed to and from the "material girl." The Beatles tried a wide variety of directions, but you never once questioned who you were listening to; it was always fresh and exciting, but distinctly them. Snoop Dogg changed from Snoop Doggy Dog to DJ Snoopadelic to Snoop Lion and back to Snoop Dogg, but his fans and non-fans alike never mistook his sound or image for anyone else.

On the other hand, Neil Young almost killed his career with an electronic album called *Trans* that alienated all but his hardiest fans, and the well-respected Chris Cornell did enough harm to his long-term career, thanks to an electronic album with Timbaland (*Scream*), that he returned to tour with Soundgarden.

Why did this happen? For both artists, the album no longer "felt" like them. Both Young and Cornell built their careers on organic music played with a band, and as soon as their music became regimented and mechanical, they broke their brands. After *Trans*, Young returned to his roots and slowly built his brand back to superstar level, but it's too soon to know what will happen with Cornell.

How do you determine what your brand is? It's easier said than done.

In order for you as an artist to successfully promote your brand, you must have a great sense of self-knowing. You must know who you are, where you came from, and where you're going. You must know what you like and don't like, and what you stand for and why, and you must have an inherent feel for your sound and what works for you.

And that differentiates a superstar from a star, and a star from someone who wants it really badly but never seems to get that big break.

The Three Pillars of a Brand

Every brand is built on at least one of the following three pillars. The stronger the brand, the more pillars are inherently used.

- **Familiarity:** You can't have a brand unless your followers or potential followers are familiar enough with who you are. They don't even have to know what you sound like to be interested in you if you have a buzz and they've heard about you enough to want to check you out. Amanda Palmer, who more people know for her social media savvy than her music, fits into this category.
- **Likeability:** Your followers have to like you or something about you. It could be your music, or it could be your attitude or your image. You could even say how much you hate your fans and do everything to ridicule them, and that irreverent manner could be just the thing they like about you. It doesn't matter what it is, but there has to be something they like. Most artists fall into this category.
- **Similarity:** Your fans have to feel either that you represent them in a cause or movement (like a new genre of music) or that someday they can be you. Female Olympic athletes usually don't do well in this category because their sleek and muscular look is so far beyond what ordinary girls or women can attain that they can't relate to them. On the other hand, young girls love Taylor Swift because they feel like she could be their best friend from next door.

If you have those three things along with a product that consistently maintains its quality (your music), you've got a brand (see Figure 8-2). Trying to intentionally manufacture your brand so it absolutely complies with these pillars usually doesn't work (people usually see right through that), but always keep in mind that this is how your audience views you, although none of them may even realize it.

Five Easy Steps to Creating Your Brand

While a true branding campaign can take a great deal of time and money, there are a number of easy steps that every artist, band, songwriter, producer, engineer, or indie label can take right now to go a long way to

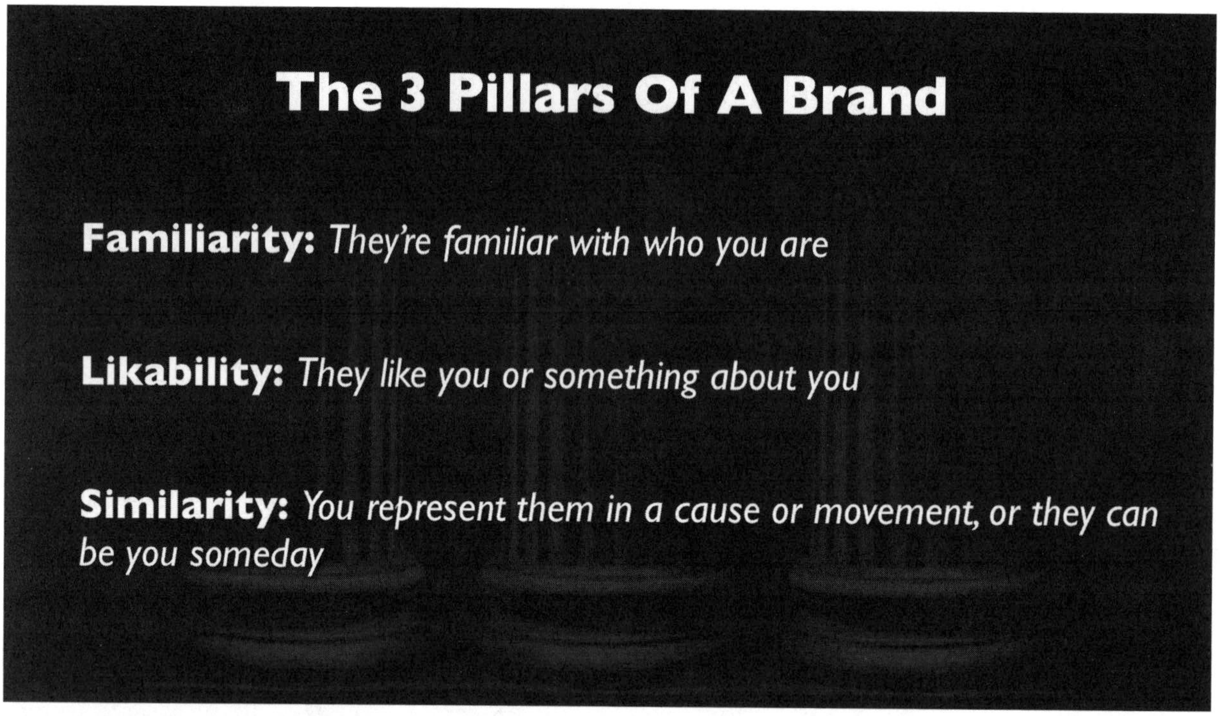

The 3 Pillars Of A Brand

Familiarity: *They're familiar with who you are*

Likability: *They like you or something about you*

Similarity: *You represent them in a cause or movement, or they can be you someday*

Figure 8-2: The Three Pillars of a Brand

establishing a brand. These steps seem almost too easy, but doing them well requires some thought.

1. **Select a name you're comfortable with.** If you're branding a band, then you already have a name, but if you're branding yourself, make sure that the professional name you use is one that you're comfortable with. In other words, don't use Ronald if all your friends call you Ronny. Use the name that you're comfortable introducing yourself with. That includes nicknames as well.

2. **Create a description subtitle.** The subtitle describes what you do in very few words. Chevy uses "Like a rock" to show it's reliable, and Allstate uses "You're in good hands" to emphasize customer support. A band could use "'50s rock with a flair" or "maximum rock," while a musician might use something mundane but effective, like "12-string guitar player from Memphis." A subtitle is not a requirement, but it helps get the point across to people who don't know you when you're just starting out.

3. **Select a graphic or photo that defines you.** For some this is a logo, but for others, it's just a great photo. A great photo is key, as this is not a place to skimp. Spend the money for a professional photographer, ideally one who specializes in music-related photos. Selfies or

photos by your friends (unless they're truly very good at photography) won't cut it.

> TIP: *While you're at it, have the photographer take an "action shot," where you're doing something other than posing. A great action shot is more likely to get you press coverage because it's what frequently catches an editor's eye.*

4. **Select a color.** Select one or two colors (no more) and then use them across all online and traditional media, with no exceptions. That means the same colors will appear in your main photos, website, social profiles, YouTube page, flyers, posters, and business cards.
5. **Select a font.** Choose a font for your name and subtitle and use it everywhere, both online and off. Remember that the font has to work with your image, so you wouldn't want to use something traditional like Times if your sound and image is ultra-modern.

You'll be surprised just how far your image can be developed just by using these five simple steps. Because they set the tone for your career, make sure you give each one ample thought; you want to keep each one in place for a long time. Nothing is more confusing to a fan base than when the branding elements keep changing.

A Quick Look at Sponsorship

Sponsorship is better thought of as "cobranding," since both the artist and the sponsor's brand image are tied together (a point many times overlooked by the artist). This can frequently put the artist at odds with his or her fan base, with cries of "sellout" in the air and on the blogs.

For that reason, sponsorship is another double-edged sword for the M4.1 artist. While it might be a source of tour support, the artist runs the risk of losing credibility with fans. This credibility gap can come if the sponsor is a large, faceless conglomerate that's difficult to relate to or is at odds with the sensibilities of either the artist or, worse, the fan.

For instance, if an artist is sponsored by a beer company but everyone in the band is in Alcoholics Anonymous, that can be a problem sponsorship. If sponsorship by a beer company goes with the band's hard-driving, partying image but goes against the mores of its fans, that too can be a problem. However, a biker band that's sponsored by the local Harley dealer, or by Harley-Davidson itself, or by the biker bar they play at, could be an effective cobranding.

—Larry Gerbrandt

Ultimately, an artist almost always risks his or her credibility in a sponsorship deal of any magnitude. Consider the risks carefully before entering into such a deal, no matter how small.

BRANDING

An artist's brand is consistency in persona and sound.

Creating a brand begins with five simple steps.

Sponsorship co-brands the artist with the sponsor.

Sponsorship runs the risk of losing fan credibility if it's at odds with the artist's image or fan sensibilities.

Any sponsorship must have perfect image symmetry between artist and brand to be successful.

OTHER AVENUES FOR SOCIAL MEDIA

Many music discovery sites, like Bandcamp, Nimbit, and ReverbNation, help your marketing by allowing you to set up a widget with upcoming concert dates, press releases, photos, videos, and stores to buy your music. They also allow you to set up a virtual "street team," where your fans can go out and promote your music for you.

Most of these promotional features are provided for paying members of the particular site, but many of the free promotion features are great for someone who needs to promote music but has little money.

DON'T DEPEND ON YOUR SOCIAL NETWORK

It's too easy for today's artist who only dabbles in social networking to get complacent and comfortable with the abilities of a single social network, but that can spell disaster for maintaining your fan base if you're not careful. As those artists who formerly depended upon MySpace now know, what's hot today can become ice cold tomorrow.

Other negative scenarios also exist that can be far worse than the network falling out of favor.

Scenario #1: Let's say that you've cultivated a huge following on Facebook. What would happen if Facebook was purchased by Google (a stretch for sure, but a good example), which decides that all it wants is the underlying technology of the network and shuts the rest down? If you didn't capture the email addresses of all your followers, you'd lose them to the nothingness of cyberspace. Don't laugh—something similar with another platform has already happened.

Scenario #2: What would happen if Facebook (I'm picking on them because they're the big dog on the social block) changes its terms of service and now charges you $0.25 for every fan past 100? If you've built an audience of 80,000 fans, it's going to cost you 20 grand to continue. They've already instituted something similar in that you now have to pay in order to reach the entirety of your followers (you can reach about 3 percent or so for free), which means you're now unable to access that large fan base that you've worked so hard to develop.

Scenario #3: This one actually did happen. In June of 2013, MySpace shut down its "classic" platform in order to migrate to a new one with a better feature set. The only thing that MySpace didn't do was inform its members that they were going to lose their entire MySpace following when that happened. Artists who had stayed loyal to the service woke up one day to find that all the fan data that they worked for years to collect was gone, and there was no way of getting it back.

That's why it's imperative that you harvest as many email addresses as you can for your own mailing list so you can keep your social communication under your control. If you rely on an external network, sooner or later you're going to get burned. It's the nature of the Internet to constantly change, and it's too early to get a feel for the lifespan of even the largest sites and networks. So play it safe—develop that mailing list.

There's More to Social Networking than Facebook

When it comes to social networking, the first network we think of is Facebook, closely followed by Twitter. But even though Facebook is still on top, it no longer dwarfs everything else. There's a lot of competition, and its coming from parts of the world that you might not be aware of. Here they are, complete with the number of active users:

1. Facebook: 1.4 billion
2. QQ: 800 million (China)
3. WhatsApp: 700 million
4. QZone: 600 million (China)
5. WeChat: 500 million
6. LinkedIn: 350 million
7. Skype: 300 million
8. Google+: 300 million
9. Instagram: 300 million
10. Baibu Tiaba: 300 million (China)
11. Twitter: 300 million
12. Viber: 250 million
13. Tumblr: 200 million
14. Snapchat: 200 million
15. LINE: 200 million (Japan)
16. Sina Weibo: 150 million (China)
17. VK: 100 million (Russia)
18. Reddit: 100 million
19. YY: 100 million (China)
20. Taringa: 75 million (Latin America)

As you can see, there are plenty of social media sites that aren't well known in the United States but are popular in other areas of the world. That doesn't mean they're any less powerful for getting your message across. Ask your fans if there's another network that they visit often, and be prepared to jump in if the answer is yes.

OTHER SOCIAL NETWORKS

Don't rely on a single social network.

Own as much data as you can away from any social network.

Explore other social networks to expand your social reach.

TEN LOW-COST, HIGH-TECH PROMOTION IDEAS

Never leave promotion to someone else. You must always be actively involved on at least an oversight level to be sure that not only is the promotion going as planned, but it's something that's beneficial to your image as an artist. This even includes employing a publicist, since he or she takes cues from you. Especially don't depend on a record label, particularly in these days when so few staff people do so many jobs. It's up to you to develop the strategy, or it might not get developed at all.

That being said, here are a number of low-cost M4.1 ideas that you can do to get your promotion started:

1. **Set up a Facebook page and be sure to stay active.** It won't do you much good if you just set it up and never update it. The only way it's worth your fans visiting is if you keep the updates coming as often as possible.

2. **Every time a Friend request is exchanged between you and other Facebook users, send them a note back thanking them**, and ask if you can include them in your group of friends outside of Facebook. Ask them to "Please reply with your email address if that's okay." This is a great way to build your tribe, but make sure they can easily opt out if it's not their cup of tea. It's not too beneficial to have all those Facebook Friends if you can't contact them outside of Facebook.

3. **Always have a "Press" section on your website** that contains the following:
   • High- and low-resolution color and black-and-white photos
   • Logos
   • Biographical information
   • Quotes from the media

- Links to any interviews
- Links to music
- Links to videos
- Social media addresses and links to Facebook, your blog, Reverb-Nation, and so forth
- Scans of three or four of your best press clippings
- A press-release section
- A discography
- A list of upcoming gigs
- A fact sheet with bullet points of interesting artist facts
- Scans of a promo flyer and poster
- Web-ready graphics and banners
- Publicist, agent, label, or artist contact info

Having this information easily available will increase the chances of getting media coverage. It's a fact that the easier you can make it for a blogger, writer, or editor, the more likely you'll get covered.

4. **Backlinks are important.** Any time you're mentioned in a club listing, on the site of a band you're playing with, or anywhere else, make sure that the post links back to your site. People won't do this automatically, so make it standard operating procedure to ask.

5. **Encourage fans to tag you** and your content on sites such as Flickr, blogs, Digg, and StumbleUpon, and then make that data available on your site.

6. Even though you may have a presence on Facebook, **you still need a website**. It's still the best place to gather your tribe and communicate with them. Make sure that you follow the "Keys to a Successful Website" sidebar for creating the best website experience for your fans.

7. **Engage your fans.** Ask them questions. Polls and surveys are free (that magic word again) and easy to set up with sites like Polldaddy and SurveyMonkey.

8. **Develop a press-release mailing list of music writers and editors** from all local and regional newspapers, magazines, specialty papers, radio stations, online radio stations, and music blogs that (especially) cover the type of music you play. (You can do national and international later, when you grow into it.)

Remember that it doesn't do you much good to send something to a blog or magazine that specializes in metal if you're a folk singer, so don't even think about anything outside your genre.

Once your list is complete, send out a short email for any major gig, event, or song release, but don't make it too frequent or you won't be covered—ever. Include links to your website and an offer for a free press pass to a show. About once a month is a good frequency. If you get a mention, be sure to send an email or even a handwritten note to say thank you.

9. **Create your own YouTube channel.** Make sure to post new videos frequently, and encourage fans to post as well.
10. **Create a special insider email list** for a few fans, key media, tastemakers, and bloggers for sending pre-announcements to those people who love to know things first . . . and like to tell others.

KEYS TO A SUCCESSFUL WEBSITE

- Make sure your or your band's name is in every one of the following: the url, title, website description, and first paragraph of text.

- Keep your keywords to a maximum of five and be sure that they relate to the content on the page.

- Delete any Flash animation. Yes, it looks great, but iOS devices and search engines can't read it, and it's pretty dated. You want fans to find you, right?

- Make sure there's an easy way for people to give you their email addresses. Make sure they know what to expect from signing up.

- Keep your content relevant to your keywords. Don't use Katy Perry as a keyword unless you actually have something about Katy Perry in the body text of your page; otherwise, Google might penalize you.

- A blog tied to your site is a great way for easy updates and a great way for your fans to interact.

- Keep the copy of each page to between 150 and 500 words.

- Make sure there are no page errors (broken links). It frustrates your visitors, and you'll get penalized by Google as well.

BUT YOU STILL MUST HIT THE STREETS
The Internet provides ways to interact with fans that were unthinkable

even back in the M2.0 days, but they're still no substitute for the hard work that goes with being a musician.

If you want to succeed, you've got to build and maintain your audience over a period of years, and for that you've still got to hit the streets. This means that you have to play live, you have to be ready to promote traditionally as well as online, and you still have to sell yourself, your music, and your merchandise one fan at a time. Getting reviews and doing press and interviews will never go away.

All the attributes of M4.1 must be seen as an adjunct to the traditional work that is the business part of the music business. Sure, social media is quite powerful and more necessary than ever, but so far, no one has made it as a result of M4.1 only. It's possible to have great visibility, a lot of "Friends" and downloads, and still not have anything other than a brief career (remember the turntable hits we spoke of before?). So even as traditional street marketing decreases in importance, it's still vital for long-term success.

TEN LOW-COST, LOW-TECH PROMOTION IDEAS

Promotion doesn't have to cost money to be effective. Here are some promotion ideas that can be powerful tools that don't even involve a computer.

1. **Don't underestimate the value of something free.** Fans love free items, either as part of a package (for example, buy a CD and get a T-shirt free), as part of a contest, or for just being one of the first ten fans to email. Sometimes items of seemingly little value have wide appeal. Backstage passes, seat upgrades, seats on stage, tickets to the sound check, invites to a meet-and-greet, and downloads of live songs are all prized by real fans.
2. It's surprising that this isn't done more since it works so well: **Park a van or truck that has a banner on it across from a show by a similar act.** Every fan entering or exiting the venue will be aware of you.
3. **Free or low-cost entry to show "after parties"** extends the show experience and rewards the true fan. These can be promoted along with the show, and even offered as a part of the ticket package.
4. Instead of sending a "thank you" email to a promoter, writer, interviewer, or just someone who's done you a good turn, **send a handwritten thank-you note by snail mail**. You'll be shocked how well

this works. It's unusual, it's sincere, and it's remembered. It's also very likely to be seen, since we're all getting fewer and fewer snail-mail items these days.

5. **Consider asking your fans to help you with promo.** Ask them to put up flyers or send out emails. Put a PDF of a poster or flyer online for fans to download.

6. Fans always want a chance to meet the musicians. **Consider having a meet-and-greet after every show**, but make sure that the fans know about it in advance.

7. **Find your niche and market to it.** It makes no sense to market to Adele's fans if your music isn't like hers, so don't waste your energy marketing in that direction.

8. **Make everything you do an event.** What holiday is coming up? Is it a band member's birthday? Is an anniversary near? Try a tribute to "Fans that just got laid off" or "Fans that just got hired."

9. **Use the power of your niche to widen your fan base.** Flyer someone else's show in a related genre. Sponsor somebody else's event. Consider trading sponsorships and gigs with another band.

10. **Align yourself with a cause you believe in.** Causes often have a large PR mechanism behind them that can expose your music, but it has to be something you really believe in or it may hurt you in the long run.

HIT THE STREETS

Traditional marketing can be as important as viral hits.

Sell yourself one fan and one gig at a time.

Provide your fans with the means to support you.

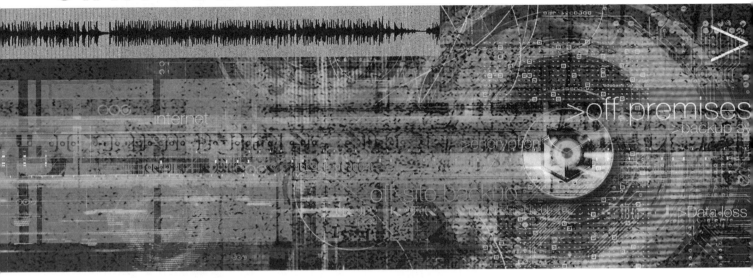

Making Money in Today's Music World

To be sure, making money in M4.1 is a lot trickier than it was in previous stages of the music business. When you're signed to a major label, there's an ever-changing sea of cross-collateralization between accounts in which relatively large sales amounts by the record label might still result in small royalty payments to you.

Yet at the same time, things are in some ways more cut and dried than before. If you're an indie artist who's without a label and who is dealing directly with the fans, you know exactly how much money you're earning and where it's coming from. No longer tied to the fortunes of a record released by a major label, and therefore to the uncertainty of a royalty statement, what you see is what you get.

Although the exact recipe for making money in today's music world is different, the ingredients pretty much remain the same. If you're looking for a magic formula, however, you won't find one here, I'm sorry to say. It still comes down to talent and a lot of work, same as it ever did.

HIT THE ROAD, JACK

As I've mentioned a few times earlier in the book, from the beginning of the modern music business, artists have always made the bulk of their money from touring, *not* from record sales. Depending on whom you speak to, this figure varies anywhere from 90 to 95 percent of a currently hot artist's total income, and even more for a former platinum-selling heritage act.

This means that for you to make money, you've got to play in front of people, and the more people you play in front of, the more you'll make. The problem is that large crowds hardly ever happen overnight, and if they do, beware. This can be a warning sign that they're interested in the spectacle of a media buzz or something other than the music you create. Any success that comes too fast will probably be short lived, as you've not spent enough time building that core fan base that's been referred to over and over in this book.

Unfortunately, developing an audience on any level is slow and time consuming. You still have to build your audience one show at a time. The formula is always the same: the more you play, the better you get at performing and the more the crowd will notice, generating bigger crowds as a result. (See my book *How to Make Your Band Sound Great* for some performance and show tips and tricks.) Things can snowball from there if you've got what it takes.

> *We often see bands that try to do too much too fast. A lot of indie labels will say, "We want the band to get in a van and we don't want them to get out of it for three years." At some point at the end of year one or two that runs its course. Virtually no band can keep on running around the country to try to build an audience indiscriminately. As much as touring is the most important thing, it has to be done strategically, concentrating on certain markets where you see the beginning of growth, then doing them often enough but not too often.*
> —Bruce Houghton

Are you playing in front of people and still not making enough money to keep it interesting or even to pay your expenses? Maybe what you're offering just isn't compelling, either musically or show-wise. People will gladly pay to see anything that they're passionate about, so perhaps they don't find you enthralling enough to pay for, or maybe even to come to see for free.

Then again, maybe you haven't found your audience yet. If that's the case, use the marketing tools outlined in Chapter 4 to build that tribe.

Either way, growing your live audience is always a slower process than it seems it should be.

> *What you still never get away from is that it's still about a song and it's still about a performance of that song. Can you play that song in front of your audience however large or small and create the "WOW Factor?"*
>
> —Rupert Perry

Describing just how to go about finding gigs, playing a show, and building your team with management and an agent is beyond the scope of this book. There's plenty of other readily available material that focuses on just that part of the biz. Suffice it to say that playing live must be part of your strategy for developing your core audience and making money over the long term.

HIT THE ROAD, JACK

Most of an artist's income after a certain level comes from playing live.

You've got to build your audience one show at a time.

It always takes longer than you think to grow your audience.

Use social media marketing techniques to find and build your fan base.

MERCH IS YOUR FRIEND

Performing live is only one ingredient of the recipe, however. Merchandise (other terms include swag and merch) is a significant component for supplementing your income. It's always been an important portion of the income of an artist but until recently was considered just an ancillary revenue stream. Today, it's an essential part of most artists' earnings.

It used to be that merch required a sizable capital outlay in order for an artist to get in the game. You had to buy enough to get some sort of economy of scale, but then you also had to worry about storing the inventory. And what if the item didn't sell? What do you do with 4,835 custom key chains or 492 pairs of branded underwear? Luckily, there are now alternatives that make the buy-in easier on the pocketbook than ever.

Today, CafePress (cafepress.com), Inksy (inksy.co), Zazzle (zazzle.com), and other similar services make it easy to provide quality merch of all kinds without worrying about either the up-front money or the inventory.

These companies (and there are many others) provide a host of items that they'll manufacture to order, and they'll even allow you to show examples of merch on your website or store. In other words, whenever an order is placed, that's when they'll make the item. They'll even drop-ship it to the customer for you so you don't have to worry about shipping and inventory. All this comes at a cost, so your profit won't be as high, but it's an easy and inexpensive way to get into the merch business.

So what kind of merch should you have? You can now get a huge variety of items branded with your logo, but typical merch items are:

- T-shirts (probably the number one item ever for a musical artist)
- hats
- sweatshirts
- coffee cups
- posters
- bumper stickers (a high-profit item because they're cheap to make)
- mouse pads
- bags (timely now, since people use them instead of paper or plastic at the supermarket)

Surprisingly, the top sales items have the highest profit margin and are also the least expensive to make—stickers and patches. A single-color sticker typically costs around $0.20 and typically sells for $1.50, while a patch costs around $0.55 and typically sells for $4, which means both have a markup of over 600 percent! Sadly, most artists and bands overlook these simple and inexpensive merch pieces.

Just about anything you can think of can now have your logo on it. Of course, that doesn't necessarily mean that just because you can make it available, it's a good idea. It's still best to narrow things down, since offering too many types of items can actually prevent willing customers from buying anything because they can't make up their minds. Keep

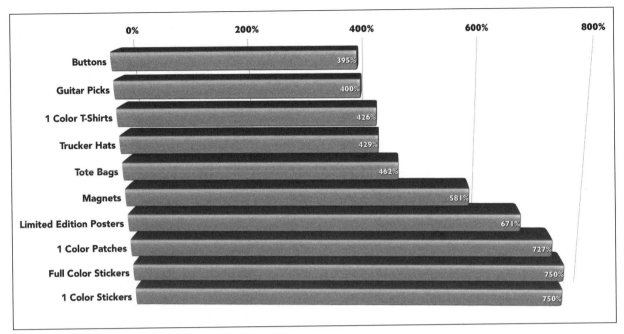

Figure 9-1: Top 10 Merch Pieces with the Best Margins

the number of types of items to a maximum of two at first, and be sure that they will sell before you add more options.

Another interesting idea is to offer a tour book of photos (like what you can get from blurb.com). Once again, it's on-demand printing, and companies offer a number of professional templates to make the design easy.

Don't forget that, in the end, branded items like T-shirts, hats, beach towels, and stickers are for marketing you as an artist, so be sure that the design looks professional. If you're going to spend hard cash on your product, this is the place to do it. Find a pro or an advanced hobbyist to design it for you. Don't forget that the true reason for selling merch is that if enough people see your intriguing logo on a T-shirt, coffee mug, or bumper sticker, some of them will be interested enough to check you out.

Price It Right

Whatever you choose to sell, be sure to price it right. The obvious temptation is to price an item too high to try to make a large profit. Don't fall into this trap. Price things low enough to cover your expenses and make a reasonable profit. Remember, these items are promotional; it's better to sell more at a lower cost than a few at a higher cost.

Above all, be sure that your costs are covered. Make sure that any pricing includes the cost of shipping, sales taxes (don't forget those), and any labor or sales costs involved (many artists will pay someone 10 percent or more of the sale's gross for manning the merch booth). Also don't forget that some venues will take a commission of between 20 and 25 percent.

A good formula for pricing might be your costs (all of them) plus anywhere from 50 to 100 percent. If you're sure the market will bear a higher price than that, go there, but make sure that you test the price first. Try a lower price at one gig and a higher one at another and see which sells better. Sometimes a higher price sells better because the customer perceives a higher quality.

Make sure you round it up to a reasonable number. If you use the formula of costs plus 50 percent and it comes out to $6.38, round it up to $7.00. Stay away from change. It's easier on everybody.

The Secret to the Merch Table

Even though merchandise is a major revenue stream for the M4.1 artist, most musicians have a natural aversion to selling it (or selling anything for that matter). Yet one simple act that doesn't directly involve selling can help you greatly increase your nightly take from the merch table.

By just announcing during and at the end of the show, "After our show, we're going to be hanging out at the merch table, so come over and say 'Hi,'" without trying to specifically sell anything, you bring your fans that much closer to an impulse buy.

By giving people the ability to casually chat with you, it becomes a low-pressure way of getting people to look at your merchandise, which is always half the battle.

This one simple act can make a big difference in your merch sales, and that's the one place that you can be assured of making money these days, especially if you're just starting out. Remember, you don't have to physically sell anything yourself, just be there and talk to fans. Can you imagine what the sales would be like if Bono did that after a U2 concert?

Credit Card Transactions Made Easy

More and more we're living in a cashless society. People are more likely to make a purchase with a debit or credit card when they want something, especially if they're short of cash. Of course, this can be a drag at a gig when you're selling CDs and merch and have to rely on the Benjamins because of the hassle of taking credit and debit cards.

While the ability to take credit cards for merchandise purchases at a gig can make transactions easier, it can also eat into your profits. First of all, you have to enter into a long-term contract with a bank, then pay for the card reader, and in many cases pay a monthly subscription fee. Then, after a purchase, you have to wait for the money to hit your account, with the bank taking its piece through processing and transaction fees that are like the phone bill—lots of small fees for each transaction that no one can seem to explain.

Typical Transaction Costs

Transaction costs are frequently overlooked, and they are the secret expense that eats your profit.

All credit cards charge you multiple fees. First of all, there's a monthly transaction fee that's a minimum of $20.00 (usually more), a "gateway" fee of between $5.00 and $20.00 for ecommerce, an authorization fee, a customer service fee, and a monthly minimum transaction total. Slip below that total and you're charged a penalty.

Then there's the transaction costs per sale, which can go from $0.20 to as high as $0.35 (it's usually higher for an Internet transaction), plus a charge of between 1.5 and 3 percent of the total of the sale.

Add all that up, and it means that if you make only a dozen or so sales a month, you might actually lose money. Even if you've met your monthly minimum, you still may be making less than a dollar per sale, thanks to the transaction costs involved.

Square and PayPal to the Rescue

That's all changed recently as a service called Square (squareup.com), followed by PayPal Here (www.paypal.com/here), has slowly but surely made a big impression on large and small touring merchandising entities alike.

With a card reader that attaches to a smartphone or tablet (see Figure 9-2), you can now have your customers easily pay with the card of their choice. What's more, it's paperless. You swipe the card, the customer uses a finger to sign for the purchase on the screen of your tablet device, and the customer receives an email receipt later. Square takes a flat 2.75 percent transaction fee, and PayPal Here takes 2.7 percent, which winds up costing less than most traditional credit card processors.

The novelty of signing with your finger is so cool that many acts report that their sales have increased just because people want to try it out! The best part is that you're immediately mailed the Square or Paypal Here reader as soon as you sign up online. The transaction software is free.

Figure 9-2: The Square Reader

MERCH IS YOUR FRIEND

Merch is an essential part of your income.

But don't forget that it's promotional, too.

Invest the money for a great design.

Use a company like CafePress, Inksy,
or Zazzle to avoid up-front costs.

Limit the number of merch items to one
or two at first.

Make sure all your costs are covered.

Price to cover your costs plus
at least 50 percent.

Meet and greet at the merch table
to increase sales.

Use Square or Paypal Here for
credit card transactions.

THE MANY WAYS TO ASK FOR THE SALE

It's one thing if you're selling either music or merch through one of the many online distributors, since their prices are set as are their sales methods. It's another thing entirely if you're trying to sell product on your website. There, the way you ask for the sale directly affects how many sales you'll actually make.

Amp Music Marketing ran a study regarding "call to action" buy buttons. They decided to test a number of buttons to see which was most effective when it came to selling music. Site visitors were given these choices:

"Get The Music"
"Download The Music"
"Buy The Music"

It turns out that the most effective was the most direct, "Buy The Music" (album, CD, etc.), while "Get The Music" was the least effective. It seems that consumers relate "Get The Music" to a bait-and-switch in which they're lured into clicking only to find that there's something additional asked of them.

When it comes to sales, sometimes the very best technique is the most direct. Ask plainly for the sale. If your fan or customer really wants to buy from you, you're doing him or her a favor by making the process streamlined and easy. If your fan or customer is unsure, you're not helping the cause by being ambiguous.

And another thing. Keep the item choices to a maximum of three (two works best). If given too many choices, the customer is likely to throw his or her hands up in the air in frustration and not buy anything!

TEN SALES TIPS

Here are ten sales tips to always keep in mind:

1. **Ask for the purchase.** Never forget that even though you're selling yourself, you're still in sales.
2. **Sell a package.** With a ticket you get a CD, with a CD you get a T-shirt, with a T-shirt you get a ticket. The idea is to make each purchase something with added value.
3. **Sell merchandise at as an affordable price as possible.** Until you're a star, you should be more concerned about visibility and branding than revenue. If you want to spread the word, price it cheaper.
4. **There are other things to sell besides CDs and T-shirts.** Hats,

a song book, a tour picture book, beach towels—get creative, but choose well. Having too many choices may actually reduce sales as a result of buyer confusion. You can now sell a variety of branded merchandise with no up-front costs using CafePress.com, Zazzle.com, or other similar websites.

5. **Begin promoting as soon as possible.** That allows time for the viral buzz (a.k.a. free promotion) to build and ensures that you'll get a larger share of your fan's discretionary spending.

6. **Capture the name, email address, and zip code** of anyone who makes a purchase, particularly ticket buyers.

7. **Always give your customers more than they expect.** By giving them something for free that they did not expect, you keep them coming back for more.

8. **Give it away and sell it at the same time.** In the M1.0 to 2.5 days, you used to give away a free track to help sell other merchandise, such as the album. Today, people expect to get music for free, but that doesn't mean you can't sell it at the same time. Many people will make the purchase just to lend their support.

9. **The best items to sell are those that are the scarcest.** Autographed items, special boxed sets, limited-edition vinyl that's numbered—all these items are more valuable because of their scarcity. If the items are abundant, price them cheaper. If the items are scarce, don't be afraid to price them higher.

10. **Sell your brand.** You, the artist, are your own brand. Remember that everything you do sells that brand, even if it doesn't result in a sale. Just the fact that people are paying attention can result in a sale and more revenue down the road.

CROWDFUNDING

One of the most difficult aspects of being an artist is finding funding for your project. Regardless of where you're at along the ladder of success, if you don't have the resources for recording or marketing, you'll be severely hampered in the process.

Crowdfunding (sometimes called fanfunding) has become a popular way to finance recording projects thanks to sites such as Kickstarter, PledgeMusic, Indiegogo, RocketHub, and Sellaband, among others. Regardless of which site you use, the idea is the same—it allows your fans to pool their money in order to fund your project.

Here's how crowdfunding generally works: The artist sets a monetary goal and the length of time to reach it. Then, the artist creates different levels of rewards based on the amount a fan contributes toward the project, very much like the multitiered product offerings by Trent Reznor and Josh Freese described in Chapter 4.

While this sounds like a great way to fund your project, it does take a moderate amount of planning and effort as well as a significant amount of time before you see any cash. More importantly, most funding platforms require that the entire goal be hit before the artist sees any of the money, and they take anywhere from 5 to 10 percent of the total as well. It does work, though, with high-visibility artists such as Public Enemy, Jonathan Davis from Korn, Rockwell, and Marillion having been successfully funded.

The Four Tiers of a Crowdfunding Campaign

In crowdfunding, a funding tier is a level of investment, going for as little as $10 to increments such as $25, $50, $100, $500 and more.

One of the most important elements of a crowdfunding campaign has to do with the rewards that an investor receives for putting money into the project. Just getting an album credit or their money back usually isn't enough.

Yancey Strickler of Kickstarter offered these suggestions in a blog post on Hypebot to make the campaign a bit more enticing:

1. **The Basic Reward:** If nothing else, the investor should receive a copy of the recording, be it a CD or a free download, along with a written credit on the project.
2. **Limited Editions:** For either the first 100 investors or the next-higher tier, the investor receives a deluxe edition that's individually numbered and personally signed.
3. **Share the Story:** The next-tier investor would receive something even more exclusive, such as pictures or videos from the studio, used guitar strings or drum heads, the coffee cup used by the artist, or some other personal item.
4. **The Creative Experience:** Bring the investor into the process itself by asking for his or her opinion on which version of a song or photo to release, bringing him or her into the studio for background vocals or handclaps, or just inviting him or her to sit in on a recording, photo session, or video. The idea is to give an investor at the highest level a once-in-a-lifetime thrill.

None of these cost very much, yet they could mean the difference between someone investing or not, or investing in a more costly tier.

The Five Rules for Crowdfunding

If crowdfunding is something that you'd like to pursue, here are five rules to help your campaign be successful:

1. **Choose an attainable goal.** Everybody would like a $100,000 budget to work with, but unless you have a large fan base to begin with, you're probably dreaming if you think you can raise that amount. Even the once huge-selling band Public Enemy had to cut their goal from $250,000 to $75,000, so be realistic in both what you need and what you can raise.

2. **Concentrate on low price points.** Kickstarter's data indicates that $50.00 is the optimum investment point, closely followed by $25.00. While most artists include amounts in the thousands as well, don't count on these being filled.

3. **Make sure the reward is sufficient.** Remember that you're not getting a donation, it's an investment, and your investors will expect something in return. Probably the biggest reason that music crowdfunding campaigns fail is because the rewards aren't enticing enough. Once again, check out the examples of successful tiers by Trent Reznor and Josh Freese in Chapter 4.

4. **Keep the campaign short.** Kickstarter has found that the optimum campaign length is 30 days, with longer campaigns performing significantly worse. The largest periods of investment come right in the beginning and right before it closes, with everything in the middle a somewhat "dead period." If that's the case, you might as well make the campaign short since there's no advantage to dragging it out.

5. **Account for the costs.** Make sure you take into account the cost of the rewards, transactional costs from the payments, and the fee taken by the crowdfunding site.

Kickstarter also has some great additional info and data on their website that's worth checking out.

The Concept of "Fuelers"

RocketHub provides some insight into crowdfunding and how to take advantage of their service on the *Success School* portion of its website, and it's there they introduce the concept of "fuelers." In RocketHub parlance, fuelers are contributors to your crowdfunding project and can be broken down into three categories, explained like this:

> *The vast majority of your Fuelers will be people you already know. They are your friends, family, and fans. These are people who already know and trust you. For most projects, the number of strangers who become Fuelers is fairly low. That being said, all Fuelers will fall into one of the following three categories:*

Category #1, the Committed, will be populated with your First Degree Network of friends and family. These are folks who will support you every time, regardless of the project or its quality. Your parents are likely a good example.

Category #2, the Inspired, will be populated with other friends and family members, your Second Degree Network. These are people whom you invite to the project page. They are not committed to contributing when they arrive, but after watching your video or reading your project description, they decide that you are up to something great! They become inspired to support you. Some strangers may fall into this category, but a friend you see occasionally is likely a better example.

Category #3, the Shoppers, will be populated with everyone else (i.e., your Third Degree Network). In order for your project to grab friends-of-friends and strangers, you'll need to grab the shoppers as well. The best way to do this is by creating rewards that are interesting and/or a good value.

> If you think about it, the fueler concept also applies to an artist's or band's audience.

The Committed are your "tribe" (as bestselling marketer Seth Godin calls them). These are your most passionate fans, who will go to any lengths to attend a show or buy a product.

The Inspired are your "casual" audience, the ones who like you but don't love you. It might take only a single great song to push the casual fan into the Committed category.

The Shoppers are the part of the audience that really likes your genre or even subgenre of music but that either hasn't been properly exposed to you or just hasn't caught the fever yet.

Your first job as an artist is to take care of your most passionate members (the Committed, or your tribe), since they frequently bring the Inspired or casual fan into the tribe just with their enthusiasm.

Spending too much time on the Shoppers of the audience can take too much attention away from the fans who really matter, and you may never win them over anyway. In short, take care of the fans who are already in your corner first. If treated well, they may be your fans forever.

CROWDFUNDING

Allow your fans to pool their money to fund your project.

Set an attainable monetary goal.

Make the incentives enticing for investors.

Embrace your "fuelers."

CHAPTER 10

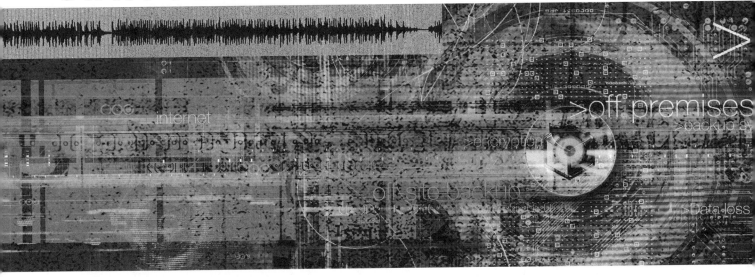

The New Distribution

For the artist or band, distribution has never been easier or more diverse than in the M4.1 world. You now have numerous ways to get your music into the hands of the consumer, but these additional choices also require a new distribution strategy.

Before M2.5 (and before iTunes), distribution was strictly a retail process in which the customer purchased directly from a brick-and-mortar retail store. Yes, there were things like record clubs and, later, online CD retailers such as Amazon, but the bulk of the sales were made through retail stores.

Starting in M3.0, however, the artist was presented with new possibilities that went beyond the traditional brick-and-mortar retail. These included online digital download distribution sites, such as iTunes and Amazon MP3, digital and CD sales made directly to the customer online, and a hybrid of the above, such as CD Baby and TuneCore.

Today, those distribution possibilities have expanded to include online streaming services like Pandora, Spotify, and Apple Music. Let's take a look at some of the current available options, as well as a new way to think about distribution.

DIGITAL, VINYL, OR BRIGHT, SHINY DISC?

In the recent past, there have always been multiple containers (a container is the way the music is packaged for distribution) of music that an artist or label could use to get its music into the hands of the consumer.

First there were vinyl singles and vinyl albums, then vinyl albums and cassettes, then CDs and cassettes, then digital downloads and CDs, and now we can add streaming digital music to the list. With the recent resurgence of vinyl, an artist has four container options for distribution of his or her work. Let's take a look at the pros and cons of each.

Music Format Pros and Cons from the Artist's Standpoint

Music Container	Pros	Cons
Digital Streaming	No container manufacturing cost Minimal distribution cost No costs for graphics/liner notes High promotional value Large and growing market Fast release to the marketplace Piracy virtually eliminated	No collectible value No resale value Intangible worth Difficult to get traditional airplay Low royalty rates
Digital Download	No container manufacturing cost Minimal distribution cost No costs for graphics/liner notes High promotional value Large market Fast release to the marketplace	No collectible value No resale value High rate of piracy Intangible worth Difficult to get reviewed Difficult to get traditional airplay Sales declining Vulnerable to obsolescence as digital formats evolve
CD	Tangible worth Potential revenue stream Collectible value Opportunity for added value	Cost of container manufacturing Cost of container distribution Decreasing market size Limited sales outlets Slow into the marketplace due to manufacturing time Difficulty getting paid by distributors

Music Container	Pros	Cons
Vinyl	Tangible worth Potential revenue stream Collectible value Opportunity for added value Market size increasing but limited	Cost of container manufacturing Cost of container distribution Hidden costs, such as breakage Small market size Limited sales outlets Unlikely to get reviewed Slow into the marketplace due to manufacturing Difficulty getting paid by distributors

As you can see from the chart, each of the current music containers has an assortment of pros and cons. This is not to say that one container is better than another in our current music world, but it helps to be aware of the benefits and disadvantages of each.

Digital Streaming

As stated earlier, the basic premise of Music 4.1 is that streaming is now the dominant music distribution method as consumers discover that being able to listen to a library of millions of songs anytime and anywhere is much more cost effective than buying a single song at a time. After all, why pay $10 a month to own only 10 songs when, for the same amount of money (or less), you can get an enormous selection to choose from, not to mention saving all that storage space on your computer or phone?

Even though streaming is just gaining traction, it's actually been with us almost since the beginning of digital music. Rhapsody can claim the tag of the original streaming service, having begun in December of 2001 and actually predating the introduction of iTunes by 18 months.

While many other services have come along since then (most notably Pandora), it wasn't until Spotify was introduced to the United States that paid streaming music began to take off, mostly because of its early integration with Facebook. The service was already a success in Europe, having begun in Sweden, where it grew to become the predominant distribution method and obliterated the download market in Scandinavia. As of the writing of this book, Spotify now boasts 75 million users and 20 million subscribers (they use a freemium model) and is available in 58 countries.

There are more than 30 other subscription services in the world, with Pandora, Deezer, and Slacker among the most prominent. With Apple Music and YouTube Red entering the streaming arena, there's more competition than ever, and with that also comes the possibility for more growth.

As of the writing of this book, the IFPI estimates that there are 41 million paying streaming music subscribers worldwide who bring in about $2.3 billion a year. That figure is expected to rise to 250 million subscribers bringing in cumulative revenues of $16.4 billion by 2020 (according to a study by PSAM), a figure that could indeed lead to a rejuvenated music industry should it come to pass.

One of the problems for all music services is the cost of the content, as payouts to writers, performers, publishers, and record labels account for between 60 and 90 percent of their revenue, not to mention the large advances paid out to the record labels for the rights to use their songs.

This has led many services to appeal for a decrease in royalty rates, only to be met by strong opposition from artists and labels, who feel that the rate is not high enough as it is. While this might be an issue today, should subscriber numbers and revenues increase as predicted, these royalty rate issues may well be a thing of the past. Streaming services and their payouts will be looked at more closely in the next few chapters.

Digital Downloads

A digital container has no manufacturing costs, so there are few additional expenses after the initial production of the music. Because there is no physical container, there's no need for disc and album artwork or liner notes, so there is no additional expense or time required for manufacturing other than typing in the metadata.

Both downloadable and streaming music make it easy for numerous services to distribute an artist's digital song for anywhere from free to a nominal charge (either a yearly or a submission fee, all well under $100).

It's relatively fast to distribute a digital container, making it instantly available on your website (although it may take two to six weeks to go live for some online distributors, such as iTunes). If you want to use a digital song (or songs) as a promotional track, again the cost is minimal because there are no manufacturing costs to recoup.

Though the digital download was the container of choice in the first era of digital music, it has some down sides. The fact that any attempt to monetize digital downloads is hampered by the ease of piracy has been discussed ad nauseum, so I won't go beyond simply making the point. Much of that problem is actually being alleviated as digital streaming takes hold.

Perhaps a larger issue is that digital's worth is intangible, since it's not something that you can physically hold in your hand. This fact has given a whole generation of consumers the notion that music is free, which is difficult to overcome. Indeed, a digital song has no collectible value. It won't be traded or prized, and you can't resell it, which is why the perception remains that it should be free.

Another serious consideration is that digital download formats such as MP3 and AAC are subject to obsolescence as new formats are introduced and evolve and as the world's taste changes to streaming.

While today digital format obsolescence doesn't seem to be much of an issue in the consumer world, it's become a serious problem in the professional audio world, with early digital masters becoming unplayable as many older formats become outdated or discontinued. Digital file-compression formats such as MP3 and AAC were initially used for distribution because bandwidth was both expensive and in short supply. With bandwidth no longer an issue for music, we're already seeing files getting larger because listeners are demanding higher quality.

As a result, bit rates of downloads have gradually increased from a norm of 128 kbps, when the formats where first introduced, to 320 kbps and higher. Lossless formats, such as FLAC and AAC+, have also gained momentum, which can mean that releases done in the current MP3 format and bit rate may have to eventually be rereleased in a lossless, higher-bit-rate format.

In fact, the day is coming soon when bandwidth will be high enough that the music doesn't have to be compressed at all, maintaining its original 44.1k or 48kHz (or higher) AIFF or WAV format used during production. (Musicians, engineers, and producers everywhere will rejoice at the sound improvement.)

To a degree, that trend has already begun, with sites like HDtracks (hdtracks.com), Acoustic Sounds (store.acousticsounds.com), iTrax.com, and many more now offering full high-resolution (96kHz/24-bit and above) PCM, FLAC, and DSD files for download. Artist Neil Young even introduced Pono, his high-res music service (which never resonated with the public). iTunes stepped up its high-res game by quietly launching its Mastered For iTunes program (affectionately known as MFIT by record labels), which accepts up to 96kHz/24-bit AIF or WAV master song files (any file that's 24-bit is technically considered high-resolution).

As with standard-resolution files, iTunes does all the encoding to AAC, but the result is a better-sounding digital file thanks to starting the process from a higher-resolution master.

In order to better facilitate the MFIT program, Apple has released a suite of tools for the mixing and master engineer to be sure that the file being submitted to iTunes is the highest quality, and to check the encoding with a virtual "test pressing" before the song goes live. Go to apple.com/itunes/mastered-for-itunes/ to download the MFIT tools.

CD—The Bright and Shiny Disc

Getting reviews isn't the only reason to consider having CDs in your distribution strategy, since there are still clear advantages for replicating them, even in M4.1. Even though CD sales have fallen off the cliff (CD sales are only about 15 percent of what they were in 2000, and they're declining steadily), they will remain a viable music container for at least a few years to come. Indeed, some music lovers still prefer buying a CD to any other format.

CDs are still viewed as an item of tangible worth by buyers because of their physical nature and the fact that they include graphics and liner notes. For many, there is an added collectible value if the CD is numbered or in short supply, and there is the ability to add value to the unit by including something additional in the packaging, such as show tickets or any number of premium items (see the section called "The Wisdom of Trent" in Chapter 4).

All this adds up to a clear revenue stream for the artist that can surpass anything that a digital download can provide. Of course, that's assuming your music is something the fan wants to buy in the first place, but we're assuming a bare minimum of popularity of the artist throughout this book.

We may never get to the point where we don't want to press physical product. In fact, I'm a believer that physical product acts like a souvenir of the band. If bands think of a CD that way and package it as such, they might find some increased success with it.

—Bruce Houghton

Even with costs ranging as low as $0.60 for a basic CD package (in large quantities, of course), manufacturing still represents a substantial up-front cost that the artist must bear, which is a clear disadvantage. Add the costs of graphic design for the disc artwork and jewel-case trays, with the time the design, manufacturing, and shipping takes before the product gets to market (two weeks minimum but likely much more), along with the difficulty one can have getting paid by distributors, and CDs soon become a music container that many artists prefer not to deal with.

The Round Piece of Plastic Known as the Vinyl Record

After the CD was unleashed on the public in 1982, it seemed as though the vinyl disc would soon be headed the way of the horse and carriage, but it never totally went away and has had a revival of sorts in recent years. In fact, the remaining vinyl mastering houses and pressing plants are busier than ever, running 24/7 to pump out product, with a backlog as long as four months. In fact, vinyl sales continue to increase, with sales in 2015 up more than 38 percent over the previous year.

Why has vinyl realized a resurgence despite the recent technological breakthroughs? Many claim that the audio quality is still superior to CDs (although that greatly depends upon the stylus and turntable involved), in spite of the fact that a vinyl record loses fidelity with every play. Others still love the cardboard album covers for their artwork and easily readable liner notes. Vinyl has a substantial collectible value and can be priced as such, giving the artist an additional revenue stream. In fact, a record is often an integral piece of the premium package offered by an artist.

But pressing a record does have its down sides as well. Aside from the obvious graphic design and manufacturing costs and the manufacturing delay to market, there's the additional issue of breakage, or the fact that some records break or warp during shipping. In a typical recording contract during M1.0, breakage was normally calculated at 10 percent of the total records pressed, and that amount was deducted off the top of the gross income. While breakage might have been that high at the time (which is debatable), the actual amount is closer to 2 percent, and it must be accounted for when budgeting.

Finally, a vinyl-only strategy is probably a loser today because, even though the market is growing, it's still relatively small. Then there's the fact that it's unlikely to get reviewed due to the fact that most reviewers don't own a turntable. That said, a vinyl product can play a huge part in the overall merch strategy of an artist.

Could the Cassette Make a Return?

It looks like another format that was left for dead may make a dramatic comeback. Believe it or not, the cassette tape is selling better than it has in years, and new tape decks are once again being manufactured.

According to National Audio, the largest of the companies still involved in cassette manufacturing, the company sold nearly 10 million units in 2014 (remember that vinyl only did 13 million with a lot more hoopla about it).

Of that number, a surprising 70 percent were actually production copies made for two of the three major labels, Sony and Universal, along with a few small indie labels. The other 30 percent were blank tapes. The company saw such an upturn in cassette sales that it persuaded Teac/Tascam to reintroduce tape machines that were long out of production.

So who's buying most of the tapes? Just like with vinyl, it's the under-35 crowd who's gravitating back to the format. After listening to digital music all their lives, many have found that they prefer the sound of analog after all.

It's too early to tell whether this is a dying gasp or a real resurgence, but it's something to keep an eye on. That said, it's doubtful that, like vinyl, the format will ever make a serious dent in the bottom line of overall music industry revenue.

MUSIC CONTAINERS

Digital streaming has vastly decreased pirating.

Digital streaming subscription is predicted to grow quickly.

But the content costs for streaming services are enormous.

Digital download sales are decreasing but remain a large part of the total industry revenue.

Digital has the cheapest distribution.

Many buyers still buy only CDs.

Vinyl is undergoing a resurgence in popularity.

Vinyl is subject to breakage during transit.

COLLECTIBLES

We've spoken about the CD and the vinyl record as being collectibles, but just what does that mean?

A collectible is an item (usually a nonessential one) that has particular value to its owner because of its rarity and desirability. Antiques, paintings, and coins are collectibles because of their rarity, which makes them highly desirable. Do you see the conundrum with digital music?

Because digital music is so easily accessed and available, there's no rarity involved. It isn't something that you can display, show your friends, or resell, so there's virtually no collectibility factor either.

Vinyl records and CDs, on the other hand, are collectible in their very basic form. In a premium package consisting of CDs, vinyl, downloads, Soundcloud or Spotify streams, DVDs, and so on, everything but the digital download and streams becomes a collectible, especially if it's signed by the artist. With the market for CDs rapidly diminishing, the discs may eventually become as rare as vinyl. With value-added content, such as concept graphics and liner notes, they still remain a must-have to true fans.

There are still a few music genres and demographics where fans prefer physical to digital, but unless those items are accompanied by some tangible merch, they're becoming an increasingly difficult sell. This might be caused by fans either lagging behind in terms of technical sophistication or being part of an older demographic, but it might also be an indication that the fans of these genres have a greater affinity for collectibles, which should not be underestimated.

COLLECTIBLES

The rarer it is, the more valuable it becomes.

CDs or vinyl can be a collectible.

Digital music is not collectible because it's not a physical product.

DIGITAL MUSIC DISTRIBUTION

Digital distribution is, of course, the backbone of M4.1, whether it's paid or free, and there seem to be more and more options every day. Because most of these services regularly rise and fall in popularity,

I'll mention only the largest and most stable and how, as a genre, they might contribute to an artist's success.

Paid Downloads

The number of digital downloads is now decreasing every year, as sales have continued to decrease as streaming has caught on. Paid downloads (meaning a downloadable song that you buy and own) is still a major revenue stream for an artist in M4.1 as just slightly under 1.33 billion digital downloads were purchased in the United States in 2014, according to the RIAA. In fact, about a third of US consumers purchased a download in 2014.

Although the payment to an artist for a download varies from site to site, the average is around $0.091 per song downloaded (about the same as a mechanical publishing royalty) and $0.915 per full-album download when a record label is involved (if the artist has a 15 percent royalty rate). This rate grows to around $0.70 per downloaded track and $7.00 if an artist or band deals directly with the distributor, before publishing and distributor costs are subtracted. Sometimes it pays to do things yourself.

iTunes

If ever there were a leviathan in the entertainment room of the music industry, it's the Apple iTunes store, which continues to hold a commanding 52 percent of the digital marketplace despite the fact that the figure was as high as 71 percent as late as 2012. From its ambitious start in 2003, iTunes has gradually risen to become the largest music retailer in the United States, eventually even topping retail giant Walmart (according to the NPD research group). Even though relative newcomer Amazon MP3 has garnered its share of users, NPD also states that most of them are new digital users, with only 10 percent of them never having used iTunes before.

Until April of 2009, all iTunes songs had the same price: $0.99. After much prodding by the major record labels, Apple expanded its offerings and went to a multitiered pricing system, with a limited number of songs available for as low as $0.69 or as high as $1.29. Most of iTunes's more than 30 million available songs still remain priced at $0.99. To date, more than 37 billion songs have been downloaded from iTunes worldwide.

iTunes introduced iTunes Radio in 2013, offering both freemium access, where the service is free with ads, or paid access, where $24.99 a year not only eliminates ads but gives access to iTunes Match, a feature that moves all purchased music to Apple's iCloud, where it can be accessed from any authorized playback device. iTunes Radio was folded into Apple Music when it launched in 2015.

iTunes is also the largest music distributor, with 850 million users (over 300 million on mobile) in 119 countries, all with credit cards on file. That said, the majority of these users are more active in the App Store than the Music Store these days, making those numbers somewhat deceptive when it comes to music.

Other Digital Distributors

Although iTunes is the largest digital distributor, there are a few other choices still available for downloads, although many have now suspended operations as streaming has become the music distribution method of choice. Where there were once more than 50 stores in the space, it's now down to Amazon MP3, 7Digital, eMusic, and Google Play Music in the United States, a definite sign that consumers' tastes have changed toward streaming for good.

Amazon Prime Music

Although second to iTunes in market share, Amazon's original digital music store, Amazon MP3, made only a small dent in iTunes' dominance, having risen to only 23 percent of the market (compared to iTunes' 63 percent) in 2013, according to the NPD Group. Digital music executives at record labels say the disparity between the two may have been even greater, with Amazon commanding just 6 to 10 percent of the market in any given week, with Apple closer to 90 percent.

That said, Amazon's major competition to other music distributors may eventually come from its Amazon Prime service, which has been consistently under the radar during any discussion of the future of online music.

Most people purchase a $99-per-year Amazon Prime membership for the free two-day shipping, but with that also comes the ability to watch thousands of movies and television shows, as well as access to the Amazon Prime Music service.

Although its catalog pales in comparison to iTunes and lacks current hits, Prime has a huge number of subscribers (Amazon won't provide the details), and the company has the resources to make a much larger entry into music distribution should it choose to.

Look to Amazon to become more involved in streaming outside of its Prime Music service in the future.

Streaming Is the New Download

Music streaming has been talked about to death, but the bottom line is still true—consumers now see the value in streaming music, and their interest will only grow. There's both a lot of hope and a lot of record label resistance to streaming music.

On one hand, everyone likes the idea of a steady monthly income that streaming might bring. On the other hand, how that money gets split up has labels, publishers, and artists all wringing their hands in simultaneous anxiety, hope, and fear.

But consumers are seeing the value of not condemning 20-plus gigs of hard-drive real estate to a library that provides no discovery options, and where you regularly listen to only a few hundred songs anyway.

The all-you-can-listen-to, anytime, anywhere option that streaming promises is beginning to make more and more sense to more and more people. This "access model" means more variety for less money from a consumer standpoint, but it also means smaller revenue increments for the artist, songwriter, label, and publisher.

While it's nice to have your music so widely distributed and available, the big negative for most artists and songwriters is what's seen as a paltry payout from streaming services. What's more, the rate paid varies depending on the type of service (on-demand or radio-like), how the income is derived (paid subscription or ad-based), the country the consumer is in, the device on which the songs are listened to, and even how long the consumer listens to the song (see Chapter 12 for more details).

The major labels have extracted large up-front advances from every streaming service for the license to use their songs and have demanded equity positions in the services. The problem is that creative accounting has caused most of that money to fall to the bottom line of the companies, with pennies on the dollar forwarded to its artists.

Many artists remain suspicious of how this money will be distributed in the future, but as streaming becomes a higher ratio of an artist's revenue, you can be sure that sharp attorneys and managers will make sure that recording agreements provide for a fairer distribution in the future.

Subscription Streaming Services

With a paid subscription streaming service, you pay a set monthly fee to be able to listen to as much music as you want during that time without limitation. The music is usually streamed, so you don't actually own it, but since it's available at any time, there's really no need to keep it on your computer, phone, or mobile device anyway.

With some subscription services, the music you choose is downloaded and stored on your playback device, but if you discontinue the service or are late paying, the files will no longer play. In many ways, it's as though your fans joined a service that lets them rent your music. As soon as they stop paying their monthly rental fee, they no longer have access to your music. Every time that more than 30 seconds of your music is listened to, you get paid a streaming royalty.

Other services use a "freemium" model that lets subscribers listen for free in exchange for playing commercials at designated intervals. Still another freemium model caps the free listening at a certain number of hours per month. Upgrading to the paid tier eliminates the ads or lifts the hour cap.

Behind the scenes, there are two ways that the streaming service can connect to a user: tethered and non-tethered. The end user usually isn't aware which is available because the streaming service normally doesn't put a lot of emphasis on this technical aspect.

- A **tethered stream** means the media player must be connected (or "tethered") to the Internet at all times in order to listen to the music.
- A **non-tethered stream** means the media player needs to be connected to the Internet only once a month for the service to confirm that the user has paid his or her monthly subscription fee. After one month, if the person either stops paying the fee or doesn't connect the device to the Internet to verify that he or she has paid, the songs will stop playing on his or her computer or portable player (see Figure 10-1).

The more widely known streaming services include the following:

- Spotify
- Pandora
- Slacker
- Deezer
- Apple Music

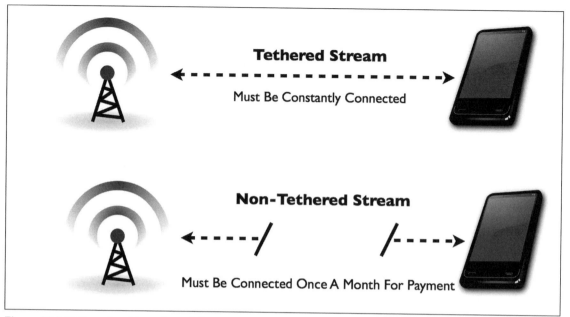

Figure 10-1: Tethered vs. Un-tethered Connections

- Google Play All Access
- Rhapsody
- Rdio
- rara
- Groove Music (formerly XBox Music)

Many brilliant business minds both within and outside the music industry have predicted that all online music business will eventually move to the paid subscription model. Perhaps that's because a widespread acceptance of subscription services is wishful thinking on the part of the major record labels, as it might solve many of their current problems, thanks to a more predictable monthly income.

That's a nice thought, but the vast majority of music consumers must subscribe in order to make up for the lost download income. Most artists signed to a record label are also not convinced that subscription is the way to go, since it's more than likely that the label will get the majority of the income, and the fact that the advances that the services pay to the major labels tend to go into the coffers of the labels instead of to their artists.

The bottom line is that streaming is growing, and with it grows the industry's financial pie. Many industry analysts predict that it won't be long before the recorded music business is healthy again, and most of that will be attributed to streaming. What's unknown is whether streaming subscribers and revenue will grow at the predicted rate.

The Digital Storage Locker (Cloud Music)

For a while, digital storage lockers where the hottest thing in digital music, and although they still exist, the feature has been quietly absorbed into more mainstream streaming services.

Digital storage lockers work on the principle that instead of storing all of your music on one desktop, laptop, phone, or tablet, you probably want the same music available on all of those devices. Having to copy and transfer all of your music files over to each device is a pain, and in many cases, you just won't have the storage space to do so anyway. A cloud music locker, like Amazon's Cloud Player, Google's Play Music, or Apple's iTunes Match, allows you to store all of your music on their online servers ("The Cloud"), which you can then access from any of your playback devices. This saves you the time it takes to transfer your files to each device as well as the storage space that would otherwise be required.

What's important to an artist is that the user pays for the privilege of using these services. Whether artists signed to record labels will see much of that revenue remains to be seen, because the language of current and past contracts may not cover this technology, but indie artists could see an immediate new revenue stream, however small.

The bottom line is that if music consumers get used to streaming their music from the cloud as predicted, digital storage locker services will become obsolete.

DIGITAL DISTRIBUTION

With a paid download, the customer owns the music.

Streaming is the new download.

In an access model (paid subscription), the customer rents music but has access to the service's entire catalog at any time.

The freemium model provides access for free with paid advertising and some limitations.

The digital storage locker allows streaming of your own music to any device you own, although it soon may become obsolete.

MUSIC AGGREGATORS

There are so many digital music sites that it's become a lot of work to submit a release to all of them, and for that reason, a number of submission services have been created not only to save you the hassle of submission but also to enable you to submit your songs to services that don't accept submissions from indie performers or indie labels. In addition, the companies will collect the royalties from the various services and forward them to you.

In exchange for these services, the companies (TuneCore, DistroKid, ReverbNation, and CD Baby are the most popular) usually charge either a small initial fee or take a small percentage of the royalties. Many of these companies can also provide bar codes and ISRC codes that identify the song, the album, and the CD and that make it easy for a physical product like a CD to be digitally tracked. OneLoad is a similar service for music videos.

MUSIC AGGREGATORS

Music aggregators save the hassle of individual submission.

They submit to different download and streaming services.

They submit to services that don't accept indie artist or label submissions.

They submit in the preferred format and bandwidth of the service.

They collect the money from digital distributors.

They take a flat fee or percentage of sales.

LICENSE OR DISTRIBUTION?

If you're not involved with a record label, this doesn't apply to you, but if you are, listen up. A recent ruling as to whether a digital download is subject to a license fee or a distribution royalty could eventually mean a lot more money in your pocket from digital download sales.

Traditionally, a license agreement meant that you gave a company the right to make copies and sell your product (this could mean music or merchandise). A distribution deal, on the other hand, gives a company the right to resell the product that you make and sell to them.

This was pretty cut and dried in M1.0 through 2.0, when sales involved a physical music product like a vinyl record, cassette, or CD. If a distributor (like a foreign label) sold records or CDs that the record company made, then it was a distribution deal. If the record company gave a copy of the master to a distributor so that the distributor could make the records or CDs themselves, it was a license deal. In today's music world, where digital products are the norm, the line between distribution and license deal becomes blurry.

In a test case, rapper Eminem's FBT Productions sued his record label, Aftermath Entertainment (distributed by Universal Music Group, or UMG), over what amounted to the definition of ownership of a digital file. FBT claimed that Aftermath owed the company more money because a digital file sold by either iTunes or Amazon MP3 is actually a license. Aftermath insisted that regardless of whether it's a CD, a vinyl record, or a digital file, Eminem's music is part of Aftermath's distribution deal. So the question became, "Is this licensing or is it distribution?"

FBT claimed that because there were no manufacturing or packaging costs (which are covered by the record label), and only a single copy was delivered to the digital download companies, then it should be considered a license, because that's what occurs with other licensing deals. Aftermath argued that a sale is a sale regardless of how it happens, and that it was therefore a distribution deal, and the terms of the recording agreement should still apply.

A lot of money was at stake here. If the court decided that selling a digital file on iTunes amounted to a licensing deal, then the record label and the artist would split the proceeds 50/50, and the artist would be entitled to about $0.30 per download. If the court decided it amounted to distribution, then the original recording agreement would be in force, and the artist would make about 15 percent, or about $0.10 on every download instead (see Figure 10-2).

In a very closely watched case, the court initially ruled in favor of Aftermath, but FBT appealed and had the ruling overturned. Then UMG essentially appealed the appeal and took the case to the US Supreme Court for a ruling. The Supremes refused to hear the case, though, and sent it back to the Ninth Circuit Court of Appeals to determine the damages; it ruled in favor of FBT.

While this reportedly meant as much as a $30 million payout to

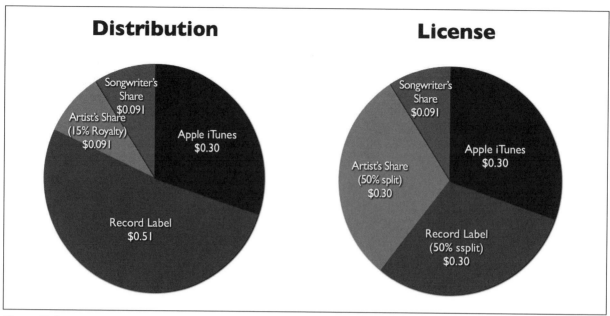

Distribution

Songwriter's
Share
$0.091

Artist's Share
(15% Royalty)
$0.091

Apple iTunes
$0.30

Record Label
$0.51

License

Songwriter's
Share
$0.091

Artist's Share
(50% split)
$0.30

Apple iTunes
$0.30

Record Label
(50% ssplit)
$0.30

Figure 10-2

FBT, the irony is that Eminem declined to be part of the lawsuit so as not to make waves with Aftermath or UMG, so he might not see an extra dime.

As predicted, more classic artists have been coming forward to sue their labels, such as the estate of Rick James, Rob Zombie, White Zombie, Whitesnake, and Dave Mason suing Universal; Michael McDonald, The Doobie Brothers, The Cars, Kenny Rogers, and Peter Frampton suing Warner Bros.; and Chuck D suing Sony, among others.

Although this ruling can change the music industry in that it means major labels could be in serious trouble if big payouts are necessary, the reality is that some artists are afraid to engage in a battle with their label, especially if they depend upon royalties from their catalog. There are enough accounting shenanigans that go on with labels already, and many artists are wary about giving them an excuse for more.

That said, you won't see this type of lawsuit filed by an artist signed after about 2003 because the labels put language in all their contracts from that time on that clearly specifies that a digital download or stream is the equivalent of a sale. FBT's suit against Aftermath did manage to increase the royalty amount for digital music for most artists, so it could be broadly viewed as a success for artists signed to labels everywhere.

LICENSE OR DISTRIBUTION

**With a distribution deal,
a distributor sells a product.**

**In a license deal, a distributor manufacturers
and sells a copy of the product
from your master.**

**Paid downloads and streams were ruled to be
a license in the FBT case.**

**New label contracts describe them explicitly
as sales, but artist digital royalty rates
have increased.**

GAMES—HIP OR HYPE?

For a while, music games such as Guitar Hero and Rock Band were hot, and mostly legacy artists made a fair amount of money from them. With that fad basically dead, another opportunity has emerged for the M4.1 artist instead.

With much of the game business turning to online rather than console games, there's more need for music than ever before. The difference is that the soundtrack to a game no longer has to be baked into the code and can in fact be dynamic.

That means it can easily change or even be selectable by the player, which means that the game now becomes more of a distribution platform for new artists. The gamer is given a number of selections to choose from, and can even purchase music by his or her favorite artist to be used as the soundtrack. The opportunity for the artist is that he or she can now collect a royalty based on sales rather than a one-time licensing fee as with console games.

If this model is adopted, gaming may soon turn into a significant source of income for many artists, with more opportunity for new artists than ever before.

GAMES

Music games will live on but won't enjoy the same popularity as before.

Console games pay a license fee for music.

Online games can pay a royalty based on sales.

Games may become a new music distribution platform.

THE NEW BRICK AND MORTAR

It's been noted in the press and various industry blogs (including my own at music3point0.blogspot.com) that sales of as few as 40,000 albums can now get you a No. 1 position on the *Billboard* charts. In M1.0 to 2.0, a No. 1 slot on the album charts would've had at least an additional zero on the end.

So why are CD sales so bad today? As stated in Chapter 2, contraction and the death of the major record retail chains, along with the demise of half of the independent music stores, have left a gap in music retail. An enterprising individual or company could take advantage of this gap, but the chances are slim that it could happen in the current economy.

That being said, there's still a network of less than 2,500 independent retail music stores to service a release. Companies like CD Baby (through Alliance Distribution) make independent CDs available to most of the remaining brick-and-mortar retail stores and distributors, as well as provide additional mastering, packaging, and graphics services and bar and ISRC codes.

Many feel that one of the reasons physical sales have been so low is because even if someone wanted to buy a CD or vinyl record, there's just no place to make the purchase anymore in most towns and many cities across the United States. The stores that remain have turned to other items, like boxed sets, artist merchandise, posters and artwork, and even novelty items as a way to stay in business.

Thanks to Record Store Day, an annual event that debuted in 2007 and is held every April, public awareness of the remaining record stores has risen. Artists have also helped support the day by releasing special vinyl editions and even making in-store appearances in the hope of promoting both the day and the stores. Record Store Day has proved to be extremely popular with the public and continues to grow every year, with more and more indie stores taking part.

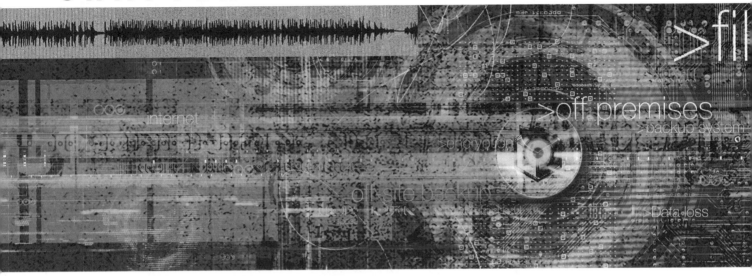

CHAPTER 11

The New Publishing Paradigm

T he topic of publishing is sophisticated enough to easily fill an entire book (and there are many books specifically on the subject), but it's an important aspect of any artist's business, so it's something we must at least touch upon here in order to understand how today's music revenue flows.

Despite popular belief, the people who have traditionally made the most money on the sale of music have been the songwriters and publishers and not the performers (unless they were the songwriters or owned the publishing companies). Let's take a look at why that happens.

THE THREE BASIC TYPES OF PUBLISHING INCOME

Regardless of the era, the songwriter and publisher have made money and continue to make money in three primary ways:

1. Mechanical royalties are paid whenever a song is digitally downloaded, a song is streamed from an on-demand service, or a physical CD or vinyl record is sold.

2. A performance royalty is paid whenever a song is played on radio, on television, or streamed over the Internet.

3. A synchronization fee is paid when music is used in conjunction with a moving picture of any kind, which includes a television show, film, commercial, video game, or YouTube video.

This payment mechanism hasn't really changed all that much in M4.1 from previous music eras, although it's managed to become even more complicated than it was. What has changed is that during M4.1, when music sales are far less than half of what they were at their peak, publishing is the one area of the music industry that has held its own. How does that happen when sales, and therefore mechanical royalties, are down, you ask?

While it's true that mechanical royalties are not nearly what they used to be now that CD sales are so low and downloads have decreased, they're offset by the tremendous increase in performance royalties because music is now played on so many more broadcasts than before. The 500-channel cable and satellite television universe, along with satellite and Internet radio, provides more opportunities for music to be played, and as a result, more performance royalties are generated.

In aggregate, people are still watching as much television as ever if not more, but they are watching it across more channels. They're watching the cable channels more and the broadcast channels less.

—Larry Gerbrandt

As record company sales have been going down since the year 2000, publishing company income has actually been going up. What's happened is that performance income (when a songwriter gets paid whenever the song is played) has gone up because there are many more places where music is played and used. Now you have tons of little cable stations and they have to all pay a small fee. As a result, you have the increase in synch fees offsetting and sometimes exceeding the loss of mechanicals. Publishing is still one of the few ways left to monetize intellectual property.

—Richard Feldman

THE DIFFERENT SOURCES OF PUBLISHING ROYALTIES

Publishing income is derived from more sources than you think, and while some of it doesn't appear significant by itself, it can all add up to a nice royalty check. Here's a simple breakdown of when a publishing royalty occurs, how it's collected, and the royalty rate:

Publishing Royalty Comparisons

ROYALTY TYPE	AMOUNT PAID
Mechanical Royalty	
Physical product (CD, vinyl)	$0.091 per song.
Digital download	$0.091 per song.
Interactive On-Demand Streaming (Spotify, Apple Music, Deezer)	$0.0001 to $0.0002 per stream (21 to 22 percent of what's paid to the record label for the sound recording if paid directly to the publisher, 17.36 to 18 percent if paid to the record label), minus any performance royalties.
Performance Royalty	
Radio	Depends on a sample survey of all radio stations, including college stations and public radio. ASCAP, BMI, and SESAC use a digital tracking system, station logs provided by the radio stations, and recordings of the actual broadcasts to determine how much a song earns.
Noninteractive Streaming (Beats 1, Pandora, iHeart Radio)	Prorated from a blanket rate of 1.75 to 10 percent of the service's total revenue, collected by ASCAP, BMI, or SESAC.
Interactive On-Demand Streaming (Spotify, Apple Music, Deezer)	Prorated from a pool of 5% of the service's gross income of the streaming service, collected by ASCAP, BMI, or SESAC.
Synchronization Fee	**Music against picture**
Television	Fee is subject to negotiation, plus survey from cue sheets that program producers provide to ASCAP, BMI, or SESAC, as well as program schedules, network and station logs, and tapes of the broadcasts to determine how much a composition earns.

ROYALTY TYPE	AMOUNT PAID
Commercials	Fee is subject to negotiation, plus survey from cue sheets that program producers provide to ASCAP, BMI, or SESAC, as well as program schedules, network and station logs, and tapes of the broadcasts to determine how much a composition earns.
Movies	Fee is subject to negotiation, with a performance royalty paid when the movie plays on television.
Printed Sheet Music	Subject to negotiation, but usually 15% of retail.
Digital Print	Any website that shows song lyrics or sheet music, flat fee or percentage of site income, subject to negotiation.
Ringtones	$0.24 per sale.

As you can see, many of the royalties and fees are variable (some of which will be covered in more detail in the next few chapters).

Synchronization fees consist of an up-front fee, which is usually negotiated by the publisher, and a performance royalty whenever the piece containing the music airs on television.

With a movie, the up-front fee is the only one that's paid for any showings in the theater, but a performance royalty is paid whenever the movie is aired on television afterward.

Likewise, both printed sheet music and digital use of sheet music or lyrics are subject to negotiation. Ringtones are still a source of income not to be overlooked even though the market for them is far below what it was during their peak.

PUBLISHING AND THE INDIE ARTIST

Can you make money from publishing if you're an indie artist? Maybe. If you're the songwriter on your band's CD or digital release, for instance, then separating the songwriting income from the sound recording income may make sense if you think the composition may have a life beyond the recording.

The reality is that to receive any kind of significant royalties from streaming or radio airplay, you really have to have a huge hit that gets a tremendous number of streams or views (50 million or more). A large income stream from this source alone happens to only a few extremely lucky indie artists.

Where you can make money is through synchronization fees, although the competition in this area today is fierce. Any time music is played with a moving picture—either on television, in a movie, or on the Internet—it requires a synchronization license. If your song is considered for a movie, you'd negotiate with the producer for a fee, which could be from $0 to $100,000 or more, depending on the placement in the film and its budget.

As with everything in the entertainment business, the higher your profile, the more you'll get paid, but if you have a song that uniquely relates to the movie, television show, or commercial (e.g., the hook of your song is the title of the movie), you can usually get a higher rate. You'll also receive a performance fee whenever it's played on television.

Still there is money to be made in synchs. At the high end, hit shows can pay as much as $15,000 to $20,000 for a publishing license, and there are tons of cable TV shows paying between $500 and $3,000. If you want to get down in the weeds, it often happens that the music supervisor blows the budget on one big song, then has to decrease the amount for all the other songs on the show.

—Richard Feldman

Getting Your Songs Placed in Movies and Television

Income from digital publishing may be small now, but it's growing larger every day as more consumers convert their listening to streaming. There's still money to be made in synch fees, although more musicians, artists, and songwriters than ever now realize this and are trying for the same thing. The problem is, how do you get your songs to the people who will license them?

Unless you live in New York, Nashville, Los Angeles, or Chicago (which is a big center for commercials), where you can network and sell yourself, your only options are to have either so much radio airplay or so much online visibility that you get noticed, or have a publisher who's actively promoting your songs to music supervisors.

Part of what a publisher does (besides collect and distribute the royalties a song earns) is promote your work. Once again, there are lots of books and articles about this to check out.

If you want to self-publish, it's also a good idea to become a member of the Association of Independent Music Publishers, where you can network with other publishers both large and small. It's well worth the $60 per year. See aimp.org for more information.

Music Supervisors: The New A&R?

Music supervisors ("music sups") are the people who select the music for a movie or television show and, therefore, have become very important in today's music business. You'll find any number of books, courses, and seminars about how to contact them and what they're looking for, but the problem is that the competition for their attention has gotten intense, from publishers, artists, and songwriters alike.

With the supply of music so high, music sups have the luxury of not only a lot to choose from, but at a cost that's been driven lower than ever before. Many artists and publishers are willing to have their music used at no cost (meaning no advance) in order to gain exposure to a wider audience, even though that audience usually doesn't know what they're listening to because it's not identified in the show.

In an effort to find new music, many music sups will actively seek out new music for their shows, and many feel that they're acting in the roll of unofficial A&R as they find previously unknown talent and give them a break. That said, while it can feel good having your music on a television show or movie (sometimes for as little as a second or two in the background of a scene), it's not the same career or financial boost it once was.

COMMON THINGS THAT MUSIC SUPERVISORS LOOK FOR

**Upbeat, happy songs
(ballads are the hardest to place)**

**Topics that express universal emotions
"enjoying life," "let's get started,"
and "things are going to be great"
(no depressing lyrics or clichés)**

Finished masters (demos don't cut it)

**New songs that sound like classic or new hits
that are in demand**

**About 75 percent of music used
is instrumental only**

THE PROBLEM WITH DIGITAL ACCOUNTING

Unfortunately, collecting performance-fee money for digital music streams is a lot more difficult than it should be. There is no standard way of electronic accounting yet, which means that online radio stations and subscription services frequently account to record labels and publishers in hard copy (though that's beginning to change). This hard copy (usually the size of several phone books for a busy publisher) must then be manually entered into the publisher's accounting system so the songwriters can get paid. This massive amount of data entry sometimes costs more than the entire amount collected.

Even if the publisher receives an electronic statement, it still must be manually entered into their accounting system as most publishing accounting software in use today isn't able to ingest this data.

To make matters worse, it's possible that a publisher is not being paid because it can't be found by the digital broadcaster or distributor (or so they say), or it's impossible for the publisher to obtain an accurate accounting of what was played. And after all that, it takes a huge number of streams and an equally large amount of accounting to show any substantial money, because the song may be earning on average around $0.001 per stream from a service like Spotify, which then has to be split 50/50 with the songwriter.

To complicate matters, streaming is divided into two different categories, the noninteractive webcaster style used by services like Pandora, iTunes Radio, and iHeart Radio, and the interactive on-demand style featured on services like Spotify, Google Play, and Deezer, and they each pay different rates (more on this in Chapter 12).

While new accounting systems are being offered by Crunch Digital and Rebeat Digital, hopefully many of the problems plaguing publishers will soon come to an end. As of the writing of this book, though, few publishers have chosen to adopt the new accounting systems, mainly due to the time and expense of porting to a new system.

WHY USE A PUBLISHER?

While many artists feel that they want to control their own publishing and just hate the idea of dividing any income, a publisher can provide a number of useful services that can make that 50 percent (the highest rate that can be legally used when splitting your royalties with a publisher) well worth it.

Besides giving you an advance against earnings if the publisher feels your songs warrant one, a publisher does the following:

- Registers the copyright for your songs so you don't have to do it
- Licenses the songs to commercial users
- Collects money from the licensees
- Pitches songs to music supervisors for film, television, and commercials
- Pitches songs to producers, A&R execs, and other potential music users
- Introduces the songwriter to artists looking for material

Having a publisher is just like having someone take care of your social networking: they'll free up your time so you can make more music, and they'll probably do a better job of administering your publishing than you can because they're pros at what they do. What's best is, in the right hands, they can make you more money than you could by yourself.

THE NEW PUBLISHING PARADIGM

The publishing side of the music industry is still making money in M4.1.

The mechanical royalty is the same for a song on a CD or a download—9.1¢ per song.

Publishing royalties from streaming are growing.

Streaming rates differ depending on the type of platform.

Everyone wants synch fees.

Music supervisors can discover new artists and music.

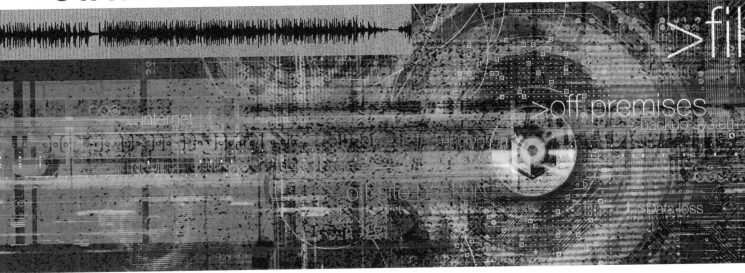

CHAPTER 12

When Music Is Your Product

While your music is your marketing, there are times when it's your product as well. As we've seen, a CD, vinyl record, cassette, or boxed set involving one or more of each can be highly valued and sought-after collectibles for your core fans.

We've also discussed different ways to price these tangible products for either maximum promotional value (free or low-priced) or maximum profit (priced high). Even though the world is going more and more to digital, physical products on some level will always be around. There's always at least some demand, and it's just too good a potential money maker to dispense with altogether.

But Music 4.1 is about music in the digital age, specifically when it comes to streaming, so it behooves the artist to know as much about the subject as possible. After all, one day soon, streaming may make up a good portion of your income.

Unfortunately, it's not as cut and dried as CD sales (and even how the money is divided there isn't always totally clear when a record label is involved); numerous streaming scenarios make how the revenue is generated and how much it generates a seriously tangled web.

Just go online and do a search for "streaming royalties" and you'll find plenty of articles proclaiming how little the artist is making against what he or she feels is fair. Hopefully, this chapter can provide some clarity in that regard.

STREAMING ROYALTY BASICS

Streaming rates are such a morass of different percentages and possibilities that few people on the planet totally understand everything, and the ones who do are attorneys working in that narrow end of the music business. Even label and publishing execs who have been in the business for 20 or more years can be confused. That's one reason artists and songwriters frequently cite low rates on what seem to be a large number of streams. It's also why an average royalty rate is used in articles about this side of the business.

That said, let's see if we can at least make sense of why it's frequently impossible to determine what an exact streaming royalty rate is.

First of all, there are two basic variables to remember that everything streaming works from:

1. **There are two kinds of streams—noninteractive or webcast (Pandora), and interactive or on-demand (Spotify).** On-demand pays more because it generates more money.
2. **There are two tiers for each stream—premium (paid subscribers) and freemium (ad supported).** The paid tier generates a higher revenue per subscriber than the free, ad-supported tier.

With this in mind, there are two different copyrights for each stream (the same as for a CD, vinyl record, or download), regardless of the tier:

1. **A sound recording royalty** (that the owner of the sound recording gets)
2. **A composition royalty** (that the publisher and songwriter get)

You can think of the sound recording as what you hear played on Pandora or Spotify (or a CD, vinyl, or download for that matter), while the composition is the notes and lyrics on paper.

Within those parameters are a tremendous number of variables, all of which affect the payout for both the sound recording and the composition. Let's explore the different types of streams first.

STREAMING ROYALTY BASICS

Physical product containing music will always be around.

There are two types of music streams that pay at different rates.

There are two tiers that pay different rates.

Each stream (or CD, vinyl record, or download) has two copyrights: sound recording and composition.

THE DIFFERENT TYPES OF STREAMS

What most artists and bands don't realize is that there are two types of streaming services, and they each operate differently and therefore pay at a different rate.

Noninteractive Streams

The first type of streaming is called a noninteractive or webcast stream and comes from either a platform that acts as an online radio station, like iHeart Radio or any traditional broadcaster with an online presence (like your local radio station), or a service like Pandora, where the user has a certain amount of control over what plays but can't directly select a song or make it repeat. Streaming platforms in this category include services like Pandora and Last.FM. SiriusXM and the music channels on cable television also fit into this category.

All noninteractive streaming services must obtain a congressionally created "compulsory" license with the rate set by an entity called the Copyright Royalty Board (CRB), which I write about in more depth later in the "How Royalty Rates Are Set" section. The CRB recently set the rates for 2016 and beyond for radio broadcasters with terrestrial radio stations at $0.0022 per stream. Noninteractive platforms like Pandora pay $0.0022 per stream from a paid subscriber and $0.0017 per stream on the free tier.

SoundExchange

The sound recording royalties from noninteractive services are paid directly to an independent nonprofit performance rights organization called SoundExchange, which was created by the Library of

Congress specifically to collect from services like Pandora, SiriusXM, and cable TV. SoundExchange collects the fees for the actual performers on a recording (not the songwriters) and for the song's copyright owners.

THE PERFORMANCE ROYALTY DILEMMA

SoundExchange collects royalties and distributes them to artists and featured performers when their songs are played on noninteractive services like Pandora, SiriusXM, and cable TV.

While this is a standard royalty feature of Internet radio, the same doesn't apply to traditional terrestrial radio, which pays the performers nothing. Terrestrial radio pays only the songwriters and music publishers, and not the artists, when a song is played.

The most played song ever on American broadcast radio is The Righteous Brothers' "You've Lost That Loving Feeling," which has been played more than 8 million times, yet The Righteous Brothers never saw a dime for any of these plays. The writers (Phil Spector, Barry Mann, and Cynthia Weil) have been paid handsomely, however.

New legislation is frequently brought before Congress to try to incorporate a royalty for the artist, but the bills are always squashed or defeated, thanks to the massive lobbying efforts of the National Association of Broadcasters, who represent radio and television stations in the United States.

Europe has a much fairer system, however, and the artists have always been paid for any airplay their recordings have received. This is collected and distributed by numerous associations that are the equivalent to BMI or ASCAP, such as the PRS in the UK and GEMA in Germany.

SoundExchange distributes these royalties at a rate of 50 percent to the owner of the sound recording copyright (which could be the record label or you, if you're DIY), 45 percent to the featured artist, and 5 percent to a fund for nonfeatured artists and singers who performed on the recording (see Figure 12-1).

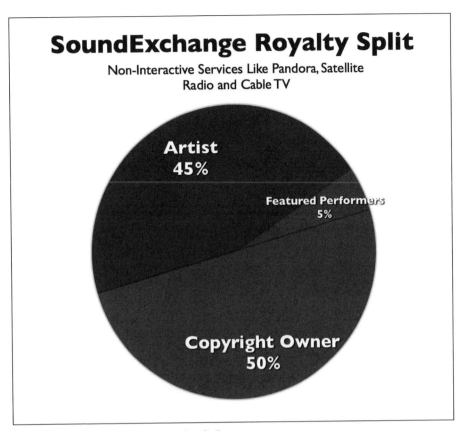

Figure 12-1: SoundExchange Royalty Split

Every artist and musician should register with SoundExchange. Go to soundexchange.com for more information.

The AMP Act

It should be noted that a new bill in the US House of Representatives has been introduced to give producers, engineers, and mixers a mandatory piece of the royalty pie. The Allocation for Music Producer Act, or AMP Act (H.R. 1457), is designed to correct an injustice that continues to carry on for all producers and engineers except the elite.

It's been standard since the late '60s for producers to get a royalty on the records they produce, but they had to negotiate their own deals with either the record label or the act they were working for. Engineers rarely had a deal for royalty points, and when they did, it was for a substantially smaller amount than the producer.

The AMP Act would create a statutory right for producers and engineers to receive royalties from digital sales and streaming, which would be handled through SoundExchange. Two percent would be set aside for the producer and engineer, which would come out of the artist's 45 percent.

So many producers and engineers have been responsible for making some major hits what they are, yet there are many cases of them not even being credited, let alone paid for the success of their work. The AMP Act hopefully will be voted into law to finally make it happen.

Interactive Streams

Interactive or on-demand streams are treated differently from the radio-style streams in that the rate is considerably higher (between $0.005 and $0.009, depending on how much the listener pays per month, among other factors). Services that provide interactive streaming include Spotify, Google Play, Tidal, Apple Music, and Slacker.

The down side here is that if you're signed to a label, money from interactive streams is paid directly to them. You'll then be paid by the label based on the royalty amount negotiated in your agreement with them. For instance, if you negotiated a 15 percent royalty rate, then you'll be paid 15 percent of $0.005 (using that number as an average), or $0.00075 per stream.

If you're not with a label, the money will be collected by SoundExchange or an aggregator like TuneCore, Ditto Music, or CD Baby if they distributed your songs to the online streaming services.

Streaming Type	Royalty Paid
Interactive On-demand	$0.005 to $0.009 (average depending upon the tier)
Commercial Broadcasters	$0.0022
Noninteractive	$0.0022 (paid tier) $0.0017 (free tier)

On top of the royalty paid to the artist and label, there's also a publishing royalty that varies yet again from the above rates, which we'll cover in the next section.

You can see why artists, bands, musicians, and even record labels can be confused about how much they're receiving from streaming. As The Temptations once sang, it's a "ball of confusion."

THE TWO DIFFERENT KINDS OF STREAMS

Interactive on-demand streams pay more per stream.

Noninteractive streams pay less than interactive streams.

Free and paid tiers pay different rates.

The royalty rate received by the artist is reduced when a label or an aggregator is involved.

Register with soundexchange.com to get paid if you're an artist or musician.

MAKING SENSE OF STREAMING INCOME

By now, we've all read the horror stories of the artist or songwriter making what seems to be an incredibly small amount of money after millions of streaming plays. What's more, it seems even more outrageous when you see that the amounts paid look random, with not many of the tiny payments at the same rate.

Hopefully, here's a way to make sense of those payments based on what was just presented in the previous two sections.

A Million Isn't What It Used to Be

Back in the days of vinyl, cassettes, CDs, and even downloads, a million was a substantial number that amounted to a lot of money in sales. Today, a million doesn't mean what it used to, especially when it comes to streaming. In fact, a million streams barely registers on the industry's radar these days; they begin to take notice at 10 million, and 50 million is considered a minor hit. Major hit records routinely rack up hundreds of millions of streams and views.

That's why it's important to keep the "million" figure in perspective when discussing streaming. It's a good starting place, but not as impressive a number as it once was.

The Sound Recording Royalty

As stated earlier in the chapter, every time a song streams, a royalty is generated for the owner of the sound recording. This is usually the record label, but it can also be a DIY artist without a label.

Sound Recording Rate Variables

Before the royalty is even paid to the artist or label, the royalty rate has lots of variables, some of which we've covered already:

- The type of service (on-demand or webcast)
- The type of tier (free or paid)
- US or foreign (where the listener is accessing the song from)
- Calculation variables

The last two points aren't frequently brought up in sound recording royalty discussions but are equally as important as the type of service and its tiers. Let's look at the country variable first.

Each country may have the same tiers, but each may pay at much different royalty rates. This is because many services charge the consumer different rates to subscribe in different countries (usually lower than the United States) because that's all the market will bear. For instance, an Apple Music subscription costs $9.99 per month in the United States but only $2 (120 rupees) per month in India and $3 (169 rubles) per month in Russia. The royalty rate paid on the sound recording will reflect these lower amounts for streams in those countries.

This is one reason why a million streams for one artist may generate more or less money than another. If most of your streams come from outside the country, chances are your royalty check is a lot lower than an artist with streams mostly from inside the United States.

Another unmentioned variable is that some services calculate their royalties on more than streams. Take Spotify, for example. One of the little known facts about the service is that the artist's market share is also taken into account when determining the monthly royalty. As a result, an artist with a huge hit effectively gets paid a bonus for her increased market share that month.

The Middleman Factor

It's been stated before but again frequently overlooked: there's almost always a middleman between the streaming network and the artist. Most of the time, it's a record label that's collecting the revenue and then paying the artist at the royalty rate set forth in their label agreement. For digital royalties, this usually ranges anywhere from 15 to about 22 percent, but you can see how the majority of the income that was generated doesn't make it to the artist in this case.

This is the same to a lesser degree for the DIY artist. Most services will accept song submissions only from major record labels or large indie labels. As a result, most DIY artists are forced to use an aggregator like TuneCore, CD Baby, or DistroKid.

Some of these aggregators charge a flat fee per song or album for uploading to the various digital services, some charge a yearly fee, and some charge a percentage of the streaming royalty that's earned. This can be another finger in the pie that the DIY artist isn't prepared for.

An aggregator provides the convenience of not only distributing your music to multiple services at once but also collecting the money for you as well, but that service does come at a price. If you're really in a DIY state of mind, consider forming your own label and affiliating with the Merlin Network indie label association (merlinnetwork.org) as a way of submitting to each service separately.

SOUND RECORDING ROYALTIES

Royalty rates are different for on-demand and noninteractive services.

Royalty rates are different for freemium and premium tiers.

Royalties for foreign streams differ from those in the United States.

Some services calculate their streams using different criteria.

There's usually a middleman involved who shares in the income.

The Performance Royalty

Just like when it's played over the radio, when a song is streamed, a performance royalty is generated. It's almost always collected by one of the performing rights organizations (PROs), like ASCAP or BMI, and then distributed to the publishing company and songwriter.

Performance Royalty Rate Variables

There are a staggering number of variables when it comes to the different performance rates paid on a stream because there are a lot of different streaming services, and each has a slightly different way of determining the royalty it must pay. Just this section alone could take up at least several chapters, but because this isn't a book on publishing, here are some of the situations you should know about in which the performance royalty rate might vary, along with a short explanation of each:

- **On-Demand Nonportable**—Subscription services accessible via desktop computers that only play music when a live Internet connection exists.
- **On-Demand Nonportable Mixed Use**—Subscription services accessible via desktop computers that can play music whether the computer is online or offline.
- **On-Demand Portable Mixed Use**—Subscription services accessible through portable devices, like mobile phones.
- **On-Demand Bundled Subscription**—Subscription sold together with another product (like a cellphone) for one price.
- **Free Nonsubscription Ad-Supported Services**—Services that offer streaming music to end users for free.
- **Paid Locker Services**—Services that provide continuous access for Internet-connected devices to recordings previously purchased by the end user.
- **Purchased Content Locker**—Services offered for free to purchasers of permanent digital downloads, ringtones, or physical records from a qualified seller that allows the purchaser access to digital versions of the purchased content from an Internet-connected device.
- **Limited Offering Subscription**—Subscription services that offer a very limited catalog of music (like from a particular genre or playlist), or services that offer streams of preprogrammed playlists.
- **Mixed Service Bundle**—The sale of downloads, ringtones, locker services, or limited offerings together with nonmusic products (like a cellphone or Internet service) for one price.
- **Music Bundle**—The sale of two or more products together for one price, like a CD, digital download, and ringtone.
- **Foreign On-Demand Free Tier**—The payment received from a foreign PRO on streams from an on-demand service's free tier.

- **Foreign On-Demand Subscription Tier**—The payment received from a foreign PRO on streams from an on-demand service's paid tier.
- **Foreign Webcast Free Tier**—The payment received from a foreign PRO on streams from a noninteractive service's free tier.
- **Foreign Webcast Subscription Tier**—The payment received from a foreign PRO on streams from a noninteractive service's paid tier.
- **Satellite Radio**—The payment received from SiriusXM streams.
- **Cable Television**—The payment received from the music-only channel streams offered by cable television providers.

The average composition royalty rate per stream is around $0.0005, according to Audiam.

The Streaming Mechanical Royalty

In the case of on-demand streaming services like Spotify or Apple Music, there's an additional royalty generated on the composition called a streaming mechanical. The streaming mechanical royalty is relatively new and was created on the premise that on-demand streaming closely resembles a permanent download because the user has such a high level of control.

When the Copyright Rate Board ruled in 2008, it mandated that the streaming mechanical rate would be around 21 percent of what's paid to the record label for the sound recording if paid directly to the publisher, or around 18 percent if paid to the record label (depending on a set of variables too deep to get into here). That means that the average streaming mechanical rate per stream is somewhere around $0.0067, according to the digital music accounting firm Audiam. As a general rule, the owners of a sound recording often end up with five or six times more revenue than the owner of the musical composition on a particular song stream.

How Royalty Rates Are Set

As you've seen, there are a lot of rates for different services and different tiers, so it helps to understand how those rates came about.

The sound recording rates that an on-demand service like Spotify pays are based upon what the major labels and large indie label organizations like Merlin have negotiated with the service. The deal usually has three separate points: an advance, the per-stream rate that the service will pay, and in many cases, equity in the streaming service (yes, the major labels own 18 percent of Spotify).

Sometimes there may be a fourth component as well, where the label receives a piece of the ad space on the free tier. This can be used by the label to promote its artists or resold to a third party.

The down side of this royalty structure is that most of what the labels receive never trickles down to the artists. The advance (which is usually in the hundreds of millions) goes to the label's bottom line, as does any revenue from reselling the ad space it receives. Finally, if the streaming service is sold at a later time, any profits derived from the sale have been kept by the labels and not passed on to their artists, although both Warner Music and Sony Music have pledged to do so in the future

The royalty rate for both the sound recording and performance for a noninteractive webcast service is set by a panel of three judges, called the Copyright Royalty Board (CRB), appointed by the Library of Congress. Every five years, the CRB reviews submissions from streaming services, record labels, and publishers in order to reevaluate the royalty rate that applies to noninteractive services.

MAKING SENSE OF STREAMING INCOME

A million streams or views is just barely in the game.

An on-demand stream generates three royalties.

There's usually a middleman who takes a good portion of the streaming income.

Sound recording rates for on-demand services are set by negotiation.

The royalty rate for noninteractive streams is set by the Copyright Royalty Board.

STREAMING ROYALTY EXAMPLES

As you can see, quite a number of factors determine the streaming royalty rate, which in turn determines how much a stream pays out. Here's a look at some examples of how much a million streams might generate. Let's look at Spotify first.

1 Million Spotify Streams Example

```
1,000,000  streams
 x $0.005  average rate per stream
   $5,000  royalty to the owner of the sound recording (hopefully
           the artist)
```

The royalty rate could be more if the majority of the streams came from listeners in the paid tier or if the total amount of streams represented a high market share that month, but it could also be lower if most of the streams came from listeners in the free tier. Spotify claims that the royalty could go as high $0.01 (a full penny), but most artists and labels find it to be lower in reality.

Now, if you're with a record label and your deal split is 15 percent of the revenue (it might be more), that means you'd only get around $750 from that amount of revenue collected.

```
$5,000  revenue from Spotify
 x 15%  artist royalty rate
  $750  paid to artist
```

On an interactive stream like Spotify, a streaming mechanical royalty is also paid. This is about one-fifth or less of the rate of the sound recording royalty. In this case, it would be about $0.00067.

```
1,000,000  streams
x$0.00067  mechanical royalty per stream (average)
     $670  to the copyright owner (hopefully the songwriter)
```

This amount is collected by the record label, who then distributes it to the publisher, who then distributes it to the songwriter.

```
$670  total mechanical royalty from Spotify
-50%  publisher's cut
$335  paid to the songwriters
```

But what if there were a total of three writers on the song, all with an equal cut? Each songwriter would then get a third of that total.

$335   total royalty paid
÷ 3   songwriters
—————————————
$111.66   paid to each songwriter

Now you can see where the "My song had a million streams and all I made was a hundred bucks" claim comes from.

But wait, what if the artist/songwriter still owes the label $25,000 from her royalty advance or for recording costs. The label will apply that money against the money owed instead of sending it to the publisher.

$25,000   owed to label
– $670   revenue from Spotify
—————————————
$0   paid to the songwriters (although the balance
       owed is now $24,330)

There's still the performance royalty income that's paid to a PRO, which then distributes it to the songwriter and publisher.

1,000,000   streams
x $0.0005   performance royalty per stream
—————————————
$500
– 14%   administrative costs by the PRO (approximately)
—————————————
$430   or less performance royalty to the publisher
       (hopefully the artist)

It's difficult to predict the royalty amount because it's based on the deal that the PRO has made with the streaming service (in this case Spotify), but it still adds up to about one-fifth or less of the sound recording rate.

$430   revenue from the PRO
– 50%   publisher's cut
—————————————
$215   paid to the songwriters

$215
÷ 3   songwriters
—————————————
$71.66   paid to each songwriter

If the songwriter owns the publishing, then all that income would be paid directly to him. If the songwriter is signed to a publisher, then the publisher would be entitled to as much as 50 percent. In this case, there are three songwriters, each with an equal ownership in the song.

Total Revenue Generated by 1,000,000 Spotify Streams

$5,000	from the sound recording royalty
$670	from the streaming mechanical royalty
$430	from the performance royalty (3 writers)
$6,100	total revenue

Revenue on 1,000,000 Streams Paid to the Artist/Songwriter

$750	from the sound recording royalty
$111.66	from the streaming mechanical royalty
$71.66	from the performance royalty (3 writers)
$933.32	total revenue

Here's the problem: both the payment for the sound recording royalty and the payment for the streaming mechanical royalty are paid to the record label. If the artist owes the label any money for advances or recording costs, this amount will go to pay down the debt first (recoupment, as it's called). Given that record labels aren't exactly known for their transparency, it could take a long time before the label debt is recouped, and even longer still until the artist sees his first payment, because labels are notoriously slow at paying and getting slower all the time.

1 Million Pandora Free-Tier Streams Example

Now let's check out what a million streams on Pandora's free tier might generate:

1,000,000	streams
x $0.0017	per stream
$1,700	royalty paid to SoundExchange for the sound recording owner (hopefully the artist)

Once again, a certain percentage of streams will come from the free and paid tiers, so there will be a mix at each rate. As a result, the average will be somewhere between $.0017 and $.0022 per stream. If the artist is signed with a record label, the label will take its cut. If the artist uses an aggregator like CD Baby, they'll take a percentage as well.

After SoundExchange collects the sound recording royalty, it deducts about 5 percent for operating expenses.

$1,700   sound recording revenue from Pandora
– 5%   SoundExchange operating expenses
$1,615   to be distributed

$1,615 sound recording revenue from Pandora after SoundExchange expenses

x 50% to the sound recording owner (artist or label) = $807.50
x 45% to the artist = $726.75
x 5% to the featured players on the song = $80.75

When it comes to publishing, ASCAP, BMI, or SESAC collects the royalty and distributes it to both the publisher and the songwriter, but the amount depends upon the total income of the service, so it can't be accurately predicted. That said, it's been estimated at about one-tenth of the sound recording rate in this case.

1,000,000   streams
x$0.00017   per stream
$170   performance royalty payments paid to PRO for
            the copyright owner (hopefully the artist)

Once the PRO receives payment, it deducts an administrative fee of around 14 percent before it distributes the payments to the publisher and songwriters.

$170   performance royalty payments paid to PRO
– 14%   PRO operating expenses
$146.20   performance royalty to be distributed

There are three songwriters, so the performance royalty is divided three ways (if each has an equal percentage).

$146.20
$\underline{\div\ 3\quad \text{songwriters}}$
$47.73 \quad$ paid to each songwriter

Let's total up how much money is hypothetically generated via one million Pandora streams in the free tier, and how much the artist would make.

Total Revenue Generated by 1,000,000 Pandora Free-Tier Streams

$1,700 \quad$ from the sound recording royalty
$\underline{\ \ \$170 \quad \text{from the performance royalty}}$
$1,870 \quad$ total revenue

Revenue on 1,000,000 Streams Paid to the Artist/Songwriter

$726.75 \quad$ from the sound recording royalty
$\underline{\ \ \$47.73 \quad \text{from the performance royalty (3 writers)}}$
$774.48 \quad$ total revenue

As you can see, this is a very complex system with multiple rates and potentially multiple fingers in the financial pie. If an artist is signed with a record label, the amount of money paid out to the artist will be a lot lower than the money collected. The same with the publishing income, where the revenue is split if there's a publisher involved, after expenses are deducted by the PRO.

Most of the horror stories that you've heard come from artists and songwriters who have a third party in the middle taking a lot more of the income than the artist is getting, as we've seen above, so the income from streaming looks a lot worse than it really is.

Again, keep in mind that while a million streams sounds like a lot (as it is for most indie musicians), most hit songs get far more than that. Add that up across a catalog of music, and add in the fact that at least a tenfold increase in streaming subscribers is expected in the next five years, and we could be talking some real money that will make everyone in the industry a lot happier about streaming income than they are today.

THE REALITY OF THE SITUATION

While the payout from any single source may seem especially small, keep in mind that if a song is popular enough to garner a million plays on one service, it's probably seeing the same numbers on other services as well. That means that the artist, label, songwriter, and publisher are seeing revenue from dozens of other sources, both in the United States and overseas. That means that while one streaming source might seem low, put them all together and they become something significant.

Consider, too, that the number of users and subscribers for all services is increasing by the month, and you can see that, just like in previous eras, even a modest hit can mean some substantial income.

One last thing—while many artists and songwriters are down on streaming, especially compared to the income made from downloads, remember this:

Streaming pays forever, while a download or sale only pays once!

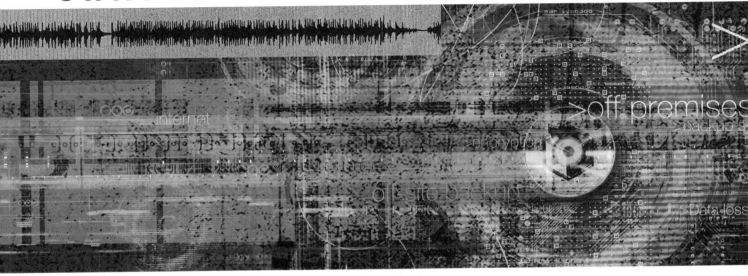

CHAPTER 13

Monetizing Video Views

For many artists and record labels, videos have become not only a great source of exposure, but a source of income as well. That said, many artists have a number of misconceptions about how YouTube videos are monetized and how much they should expect to be paid from them.

While this chapter mainly explores monetizing YouTube videos, it does look at other platforms as well, since it won't be long before You-Tube has some real competition on its hands.

MONETIZING YOUTUBE

YouTube has become an additional income source for some artists and a major one for record labels. But it's not as easy for a video to go viral as many are led to believe, and the revenue splits and potential income are fairly low, even when compared to streaming music.

How YouTube Videos Are Monetized

First of all, understand that just because your video is being viewed doesn't mean you're getting paid. Your channel must first be signed up with Google AdSense (who supplies the advertisements), then set for monetization, and then the monetize option for each video must be selected. It's only at that point that your videos can begin to be monetized (see Figure 13-1).

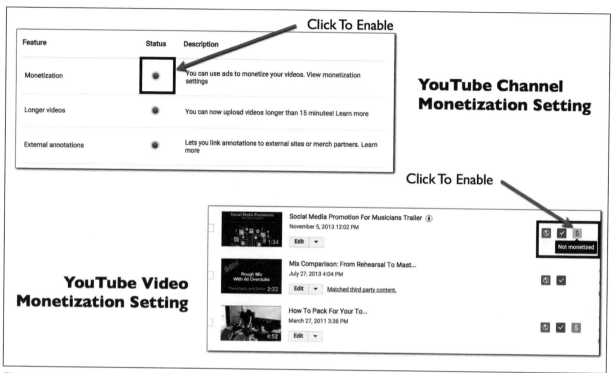

Figure 13-1: Monetizing Your Video Channel

View Variables

There's more to it than that, though, as with everything involving digital music. The commercial on the pre-roll must be watched all the way through or else it doesn't count toward monetization. If there's a banner ad across the bottom of the video, it must be viewed for at least 31 seconds before it counts as a monetized view.

There's also the fact that YouTube doesn't sell ads on all of your views, and some views on mobile devices just don't register unless the viewer uses an official YouTube app.

Another major factor is the advertiser that's placed on your video. If your audience happens to like expensive cars, jewelry, or clothing, then an advertiser would probably be willing to pay a higher ad rate, which means that each video view would earn more money.

Yet another variable is the time of year the video is viewed, as many advertisers pay more for the holiday season than in January, for instance.

And then there's the type of ad that's used on the video or channel. This can vary from a skippable video ad that runs before your video begins (a "pre-roll"), to a transparent overlay ad that takes up the bottom portion of your video, to a display ad featured to the right of your video, and more. Each pays at a different rate.

That's why payouts can range anywhere from around $2.50 to $9.00 per thousand views, which means that a monetized video with 1 million views may generate anywhere from $2,500 to $9,000. YouTube takes a 45 percent cut, however, which puts the income to the copyright holder between $1,375 and $4,950.

A generally accepted average of what to expect from a million video views is around $1,750, or $0.00175 per view, after the split with YouTube, although it's also common to see payouts as low as $0.011, or $1,100 per million views.

Don't forget that if you're signed to a record label, this is what the label takes in, and you're paid at your label royalty rate (15 to 22 percent of the net amount) minus any recoupable deductions. No wonder you're not seeing any YouTube money.

YouTube and the Labels

Record labels have found YouTube to be a nice profit center and have entire departments dedicated just to making, distributing, optimizing, and monetizing videos of their artists. That's because there can be some real money with a stable of artists who post a lot of videos.

Let's look at a hypothetical label that has 30 artists on its roster. Each artist has ten monetized videos that are getting substantial views. Let's say that the average number of views of each video is a million a month (some are going to be way more and some way less, but the figure isn't outrageous).

30 artists x 10 videos each = 300 videos
Each video gets 1,000,000 views per month at $0.00175 =
$1,750 per video
300 videos x $1,750 = $525,000

Considering that most of that money stays in-house for the label, it's a pretty nice profit center for them.

It would be great if every indie artist was capable of getting a million views a month, but most don't have the muscle or expertise of a label to make that happen. That doesn't mean you shouldn't try, though.

Make sure to monetize at least some of your videos, then optimize them as outlined in Chapter 7. Remember that it's probably a good idea not to monetize them all, because short, impromptu iPhone videos of you on tour may be more effective if they aren't cluttered with ads.

Content ID

YouTube is able to monetize third-party videos that use your music via a system known as Content ID. This works by adding a digital fingerprint to the audio and video that you upload and then scanning the YouTube universe for content that uses it without your permission.

If Content ID finds either audio or video that it thinks is being used without permission, it flags the owner of the content. The owner (which could be you or your record label) then has the option of doing nothing and leaving the third-party video as is, having the video taken down, or having advertising added to it, with most of the money earned going back to the copyright owner.

Content ID is essential for making money when a video goes viral. If someone uses one of your songs as music on a video, Content ID will flag it if it's been loaded into the system. If someone posts a lyric video of your song, Content ID will flag it. If someone uses your song as background for a cat video, Content ID is on the job.

One down side is that sometimes Content ID can flag a song or video that you own as a violation. You can then appeal the copyright claims by the system, but it could take anywhere from a few hours to 30 days to resolve.

A YOUTUBE SUCCESS STORY

Here's an example of how the tiny royalties coming from YouTube can add up. Wanting to increase their revenue from YouTube, Josh Colum and his band Secrets In Stereo signed up with Rumblefish, a company that finds licensing opportunities for artists.

Initially there wasn't a lot of money—only a few bucks per statement—but soon, Josh began to see around $10,000 per quarter. Astonished, he explored what happened.

It seems that a song called "Happy" from the band's first album was chosen by a wedding photographer who was looking for music to accompany a wedding video he made. He chose the song from a site called Animoto after listening to hundreds of songs.

After he gave the couple their video, they posted it on YouTube, where others saw it, and they also used the song for their own wedding videos. Today, the song has surpassed 250 million views, which adds up to some substantial cash for the artist and songwriter.

Rumblefish takes care of collecting the money from Animoto and tracking the views on YouTube and online video services.

Both Josh Colum and Secrets In Stereo are pretty under the radar in the music business, but they've managed to carve out a living thanks to putting their songs in the right places and having a little luck and a little virality.

MONETIZING YOUTUBE VIDEOS

You must choose to monetize your videos on your YouTube channel before you can make money from them.

Not all video views will be monetized by YouTube.

Not all videos should be monetized.

YouTube takes 45 percent of the advertising revenue.

Different ad types and different advertisers pay different ad rates.

Content ID looks for unauthorized videos using your music.

FACEBOOK VIDEO

Facebook is making a play to overtake YouTube as the number-one destination for online video. As of the writing of this book, the service has actually equaled YouTube in the number of video views per day (over 4 billion!), but it falls behind in a feature vital for content creators—a way to monetize videos.

Facebook doesn't yet have anything similar to Content ID in place, although it's rolling out a video-matching technology that may be the precursor to its own version of Content ID. Until that happens, many YouTube creators have chosen to stay put and not test the Facebook video waters.

Facebook Video Pros and Cons

Besides the lack of a way to adequately monetize videos, Facebook faces a few other equally serious problems. First of all, the number of actual video views is deceptive because Facebook counts a view if someone watches a video for as little as 3 seconds. YouTube counts a view only after 30 seconds.

An even larger problem is the process known as freebooting, where a user copies a video from YouTube and uploads it to Facebook as their own. Because there's no Content ID equivalent, there's no way for the original content owner to claim the video in order to get credit for the views. To make this even more outrageous, it's estimated that 70 percent of all videos currently on Facebook have been freebooted from YouTube.

Facebook does currently have one major advantage to posting your videos there: because it's trying to build that side of its business, it favors native videos (those uploaded directly and not using an embed code). While a standard post might reach only 2 to 5 percent of your fans, a video will reach all 100 percent and more.

Maybe you can't make money with Facebook yet (and that will surely change soon), but you can get a lot more visibility on the service by natively posting your videos there.

FACEBOOK VIDEO

Facebook has as many daily video views as YouTube.

Those views are calculated differently, so the total might be deceiving.

Facebook currently has no Content ID equivalent.

There's no way to monetize videos or get credit if someone posts your video to Facebook as their own.

The majority of Facebook videos are freebooted from YouTube.

Facebook favors video posts over all other types of posts.

OTHER VIDEO PLATFORMS

Many artists have found that other video platforms, like Meerkat, Periscope, Vine, Snapchat, and others, have been an effective way of not only reaching their audience, but increasing it as well.

Unfortunately, due to the short-term nature of the videos created by some of these platforms, it's difficult to use them for anything other than fan engagement. Companies like Gbox allow content creators to monetize these videos, but realistically, there's probably not a huge up side to doing so. Most fans are not used to videos on these platforms either having ads or being purchased, and trying to do so may actually be counterproductive.

CHAPTER 14

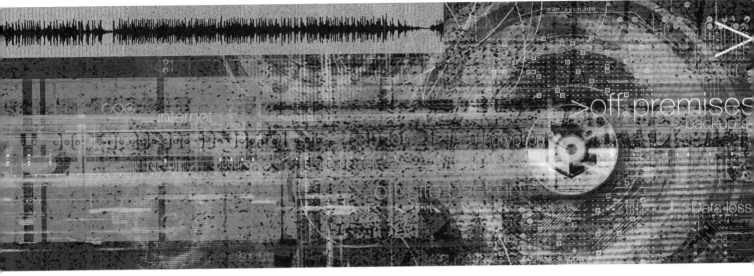

The Music 4.1 Rules for Survival

Like just about everything else, the rules to survive and flourish in M4.1 have changed from what worked in the past. In M1.0, the success path might have looked like this:

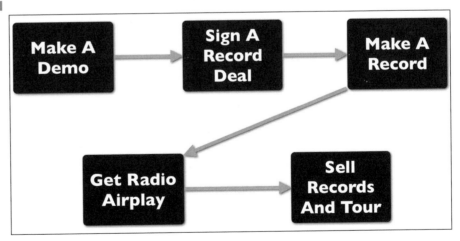

Figure 14-1

The path in M4.1 is much different; it's shorter than before but, at the same time, more complex for artists because they must do so much of the work themselves.

Figure 14-2

Although it might seem simple, since the path to the consumer is so direct, each step is much more complicated. Assuming that you've already created your music (if not, check out a few of my other books for tips), let's take a closer look.

DEVELOPING YOUR AUDIENCE

M4.1 is totally dependent upon the development, care, and feeding of your fan base. Your core fans, or "tribe," are only a piece of your total audience, though. Your audience can be broken down into the following two categories: casual fans and core fans.

Your total audience, or your fans, are fervent about a particular small niche of music that's usually a subcategory of a larger genre, which means that they love speed metal (as opposed to the much larger metal or hard-rock genres), bluegrass (as compared to the larger country-music genre), or alien marching bands (as opposed to either of the larger alien music or marching band genres).

If you're an artist in that particular niche, your audience will automatically gravitate toward you, but they still might not be your fans. This includes casual fans, occasional listeners, and people who like what you're doing but aren't particularly passionate about it.

Although this part of your audience can't be ignored, it's probably not a good idea to expend all your energy on it. They're aware of you and will probably give you a try with every release, unless they're disappointed too many times in a row. They can be turned into passionate fans, though. One "hit" song or album, a change in image, or a change in general perception, and they become the passionate critical mass needed for the breakout that turns a respected artist into a true star.

In M4.1, your most important core audience contains your most passionate fans, or your "tribe," as described in Chapter 4. They'll buy whatever you have to sell, work for free, recruit other fans, and basically do anything you ask. All they want is access to and communication with the artist, which is the basis of M4.1. But how do you develop your tribe?

DEVELOPING YOUR AUDIENCE

Your audience consists of your casual fans and your core fans.

Fans may like an artist but may not be particularly passionate.

Your core fans (true fans, uberfans, super fans, tribe) are very passionate about everything you do.

Most of your energy should be directed toward your core fans.

ESTABLISHING YOUR TRIBE

According to Seth Godin, the originator of the tribe concept, a tribe is a group of people connected to one another, connected to a leader, and connected to an idea. In M4.1, tribe members are connected to each other and to the artist via their passion for the artist's music, but the leader is the integral part of the tribe. In fact, without a leader, the tribe is only a self-organized group. As an example, a blog may have thousands of readers who never add a comment, so this makes it a group. The blogger could be the leader, but if she's the only one who posts, there's still no tribe.

We're assuming that more than three people are passionately connected to the artist, since that number is obviously essential to the creation of a tribe. The music is what connects them to the artist and to each other.

The Leader

The most important thing the tribe needs is a leader. Although the artist is the most logical leader, a representative who speaks for the artist can work in that capacity as well. In the old fan-club days, the fan-club president acted as leader, and today, he or she still could be the leader of the tribe. Unless he or she directly represents the artist, though, the tribe isn't as powerful or as dynamic as it could be.

So how does one become the leader of the tribe? The leader initiates contact with the tribe and leads the conversations. For instance, the artist/leader might send or post a tour schedule with a list of "meet-and-greets" especially for tribe members. He or she makes it easy for everyone to participate and rewards the members who do so.

Before the artist makes a new recording, she might ask the tribe what direction they'd like her to go in, and then reward the ones who respond by sending them a link to stream a special mix of the song. And most importantly, the leader gives projects to tribe members to work on. The artist might ask people to send suggestions on venues in a certain area or to pass out flyers before an upcoming gig. Remember that tribe members are passionate and truly want to be part of something. Active participation fulfills that longing.

However the leader reaches out, it must be authentic and show true caring for the tribe members. Tribe members can feel in an instant if you're just going through the motions, and the tribe will begin to dissolve. If you're posting to your fans just as an exercise because "That's the way M4.1 works, dude," then you're better off finding a surrogate leader.

The next thing that a tribe needs is a place to meet. This is pretty easy today because there are a variety of alternatives, from blogs to Facebook groups and Twitter to a custom social network on Ning. Whatever the online technology used, tribe members must be able to communicate with one another easily, or the glue that holds the tribe together will be weak. That being said, having just a simple mailing list can be enough to connect the tribe.

ESTABLISHING YOUR TRIBE

You don't have a tribe without a leader.

The leader doesn't have to be the artist.

The leader initiates contact, leads conversations, and makes it easy to participate.

The tribe needs a place to meet and communicate.

Growing Your Tribe

Now that your tribe is established, it must be carefully expanded (we'll get into some of the reasons besides the obvious in a minute). Although it might not seem like a method for expanding the tribe, how the leader treats the tribe is as integral to expansion as any external methods.

Tribes flourish from within. Word of mouth is perhaps the most powerful marketing method there is, and your tribe will champion you to anyone who will listen if you give them the slightest reason. Therefore, the first and most important way of developing the tribe is by nurturing it.

The easiest way to nurture the tribe is to transfer some of the artist's social standing onto them. To you, the artist, it might not seem like much if you have only 10 dedicated members in your tribe, tally a dozen downloads a week, and get only 15 people to your shows. But your tribe feels that you're the greatest thing since Adele or Coldplay and that they've discovered you before anyone else. In their eyes, you have a degree of prestige and status that comes with the uniqueness of your music. You must transfer some of it to them. Here are a few ways to do that:

- If a certain fan has seen you 15 times, call him out at a show. Bring him backstage for a meet-and-greet or invite him to an after-show party.
- If a member consistently posts in a helpful manner for the betterment of the tribe, develop a personal off-list dialog with the fan, offer her a free ticket to the next show, or post a picture of her on the meeting space.

Any small action, such as the ones listed above, that transfers a bit of status will make the member more loyal and vocal and will encourage other fans to take more action in hopes of reaping the same rewards.

The leader must constantly check the pulse of the tribe to hear what the members are feeling and thinking. This can be helpful in determining just what the tribe likes and dislikes about you and your music. Maybe there's a direction that you briefly touched upon on your last album that drove the tribe wild that you didn't notice, or maybe one that they hated. You might choose to follow your musical instincts instead of listening to tribal feedback, but at least you won't be surprised by the resulting reaction.

Taking the tribe's pulse also lifts the mood of its members because interaction with the leader is always appreciated and results in more participation. Showing your appreciation for their participation fosters even greater loyalty and participation and gets them invested emotionally and intellectually.

So how do you take the tribe's pulse? You ask them questions or ask them to help you.

- Ask them which piece of merch they prefer.
- Ask them about the best venues in their area, why they like them, and if they'd prefer to see you there.
- Ask them what song they'd love to hear you cover.
- Ask them who their favorite artists are (this answer is great for other elements of social marketing, as mentioned in Chapter 7).
- Ask them to judge the artwork on your next release. Then, when they respond, reward them. Give some free merch to the first ten people who respond.
- Send them a secret link to stream a track that's available only to them.
- Give a personal shout-out to some of the best responses.

All of the above makes them feel special and great about belonging and keeps the tribe's interest high.

Also remember that the tribe is composed of both leaders and lurkers. These two subgroups usually fall into the familiar 80:20 ratio (80 percent of the participation is provided by 20 percent of the tribe). Leaders are the first to respond and are always eager to participate. Lurkers remain in the shadows—interested, but not enough to engage the tribe. Getting the lurkers to participate is essential to growing the tribe. Let them know that there are benefits (such as free show tickets, after-show party invites, and exclusive merch or streams) for being more active. Above all, let them know that they'll be sorely missed if they decide to opt out of the tribe.

Even though you want the tribe to expand, don't focus on the number of members; it's not the numbers that count, but rather the quality of the experience. Focus on the members themselves, and they'll bring others to the tribe. Remember that a tribe's rate of growth depends upon two things: the level of passion of the members and the leadership's involvement. Have a high level of tribal passion and leadership participation, and the tribe will grow quickly; but have a lower level of either of the two, and the tribe will be faced with slower growth. When the tribe no longer benefits anyone, it will die.

GROWING YOUR TRIBE

Tribes flourish by word of mouth.

**How the leader treats the tribe
determines how it grows.**

**The leader must constantly check the pulse
of the tribe by asking questions or asking for help.**

The tribe is composed of leaders and lurkers.

**Getting lurkers to participate
also grows the tribe.**

Marketing to Your Tribe

Be extremely careful about how you market to your tribe. Chances are that your tribe wants everything you have to offer, but they don't want to be sold to. Make an announcement about a new release or a piece of merch, but don't oversell it.

Members don't need to know that you think your new music is the greatest thing you ever did, or that it's better than the Foo Fighters' last release. They'll decide for themselves and then sell it for you in their own conversations if they like it.

You market to your tribe simply by presenting your product to them. Just make them aware that it's available, and they'll do the rest. You can take it a bit further by offering them information about the product—the more exclusive, the better.

Instead of a sales pitch, try these ideas:

- Give them a behind-the-scenes story about the making of the product.
- Tell them where the idea for it came from.
- Tell them about all the people involved, especially other tribe members.
- Provide interviews with others involved in the project.
- Give them all the trivia involved in the project, no matter how small. True fans will eat it up. If it's a new song, tell them where it was recorded, who the engineer and producer were, how many Pro Tools tracks were needed, how long the mix took to finish, how many mixes you did, how the final mix compared with the rough mix, and

all of the hundred other fine details that go into producing a song. If you just produced a new T-shirt, describe where the design came from, why you chose the manufacturer, what the shirt is made of, why you chose the color, and so on. Get the idea?

Giving them insight that no one else has makes them feel special, will keep them loyal, and will show mere fans and lurkers the benefits of participation in the tribe.

MARKETING TO YOUR TRIBE

Present your product, don't sell it.

Give them lots of information and trivia.

Absolutely no hype!

SUSTAINING YOUR CAREER

How you sustain a career in M4.1 has changed significantly from previous eras of music. The formula is simple: maintain your connection with your audience. This could mean putting out frequent releases, blog posts, email blasts, tweets, or anything else in social media, but you've got to keep your fan base regularly engaged. Although long periods of time between releases (such as six months or a year) are not recommended, they can be overcome by constant interaction by the artist. It's only when communication grows cold that the tribe begins to dissipate. A typical consistent communication schedule might look something like the following:

- **Tweets:** at least a few times a day
- **Blog posts:** once or twice a week
- **Email blasts:** once a month, with tour schedules, release schedules, or just general info
- **Music releases:** once every six to eight weeks
- **Videos:** at least two a month, but once a week is best

Online communication isn't the only way to stay in touch with your fans. Touring will always be a part of being an artist, and it's an especially important ingredient in not only sustaining your fan base but also growing it. The more personal contact you have with your fans, the more opportunities you have to reach out and touch them. Don't forget some of the items mentioned in Chapter 5, such as meet-and-greets, after-show parties, backstage passes, and the like. Online and offline contact must all be part of the same strategic plan.

The "1,000 True Fans" Theory

The "1,000 True Fans" theory by *Wired* magazine's "senior maverick" Kevin Kelly states that all an artist needs is 1,000 true fans to maintain a fruitful, if unspectacular, career, thereby relieving the artist of the need for some of the nastier things in life—like a regular job. True fans are sometimes called superfans or uberfans, depending on whose theory we're talking about.

Kelly wrote the following:

A creator, such as an artist, musician, photographer, craftsperson, performer, animator, designer, videomaker, or author—in other words, anyone producing works of art—needs to acquire only 1,000 True Fans to make a living.

A True Fan is defined as someone who will purchase anything and everything you produce. They will drive 200 miles to see you sing. They will buy the superdeluxe reissued hi-res box set of your stuff even though they have the low-res version. They have a Google Alert set for your name. They bookmark the eBay page where your out-of-print editions show up. They come to your openings. They have you sign their copies. They buy the T-shirt, and the mug, and the hat. They can't wait till you issue your next work. They are true fans.

The idea is that if each of the 1,000 fans bought $100 worth of product every year (the figure equals an arbitrary full-day's pay), you'd have an income of $100,000, which, even minus expenses, can still represent a reasonable living for most artists. The trick, of course, is how you expand your fan base to that magic 1,000-fans number (providing that you buy the theory, of course).

I also see the rise of the musical middle-class artist that can make anywhere from a store-clerk living to $100 grand a year per band member. There'll be fewer superstars and a lot more mid-level artists as time goes on.

—Bruce Houghton

Like most theories on such things, the detractors of the 1,000 True Fans theory point out several relevant issues:

- **The $100,000 amount is the gross income and doesn't take expenses into account.** Expenses for any creative endeavor can be quite substantial and must be accounted for in any income assumption.

- **Even if you reach the magic 1,000-fan number, that doesn't mean that each will spend $100 per year.** That's true, but remember that $100 is an average number. Some fans might spend $500, while others might spend only $20. Of course, you have to present them with the products and the opportunity to spend money. If you put out a single release and don't tour, it's unlikely that you'll hit your target. If you're touring, and a true fan attends three shows and brings five friends, that could easily account for $100 right there. And if you release two albums, a deluxe box set, and newly designed T-shirts, hats, mouse pads, and coffee cups, there's an even greater chance that the true fan will just have to have whatever you're selling.

- **M4.1 presents a worldwide marketplace, so 1,000 fans don't necessarily have to reside just in the United States.** Again, this is true and can lead you to believe that developing your fan base is a lot easier than it really is. Don't forget that true fans in developing countries might enjoy your work yet not have the wherewithal to purchase anything from you. Postage and import taxes make international sales difficult as well.

- **You can expect some attrition of your new fans.** Hopefully, the attrition of your fan base will at least be offset by new members, and perhaps your fan base will even grow some in the process.

- **Other artists are competing for the same fans.** There's always competition in the marketplace for every dollar, sale, and item. You must differentiate yourself and your product from your competition to make the choice easier for the fan. For sure, you'll lose some fans during this process, but if you plan and deliver well, you'll make that number up and more.

Although the total number of true fans actually required to make the theory work (is it 300 or 1,000 or 4,000?) may be in question, the idea is that you need this hard-core group in order to sustain your career.

Whatever number you're lucky enough to develop, be sure to take care of and nurture them, because they truly want you to.

SUSTAINING YOUR CAREER

Frequent online communication is a necessity.

Too little or too much communication can be detrimental to the growth of your fan base.

Touring and face-to-face communication are equally important as your online presence.

Aim to develop a core audience (the 1,000 True Fans theory).

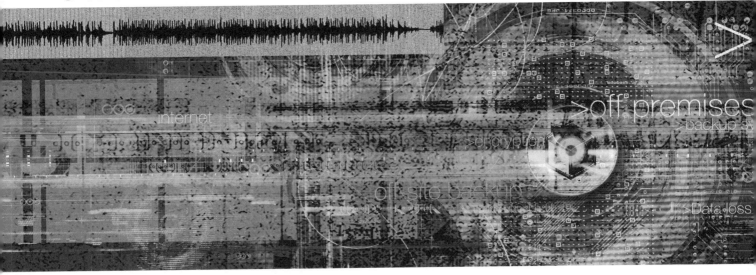

Living in Music 4.1

To many in the business, the future is now. We're already in Music 4.1, but what was the barrier that we crossed? Was it a date, a technology, or an event? Yes, it was all of those, but also a change in attitude. Let's look a little into the very near future. Chances are that much of it will have already come to pass by the time you read this.

MAKING A LIVING IS THE NEW SUCCESS

Musicians and artists will begin to see success in a different way as making a living replaces stardom as the big score. To some degree, this was always true. Most musicians are only too happy making a living by playing music, but thanks to the excesses of previous eras, far too many felt that stardom was well within their reach.

This notion has changed as a new realism about the music business has evolved:

- The realization that DIY takes a lot of work and the rewards aren't as great as in the heyday of the major labels. There's not as much revenue in the music industry pie to split as there was before, at least for now.

- The realization that social networking has limitations, just like traditional marketing, so traditional marketing and promotion can't be completely abandoned. You still need both for effective branding and marketing.
- The realization that the touring market is not nearly the gold mine it once was. Fewer venues, less money, and more competition makes gigging more difficult than ever.
- And the realization that some things in the music business never change. You still need talent, great songs, lots of hard work, and a little luck to make your mark.

There's No Such Thing as a Demo

If you're an artist or band recording your own songs, erase the word *demo* from your mind.

In these days of increasingly better recording gear at ever lower prices and great, easily accessible information on just how to use it, a demo will always keep you in the "good enough" mindset. Each song has to be approached as if it were a finished master because, these days, it's easier than ever to make some really excellent recordings, and that's what nearly everyone expects to hear. The days of producers or publishers being able to "hear through the song" (hear the final product in their head) are over. So forget about demos. They're just an excuse for a recording that's inadequate in some way.

The idea of the demo came out of practicality. Up until about the year 2000, most artists just didn't have the ability to make a record that sounded like a major release anywhere but in a "real" recording studio. Yes, occasionally an artist recorded a hit using a home studio with "prosumer" equipment, but the vast majority of songs that you'd hear on the radio had real pros with real pro equipment involved.

What would happen is that you'd make a demo that was just good enough to get a label or producer interested in taking you to the next level. Because studios were so expensive to record in (typically $100 to $250 an hour, plus engineer, tape, etc.), it was usually impossible to spend enough time to make a recording that was up to snuff with a major label release. And if you weren't located near a reasonably high-end studio, you were forced to use whatever was available. As a result, almost everyone made a demo before moving on to a deal with a label, where they got to make real records in real studios with some real pros who knew what to do.

Most of that has changed with the last few generations of affordable recording gear that is now readily available, and with the fact that the listening public doesn't care as much about audio fidelity as it once did (maybe they never did, but the record companies sure thought so). So now it's easy enough to record for not a lot of money and distribute it for next to nothing, but labels and listeners expect every recording to be as good as you can make it.

MAJOR LABEL DECONSTRUCTION

Among the many recent changes in the music business is the total disruption of the major label paradigm. Where once the music world revolved around six majors, the number has been reduced to just three.

While the influence of the majors seemed to wane during the Music 3.0 years, when social media became a fresh new way for an artist to assemble a fan base, today in Music 4.1, the major labels seem more firmly in control than ever.

To most young artists or bands, the majors still represent the idea of indentured servitude rather than the path to fame and fortune.

The path to major label deconstruction has been rather swift. The Big 6 of Warner Music Group (WMG), EMI, Sony Music, Bertelsmann Music Group (BMG), Universal Music Group (UMG), and Polygram reigned for only ten years, from 1988 to 1998. The group decreased to five in 1998, when UMG absorbed Polygram, and further consolidated to four in 2004, when Sony Music and BMG merged and became Sony BMG. In October of 2008, Sony acquired Bertelsmann's 50 percent of the venture, and the name returned to Sony Music.

Bertelsmann wisely retained many of the publishing elements it maintained prior to the merger and was renamed Bertelsmann Rights Management, understanding that the physical record business was floundering but publishing still remained strong.

In 2009, the private equity firm Kohlberg Kravitz Roberts, also known as KKR, acquired 51 percent of the company, a sign of things to come. In 2012, BMG expanded into administration and management of master recording rights with an unusual arrangement of offering artists a higher royalty rate in exchange for zero advance. The company now distributes its physical product through the other major labels.

The Sad Case of EMI

In May of 2006, EMI attempted to buy Warner Music Group, but the bid was rejected. WMG then returned the favor and tried to buy EMI, only to have it reject a $4.6 billion offer. Then, in 2007, EMI was acquired by Terra Firma Capital Partners, a private equity firm, for £4.2 billion (about $6.8 billion) that was largely financed by a loan from banking giant Citigroup.

After buying at the top of the market, EMI began to hemorrhage money almost immediately after the Terra Firma takeover, as its sales and market share fell through the floor, and several important artists, such as Paul McCartney and Radiohead, walked away when their contracts ended.

Shortly thereafter, Terra Firma was no longer able to make payments on the debt service and sued Citigroup, essentially for "forcing them to take the money" to purchase EMI in the first place. Terra Firma lost the court case in short order, and as of February 1, 2011, Citigroup became the owner of EMI, immediately writing off £2.2 billion of the debt.

In 2012, Universal Music Group acquired EMI from Citigroup, making The Big 4 into The Big 3 as a result (see Fig. 15-1).

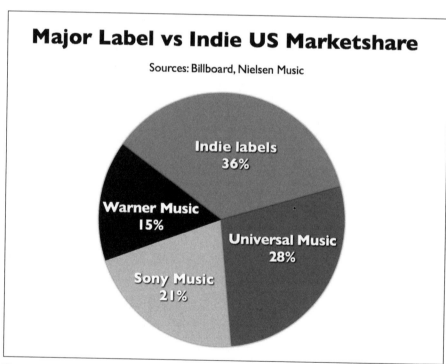

Figure 15-1: Major Label Market Share vs. Indie Labels

WMG Changes Hands

Warner Music Group (WMG, previous known as Warner/Elektra/Atlantic) was one of the most respected labels by both the music industry and artists. Once helmed by music-industry pioneers like Mo Ostin, Joe Smith, Ahmet Ertegun, and Jac Holzman, the label was known to stick by artists it really believed in, regardless of whether the first few albums sold or not, as was the case with classic legacy artists like Jackson Browne and Fleetwood Mac.

From the time that Seagram (the Canadian liquor giant) purchased a small piece of the company in 1994, WMG has been in increasing disarray, which was exacerbated in 2004 when a group of investors led by Edgar Bronfman Jr. (who became CEO) purchased WMG from the Time Warner group.

For a time, it was an uphill climb for the company. WMG struggled with sales, market share, and revenue dropping in spite of excellent digital sales. Then, in a surprise move, WMG put itself up for sale and was purchased by Russian billionaire Len Blavatnik and his Access Industries.

Today, WMG is known as the most digitally progressive of the remaining major labels, as evidenced by a 2013 deal with Clear Channel Media that saw Warner artists paid for terrestrial radio play for the first time. In return, Clear Channel received preferential rates for streaming songs through its iHeartRadio service and other online platforms.

Another example of WMG's willingness to think outside the digital box came in 2014, when it entered into an agreement with Shazam to access the company's proprietary music data. Warner hoped to find promising unsigned artists by analyzing parameters like the song being identified, location where the song was tagged, and even time of day.

In the end, the remaining major labels seem to have as much influence as ever and are in no danger of going away. They will always be needed for what they do best—taking successful artists and making them superstars.

The Major Label of the Future

In Chapter 4, we briefly looked at the joint venture, called Azoff MSG Entertainment (AMSGE), between Madison Square Garden Company (MSG) and music business mover and shaker Irving Azoff. What makes this venture interesting is that the company is divided into four divisions: artist management, music publishing, television production/live event branding, and digital branding. Couple that with the many venues owned by MSG that could host concerts for the company's artists, and you have a look at what the new world record major label could look like.

For the record, Azoff and MSG chairman James Dolan never called this venture a record label, but they don't have to. It's an outdated term for an outdated concept anyway.

The traditional record label combined talent scouting, artist development, distribution, and marketing, but each of those operations has changed substantially since the new millennium. Record labels now have fewer A&R talent scouts than ever, and in this one-failure-and-done atmosphere we live in, artist development is merely a nice term with little execution. Couple that with a dying brick-and-mortar music retail business and companies that market really well in traditional media that doesn't matter nearly as much to music consumers as it once did, and you can see that something in the way the current music business is run has to change.

Of course, Azoff brings his formidable roster of talent (including The Eagles, Christina Aguilera, Steely Dan, and Van Halen) with him, but in the future, more and more new talent will bubble to the surface through social media (think Justin Bieber from YouTube or, more recently, Macklemore, Ryan Lewis, and Jack & Jack) that a cognizant digital department could spot. The digital department could also take care of the heavy lifting when it comes to marketing, because the music consumer that a music company wants to reach today is primarily online.

And then there's management. The so-called "360 deal" recording agreement, in which a label participates in all the revenue streams of an artist, is now what major labels prefer, but AMSGE is among the best in the business when it comes to management, which labels are not. As an artist, which would you choose? Today's record labels also have publishing arms, as does AMSGE, but according to an article in the Hollywood Reporter, it will concentrate more on digital performance rights, a place where many publishers are slow to catch up.

One of the ways to expand the revenue stream from concerts is to live stream the performance as a pay-per-view event or package the show and sell it to a cable network like Palladia or Fuse, which MSG owns. Consumers are already getting used to live streaming of concerts from sites like Livestream and Concert Window, and they'll eventually adopt it as they're doing with streaming music—another win for a company like AMSGE.

When you step back and look at it, doesn't this look like a company prepared for music's future? Doesn't it look like a "label" that artists would kill to be on? It's true that physical product hasn't gone away completely, but putting brick-and-mortar distribution in place shouldn't be a problem in this new era. It can be farmed out to one of the existing major labels, just like BMG now does.

Make no mistake about it, major record labels are not going away. An artist can break online, but getting to the superstar level still requires the infrastructure that only a major label can bring. The current majors are desperately trying to change, and on some levels they're doing a pretty good job of it, but they're stilled mired in the framework of the past, just like any corporation that's been around for 50-plus years. It takes some time for that supertanker to change course.

AMSGE offers things that no major can offer, like management, integration with venues and television, and a new outlook on publishing. That's why we're looking at them as the next-generation record label, if they can pull it off.

WHEN YOU NEED A LABEL

This entire book so far has been about getting along in the new music world without a record label, but there comes a time when having a label is worth considering if you want to jump to the next level as an artist.

Record labels are not intrinsically bad; it's just that you have to weigh the advantages against the disadvantages to determine whether the time is right for you to be associated with one. You might want to consider a label if you find yourself in one of these situations:

- **If it's offering you a staggering amount of money.** If this happens, either you must be hot enough for a bidding war to have broken out, or they really believe in your future. Just remember that this might be the last money you'll ever see from the label, and it may have a significantly negative impact on your credibility with your fan base. Best to test the notion of signing with a label with your tribe just to see their reaction first, because they won't buy anything from you if they feel you sold them out.
- **If you need money for recording, touring, or any other needs.** One of the things that labels do really well is to act like a bank, using your music as collateral. Major labels still do this as skillfully as ever, but is it worth the price you're going to pay in terms of the freedom that Music 4.1 offers?

- **If you're spending too much time on certain nonmusical aspects of your career.** A label can take some of the burden of marketing and distribution off your shoulders. You still have to be involved on some level, though, or you run the risk of things getting way off course before it's brought to your attention. If you don't have a manager already, that might be a better association to make at this point than to start working with a label.

- **If you need expanded distribution.** If distribution into the remaining brick-and-mortar stores is beyond what a small indie label can provide, a major label can be your friend. Major labels have the relationships, the sales force, and the means to collect the money. If you're distributing by yourself, you'll get paid if and when the stores feel like it because you have no clout. In some cases, you won't even be able to get into the remaining chains and retail stores because you don't sell enough to get on their radar. A major label or large indie label sells the stores a lot of product, and they're trusted, so it's a lot easier for them to get the retailer to take a chance. Further, the label has some leverage in that they can always threaten to withhold in-demand product if they don't get paid.

- **If you want to expand into foreign territories.** Let's say that you have a huge following in Germany via your online efforts, but you can't service them properly because you live in Kansas City. A major label can use their overseas resources to promote you and get product in the stores there. It saves you the hassle of reinventing the distribution and marketing wheels.

- **If you need economies of scale.** Sometimes the power of a big label can be used to your advantage because they can cut a better deal with a service (YouTube and MTV come to mind) than you ever could as an indie.

- **If you need major marketing.** Another thing that a major label does well is to market you traditionally. If you want airplay on radio and appearances on television, a label may be your only hope. If you want reviews and articles in mainstream media, they still have the clout to get it done.

- **If you feel you've gone as far as you can go as an indie artist.** If you need help to push your career over the edge to stardom, then a major label or major label imprint may be the way to go. This is what they do—sometimes well, sometimes not.

Unless you have a specific need for any of the above that you're sure you can't fill any other way, it's best to stay independent for as long as you can in order to retain as much control over your music and your musical destiny as possible.

GETTING ALONG IN MUSIC 4.1

As you've read this book, hopefully you've spotted a number of concepts that have continually popped up that directly apply to the music world we live in today. Some of these principles have seen dramatic change, like the shift from the old Music 1.0 to 2.5 way of doing things, and some have remained relatively the same. Let me leave you with some additional thoughts about making music in the Internet Age.

- **It's all about scale.** It's not the sales, it's the number of YouTube views you have. A hit that sells only 50,000 combined units (album and single) may have 50 million YouTube views. Once upon a time, a sales number like that would've been deemed a failure; today, it's a success. Views don't equal sales, and vice versa.
- **There will be fewer digital distributors in the future.** Digital distribution is an expensive business to get into and maintain, so in the near future, there will be a shakeout that will leave far fewer digital competitors. Don't be shocked when you wake up one day to find a few gone.
- **It's all about what you can do for other people.** Promoters, agents, and club owners are dying to book you if they know you'll make them money. Record labels (especially the majors) are dying to sign you if you have an audience they can sell to. Managers will want to sign you if you have a line around the block waiting to see you. If you can't do any of the above, your chances of success decrease substantially.
- **Money often comes late.** It may not seem like it, but success is slow. You grow your audience one fan at a time. The longer it takes, the longer your career will likely last. An overnight sensation usually means you'll also be forgotten overnight. This is one thing that hasn't changed much through the years.
- **Major labels want radio hits.** They want an easy sell, so unless you create music that can get on radio immediately, a major label won't be interested. This is what they do, and they do it well, so if being on a major label is your goal, you must give them what they want.

- **You must create on a regular basis.** Fans have a very short attention span and need to be fed with new material constantly in order to keep you at the forefront of their minds. What should you create? Anything and everything: new original tunes and cover tunes, electric versions and acoustic versions, remixes and outtakes, behind-the-scenes videos, lyric videos, and more. You may create it all at once, but release it on a regular schedule so you always have some fresh content available.
- **YouTube is the new radio (but Facebook may soon challenge it).** Nurture your following on YouTube and release content on a regular basis (see above). It's where the people you want to reach are discovering new music.
- **Growing your audience organically is best.** Don't expect your friends and family to spread the word; they don't count. If you can't find an audience on your own merits, there's something wrong with your music or your presentation. Find the problem, fix it, and try it again. The trick is finding that audience.
- **First and foremost, it all starts with the song.** If you can't write a great song that appeals to even a small audience, none of the other things in this book matter much.

Much more could be written about what Music 4.1 has to offer and how to navigate it, especially in the realm of social media. For that, I recommend you read my book *Social Media Promotion for Musicians*. That said, I'm sure you'll agree that the music business is both exciting and invigorating in its current form. Counter to what you'll hear from old-school naysayers, it's not dying, and it's not wilting. It is constantly evolving and progressing, and those who don't progress with it will fall behind.

Hopefully, after reading this book, you'll have the tools you need to thrive in our current musical age—the age of Music 4.1.

Appendix 1: Online Tools

Below, you'll find all the sites, tools, and applications mentioned during the course of this book, as well as some additional ones that might be helpful.

BAND-ORIENTED PLATFORMS

ReverbNation (reverbnation.com)

Bandcamp (bandcamp.com)

Sonicbids (sonicbids.com)

Nimbit (nimbit.com)

RouteNote (routenote.com)

Ning (ning.com)

The Ultimate Chart (ultimatechart.com)

DistroKid (distrokid.com)

CD Baby (cdbaby.net)

TuneCore (tunecore.com)

Topspin Media (topspinmedia.com)

A&R Registry (musicregistry.com)

BLOG PLATFORMS

Blogger (blogger.com)

Typepad (typepad.com)

Wordpress (wordpress.com)

Tumblr (tumblr.com)

CROWDFUNDING

Kickstarter (kickstarter.com)

Indiegogo (indiegogo.com)

RocketHub (rockethub.com)

Sellaband (sellaband.com)

PledgeMusic (pledgemusic.com)

FACEBOOK

BandPage (bandpage.com)

My Band App (facebook.com/rn.mybandapp)

Facebook Insights (facebook.com/insights)

FanBridge (fanbridge.com)

MAILING LISTS

FanBridge (fanbridge.com)

MailChimp (mailchimp.com)

Constant Contact (constantcontact.com)

iContact (icontact.com)

GetResponse (getresponse.com)

MEASUREMENT

PeopleBrowsr (peoplebrowsr.com)

Sysomos (sysomos.com)

Radian6 (radian6.com)

Google Analytics (google.com/analytics)

Google Alerts (google.com/alerts)

WhosTalkin (whostalkin.com)

Twitter Search (search.twitter.com)

Stat Counter (statcounter.com)

Next Big Sound (nextbigsound.com)

Musicmetric (musicmetric.com)

Starcount (starcount.com)

YouTube Analytics (youtube.com/analytics)

MERCHANDISE

Zazzle (zazzle.com)

CafePress (cafepress.com)

Inksy (inksy.co)

Blurb (blurb.com)

Square (squareup.com)

PayPal Here (paypal.com/here)

QR codes (qrcode.kaywa.com)

Kunaki (kunaki.com)

MUSIC BLOGS

Hypebot (hypebot.com)

Music Think Tank (musicthinktank.com)

Seth Godin (sethgodin.typepad.com)

Digital Music News (digitalmusicnews.com)

Music Business Worldwide (musicbusinessworldwide.com)

Ariel Hyatt/Cyber PR (cyberprmusic.com)

Music 3.0 (music3point0.blogspot.com)

PUBLISHING

Association of Independent Music Publishers (aimp.org)

SoundExchange (soundexchange.com)

SOCIAL MEDIA MANAGEMENT

ArtistData (artistdata.com)

Amp Music Marketing (ampmusicmarketing.com)

Ariel Hyatt/Cyber PR (cyberprmusic.com)

STREAMING VIDEO

UStream (ustream.com)

Livestream (livestream.com)

Google+ Hangouts On Air (hangouts.google.com)

Concert Window (concertwindow.com)

SURVEYS

SurveyMonkey (surveymonkey.com)

Polldaddy (polldaddy.com)

TWITTER

Search.twitter.com

Twellow (twellow.com)

Klout (klout.com)

Blast Follow (blastfollow.com)

Tweepi (tweepi.com)

Gremln (gremln.com)

TweetDeck (tweetdeck.twitter.com)

TweetChat (tweetchat.com)

TweetWhen (tweetwhen.com)

TweetReach (tweetreach.com)

YOUTUBE

YouTube Trends (youtube.com/trendsdashboard)

YouTube Insight (available on each video and channel)

OneLoad (oneload.com)

YouTube Analytics (youtube.com/analytics)

Appendix 2: Glossary

360 deal. A record deal that enables the record label to share in the income of other aspects of an artist's career beyond recording, such as ticket sales and merchandise.

A&R. An abbreviation for *artist and repertoire*. A talent scout at a record label.

AAC. An abbreviation for *Advanced Audio Coding*. A standard compression encoding scheme for digital audio used exclusively by Apple's iTunes store.

access model. A model in which music consumers prefer to access their music through subscription platforms instead of owning their music by buying downloads.

AdSense. A Google service for supplying advertisements to a website based on many factors, such as the website's content and the user's geographical location.

after-show party. A party directly following a show that is for the band's friends and associates.

airplay. When a song gets played on the radio.

Arbitron rating. A measurement of the number of people listening to a radio station.

art. A creative endeavor that you do for your own personal satisfaction.

artistic control. Control of the creative aspects of a recording. Artistic control usually lies mainly in the hands of the producer, with input from the artist.

backlink. An outside link on another website that's connected to your page.

bar code. A series of vertical bars of varying widths in which the numbers 0 through 9 are represented by a unique pattern that can be read by a laser scanner. Bar codes are commonly found on consumer products and are used for inventory control purposes and, in the case of CDs, to tally sales.

bootleg. An unauthorized recording of a concert, rehearsal, outtake, or alternate mix from an album.

brand. A name, sign, or symbol used to identify the items or services of a seller that differentiate them from competitors' items or services. A brand is a promise of quality and consistency.

branding. The promotion of a brand.

breakage. In the days of vinyl, the percentage of records that would break in transit. This number was subtracted from the artist's royalties.

brick-and-mortar. A physical retail store, as opposed to an online store.

catalog. Older albums or recordings under the control of the record label.

cobranding. Two firms working together to promote a product or service.

collectible. An item (usually nonessential) that has particular value to its owner because of its rarity and desirability.

conglomerate. A multi-industry company or a large company that owns smaller companies in different businesses.

container. With regard to music, the package that allows the listener to consume it. Vinyl records, CDs, and MP3 and AAC files are all containers.

consultant. A person who advises a radio station about what to play, when to play it, and what on-air personalities to use.

Content ID. A technology used by YouTube to identify the owner of both audio and video uploads.

craft. A creative endeavor that you do for someone else's approval.

cross-collateralization. Royalties from one agreement used to cover the losses or advances of another agreement.

crowdfunding. A method of raising money for a project by offering incentives for fans to pool their money.

distribution network. The various retail sales outlets or, in the case of M3.0, digital music download sites.

DIY. An abbreviation for *do it yourself.*

DJ. An abbreviation for *disc jockey.* A term used in the early days of radio for the on-air radio person who played the records that the station was broadcasting. Later replaced by the term *on-air personality.*

DRM. An abbreviation for *Digital Rights Management*, an antipiracy measure that limits the number of legal copies of a digital audio file that can be made.

FLAC. An abbreviation for *Free Lossless Audio Codec*, a lossless file format used to make digital audio files smaller.

four-wall. When one management individual or company uses the clout of a larger management company in return for a percentage of the income. The manager of the smaller company sometimes shares an office with the larger management company, or is "four-walled" within the company's offices.

freebooting. Uploading a video to Facebook that has been downloaded from YouTube, often by someone who's not the owner of the content.

freemium. A business model in which a product or service is offered free of charge, but the customer is charged for advanced features or functions and may be required to view advertisements.

fuelers. Contributors to a crowdfunding project.

gatefold. An album cover that folds out.

heritage artist. A superstar act that is still active. Madonna, Tina Turner, the Rolling Stones, and The Eagles are examples of current heritage acts.

IFPI. An abbreviation for the *International Federation of the Phonographic Industry.* Represents the recording industry worldwide, with some 1,400 members in 66 countries and affiliated industry associations in 45 countries.

imprint. A project, division, or custom label of a record label, usually given to

independent promoter. A person or company not employed by a record label but hired by the label to persuade a radio station to play a record.

ISRC. An abbreviation for *International Standard Recording Code,* used to uniquely identify sound recordings and music-video recordings. An ISRC identifies a particular recording, not the song itself. Therefore, different recordings, edits, and remixes of the same song will each have their own ISRCs.

jewel case. The standard plastic case that holds a CD.

kbps. An abbreviation for *kilobits per second,* or the amount of digital information sent per second.

leader. Initiates contact with the tribe and leads the conversations.

loss leader. An item priced at a loss in order to entice people to buy another more costly product, usually at full retail price.

lurker. One who reads a blog but doesn't participate or post.

meet-and-greet. A brief meeting with an artist to say hello, answer a few questions, and take pictures.

metadata. Data about other data or content.

micropayment. A means for transferring very small amounts of money in situations where collecting such small amounts of money is impractical, or very expensive, with the usual payment systems.

millennial. A member of the generation of children born between 1980 and 2000.

MP3. The de facto standard data-compression format used to make audio files smaller in size.

M0.5. See Music 0.5.

M1.0. See Music 1.0.

M1.5. See Music 1.5.

M2.0. See Music 2.0.

M2.5. See Music 2.5.

M3.0. See Music 3.0.

M3.5. See Music 3.5.

M4.0. See Music 4.0.

M4.1. See Music 4.1.

Music 0.5. The time before recorded music, when sheet music was the only form of music distribution.

Music 1.0. The first generation of the music business, in which the product was vinyl records, the artist had no direct contact with the record buyer, radio was the primary source of promotion, the record labels were run by record people, and records were bought from retail stores.

Music 1.5. The second generation of the music business, in which the product was primarily CDs, labels were owned and run by large conglomerates, MTV caused the labels to shift from artist development to image development, radio was still the major source of promotion, and CDs were purchased from retail stores.

Music 2.0. The third generation of the music business, which signaled the beginning of digital music. Piracy ran rampant because of P2P networks, but the industry took little notice because CD sales were still strong from radio promotion.

Music 2.5. The fourth generation of the music business, in which digital music became monetized, thanks to the online digital distributor iTunes store and, later, others, such as Amazon MP3. CD sales plunged, the music industry contracted, and retail stores closed.

Music 3.0. The generation of the music business in which the artist was first able to communicate and interact with, and market and sell directly to, the fan. Record labels, radio, and television became mostly irrelevant, and single songs were purchased instead of albums.

Music 3.5. The generation of the music business in which YouTube became the principle way music consumers discovered music, and as a result, became more comfortable with streaming digital music instead of downloading it.

Music 4.0. The generation of music in which streaming music becomes profitable for the entire supply chain of the music industry, as consumers change completely to the access model of consuming music.

one-stop. A company that buys from major record distributors and sells to small retailers, who buy in quantities too small for major distributors to bother with.

paid download. A downloadable song that you buy and own.

paid search. A type of contextual advertising in which website owners pay an advertising fee to have their websites shown in the top placement on search-engine results pages.

payola. Payment in exchange for airplay. The payment could be in cash, illegal substances such as drugs, or products such as televisions or paid vacations. The practice is illegal.

pay per click. An Internet advertising model used on search engines, advertising networks, and content sites such as blogs, in which advertisers pay their hosts only when their ads are clicked on.

pay to play. In order for a band to play at a club, the club's owner demands that the band buy a certain number of tickets, which they then sell or give away to their fans. The club owner is guaranteed a minimum cash presale, while the band usually ends up losing money.

peer to peer (P2P). A type of transient Internet network that allows a group of computer users with the same networking program to connect with each other and directly access files from one another's hard drives.

performance fee. A fee paid to the performer (as opposed to the songwriter) each time a song is played on the radio, over the Internet, or on television.

performance rights organization (PRO). An organization that collects performance royalties from broadcasters or Internet streaming and distributes it to songwriters. Performance-rights organizations include ASCAP, BMI, and SESAC.

P2P. See peer to peer.

pirating. The sale of an illegal copy of a digital file, CD, CD artwork, or any other creative product in which the record label, artist, and songwriter neither take part in the profit nor are provided royalties.

pre-roll. A commercial that runs before the main video.

PRO. See performance rights organization.

producer. The person in charge of recording, from managing the budget to creatively guiding the project to completion.

promoter. A person who organizes a concert or show, including booking the venue and talent; arranging for advertising, security, and insurance; as well as a host of other duties. The promoter usually uses his or her own money to finance the project in the hopes of making a profit.

QR code. A graphic code similar to a bar code that provides a link to a website when scanned. An analog web link.

rack jobber. Someone who leases floor space from a retail store (such as a department store or car wash) and puts in "racks" of CDs or other types of recorded music for sale.

record. A generic term for the distribution method of a recording. Regardless of whether it's vinyl, a CD, or a digital file, it is still known as a record.

record club. An outdated way of obtaining prerecorded music at a discounted rate through the mail. Usually used by the consumer because there is no retail music store in his or her area.

RIAA. An abbreviation for the *Recording Industry Association of America*, a trade organization for record labels.

rotation. The playlist of a radio station.

RSS. An abbreviation for *Real Simple Syndication*, a family of web-feed formats used to publish frequently updated works (such as blog entries, news headlines, audio, and video) in a standardized format.

SEM. An abbreviation for *search engine marketing*.

SEO. An abbreviation for *search engine optimization*.

shed. A large, outdoor concert facility.

SKU. An abbreviation for *stock-keeping unit*, the number allotted to every item in a store for the purpose of inventory control.

SoundScan. The company that measures record sales. Whenever a CD or a DVD is sold, the bar code on each unit is scanned and recorded by SoundScan.

subscription service. A download service for which you pay a set monthly fee and listen to as much music as you want during that time without any limitations.

superfan. A fan who is more passionate than the average fan. Also called a **true fan** or **uberfan.**

swag. Another name for merchandise, such as T-shirts, that is sold at a concert or on a website.

technology expense. A clause in a recording agreement that subtracts a portion of the artist's royalty if a certain new technology is used in the production or sale of product.

torrent. The latest form of Internet P2P (peer to peer) file sharing. Since 2006, BitTorrent sharing has been the most popular means by which web users trade software, music, movies, and digital books across the Internet. *BitTorrents* (a term that is synonymous with *torrents*) work by downloading small bits of files from many different web sources at the same time. See also **peer to peer.**

true fan. A fan who is more passionate than the average fan. Also called a **superfan** or **uberfan.**

turntable hit. A song that receives massive airplay but has few actual sales.

tweet. A Twitter posting.

uberfan. A fan who is more passionate than the average fan. Also called a **superfan** or **true fan.**

vertical. A particular marketing or sales niche or demographic group.

webcast. A noninteractive stream from a radio-like streaming service.

WMA. An abbreviation for *Windows Media Audio*, an audio data compression format created by Microsoft.

Index